The Experience of Labour in Eighteenth-Century English Industry

JOHN RULE

ST. MARTIN'S PRESS NEW YORK

Library of Congress Cataloging in Publication Data

Rule, John 1944-
  The experience of labour in eighteenth-century
English industry

  Bibliography: p. 217
  Includes index
  1. Labor and laboring classes–England–18th
century. I. Title.
HD8389.R84   1980   331'.0941   80-23245
ISBN 0-312-27664-8

CONTENTS

2190431

Preface

1. Introduction: The Extent and Nature of Manufacturing
   and Mining in Eighteenth-century England   11

2. Uncertainty, Irregularity, Hours and Wages   49

3. Work and Health   74

4. Apprenticeship   95

5. Exploitation and Embezzlement   124

6. Trade Unionism and Industrial Disputes: The Nature
   and Extent of Trade Unionism   147

7. The Methods and Effectiveness of Industrial Action   172

8. Custom, Culture and Consciousness   194

Select Bibliography   217

Index   224

PREFACE

Several aspects of the eighteenth century have begun to receive the specialist social historian's attention: notably the history of crime, of popular recreation and of popular disturbances. The history of work has however been rather neglected. One reason for this has been the conventional concern of economic historians to single out the period 1760 to 1830 (or 1850) as the 'Industrial Revolution'. As a result the eighteenth century has tended to be split into two by the usual text-book divisions. The latter part is hurried through as a preface to the triumph of industrialisation and the factory system, while the first half is added as an under-considered appendix to the 'early modern economy' by writers whose main concern is with Tudor and Stuart England. There have been notable exceptions, for example the classic studies of T.S. Ashton and Paul Mantoux, but the effect of dividing the century has led to a distorting emphasis on change rather than on continuity. There was certainly change, but in the area of labour history much remained unchanged through the Industrial Revolution, and much even persisted long after it. The typical labour experience and response of the eighteenth century was not that of the factory proletariat, for the factory system was very much in its infancy even at the end of the century. Hand-workers and artisans had a formative role to play in the development of working-class consciousness.

This work is not offered as a monograph bringing fresh knowledge from previously unexplored archive sources; rather it has developed from ten years of teaching a final-year special subject. We offer our students (and perhaps too the intelligent reader of history in general), too little between the general textbook and the monograph. The former leaves the student hungry for further details and insights, while the latter is usually based on sources which are beyond his reach and force him to accept opinions as presented. I have tried to make extensive use of the kinds of sources which could be found in most well-established university libraries. For the most part the reader who has doubts about my interpretation can find for himself the information upon which I based it. I have also arranged the bibliography to this end by giving a substantially complete listing of primary sources and a bibliographical note on the main secondary authorities — an alphabetical listing of the latter without comment or arrangement is of little value to the student.

I have profited much from discussion with many scholars. My debt to Edward Thompson, my former research supervisor, is a large one and it extends also to those historians who were contemporaries of mine at the Centre for the Study of Social History at the University of Warwick in the middle-sixties: Eric Evans, Bob Malcolmson and Malcolm Thomas. My Southampton colleagues have always been encouraging and stimulating. Nick Gaskell of the Law Department searched through large volumes of Law Reports on my behalf, and my typist Vivian Luffman is to be thanked for her intelligent reading of my draft as well as her skill and speed in typing it. Most of all I am grateful to the sixty final-year students who chose to take my special subject over the last ten years.

University of Southampton

1 INTRODUCTION: THE EXTENT AND NATURE OF MANUFACTURING AND MINING IN EIGHTEENTH-CENTURY ENGLAND

To Daniel Defoe prosperity in an English region almost invariably indicated the presence of manufacturing:

> In the manufacturing counties you see the wheel going almost at every door, the wool and the yarn hanging up at every window, the looms, the winders, the combers, the carders, the dyers, the dressers, all busy; and the very children, as well as women constantly employed.
>
> As is the labour so is the living; for where the poor are full of work, they are never empty of wages; they eat while the others starve, and have a tolerable plenty.[1]

He was, perhaps not surprisingly for his time, prone to write about manufacturing as if it and the great woollen industry were synonymous. One is likely to learn more from Defoe about Exeter than Birmingham; Norwich than Sheffield; Colchester than Newcastle. We are nevertheless briskly reminded by his writings that England by the beginning of the eighteenth century was already an economy in which manufacturing had attained a position of importance beyond that usually associated in our contemporary world with 'underdevelopment'.

This importance, although evident from so many contemporary descriptions and from the amount of legislative concern devoted to the manufacturing interest, is difficult to measure accurately. Certainly, although a possible break in the 1720s has recently been suggested, it was a progress which was constant and, by any previous standards, rapid well before the time in which the beginnings of the Industrial Revolution are usually placed. The population of England and Wales has been estimated at 5,826,000 for 1701, and by that date the mining and manufacturing occupations may have already accounted for between one-quarter and one-third of the total adult population with the value of their output equalling that of agriculture.[2] One interpretation of a survey of English social structure made in 1759 suggests that trade and manufacturing together may well by that date have employed more workers than agriculture, although other historians have estimated that by that date 60 to 70 per cent of the population were still primarily (but not necessarily exclusively) dependent upon agriculture.[3] Precision in measurement is unobtainable, but the trend is unmistakable. By 1801 the 29.7 per cent of the population occupied in manufacturing and mining when added to the 11.2 per cent in trade clearly outnumbered the 35.9 per cent in agriculture, forestry and fishing. Between 1801 and 1811 there was surprisingly little movement: agriculture fell only 2.9 per cent while mining and manufacturing rose by only 0.5 per cent and trade by 0.4 per cent. The trend was clearer between 1811 and 1821 when agriculture fell by 4.6 per cent, manufacturing rose by 8.2 per cent and trade by 0.5 per cent.[4]

The difficulties in statistically delineating the sectoral distribution of the eighteenth-century labour force stem as much from the nature and structure of the economy as they do from any paucity of data about it. Gregory King in his famous survey of 1688 did not distinguish between the agricultural and the non-agricultural workers, while despite the perceptive analysis of his findings by Professor Mathias, there is still some difficulty in this respect in using the figures of Joseph Massie for 1759. Explicit distinctions were not made because in the economy of the eighteenth century their strict application would have been unreal. The nature of the 'putting-out' system was precisely to distribute manufacturing to the countryside, while many rural craftsmen such as blacksmiths, wheelwrights and thatchers were part of the agriculture 'industry' and indeed probably spent more time mending than making. The very different economic structure of that time makes contemporary assumptions about the dichotomy of industry as against agriculture largely meaningless.[5] Double occupations persisted in many areas throughout the century, and in others well into it. In some areas they seem to have died out very early. The picture is not therefore a simple one of a widespread and commonplace *equal* combination of agricultural and industrial employment. There was considerable regional variation and there was variation in the extent to which mixing took place: a continuum from the fully mixed in which a man might be equally dependent upon two occupations, through the seasonally mixed in which he might be employed in one or other of two occupations depending on the time of the year, to the tending of a garden which added usefully but in a strictly collateral way to the family's comfort.[6] In one form or another the mixing of manufacturing or mining activities with husbandry ones was sufficiently widespread to make attempts at a precise measurement of the manufacturing labour force unreal or even misleading.

Cornish parish registers frequently record the double occupation 'tinner and husbandman' up to the middle years of the century, although by the early-nineteenth century, smallholdings were regarded as 'collateral aids' useful to full-time miners. Within the county conditions varied. In remote rural districts like St Just or St Agnes a high proportion of miners might have had smallholdings, but the growth of mining towns like Redruth and Camborne, brought a density of settlement which could not possibly have allowed smallholding on the same scale.[7] Among northern miners smallholdings were encouraged by some employers, but Arthur Young was of the opinion that unless directly encouraged, miners were willing to give little of their substantial above-ground hours to agricultural pursuits.[8] Among the rural weavers of the West Country it seems to have been rare, but among those of Lancashire so common that those weavers who by mid-century did weave cotton full-time were complaining of competition from 'farmer-weavers' lowering rates. Even by then although the full-time weavers were in the majority, the distinction between husbandman and weaver was still not a fully effective one: one describing himself as a husbandman undertook to teach an apprentice to weave cloth. In other branches of the cotton trade weavers already formed a permanent town journeyman class in places like Manchester or Bolton.[9] The West Riding of Yorkshire has been described as representing for most of the eighteenth century 'an alliance of land and loom', but here the small farms were those of the small clothiers, those working employers who were the distinctive feature of the woollen manufacture in that district.[10] The Yorkshire clothiers were independent in that they bought their own raw material and marketed their own produce. Such men worked at home with their family supplemented by from two to six apprentices or journeymen, and smallholding was an essential part of their 'economy'. Defoe had remarked on this early in the century:

> Every clothier must keep a horse perhaps two to fetch and carry for the use of his manufacture, to fetch home his wool and his provisions from the market, to carry his yarn to the spinners, his manufacture to the fulling mill, and when finished to the market to be sold . . . so every manufacturer generally keeps a cow or two, or more for his family, and this employs the two, or three, or four pieces of enclosed land about his house.[11]

The total acreage of such holdings rarely exceeded seven and was commonly only two or three.[12] The pattern persisted until the coming of the mills, for as late as 1795 the keeping of horses and cows on small enclosures was commonplace. For the most part this added the 'comforts, without the superfluities' to the life of the smallholders, although a sizeable minority could have been described as small farmers.[13]

At the end of the century the watch and fine-tool makers around Prescott were still a scattered rural trade who occupied small farms in conjunction with their manufacturing activities, much in the manner of the rural weavers around Manchester.[14] On the other hand in the Black Country the emphasis was different. Here in 1776 Arthur Young saw about Wednesbury 'not one farm house, nothing that looked like the residence of a mere farmer', while around West Bromwich such agriculture as was carried on was 'subservient' to manufactures. The gardens which he noticed along the canals at Birmingham were no more than allotments in the modern sense, rented at a guinea a year.[15] So too were the 'narrow strips of garden' on the outskirts of London which John Thelwall recollected in 1795 as having been kept by many of the silk-weavers of Spitalfields. He remembered them as having been used to grow tulips or keep pigeons — recreational rather than material contributions to the weavers' well-being.[16]

Many of those who did combine manufacturing or mining with agricultural pursuits were still full-time industrial workers. That is they put in as long a day as was required at their industrial employment before tending to their smallholding or garden. This has been noted of the Lancashire weavers, and it was very evident in the case of miners. By mid-century the labour demands of a rapidly-capitalising mining industry were for a committed workforce. Hours were generally short: rarely more than eight and in some cases only six.[17] Young was effusive in his praises of a northern mine-owner who encouraged his miners to fill in their time on smallholdings which he allowed them to enclose from the moors and build a cottage upon:

> Now there is not a collier without his farm; each from three or four to 20 acres of land. Most of them keep a cow or two, and a galloway: raise the corn etc. they eat; are well fed, well clothed, industrious and happy. Their time is spent at home instead of the alehouse: those young fellows, who formerly were riotous and debauched, now marry, settle and become the honest fathers of a laborious and valuable race of children . . .
>
> And by this well concerted conduct, the whole colliery from being a scene of idleness, insolence, and riot, is converted into a well-conducted and decently cultivated colony: it is become a seminary

of industry; and a source of population.[18]

Several landowners in west Cornwall with interests in the mines acted in the same way towards the tin and copper miners. A description from that area in 1802 is strikingly similar to that of Young's just quoted:

> Whenever this has been tried . . . the happy effects have soon been perceived. In the course of a few years they have been able to rear up little cottage houses for their habitation, and instead of meeting them staggering from their former haunts, the brandy shops, as before, you may now see them busy in enclosing and cultivating their little fields . . . they feel themselves comfortable in their little homely cots, surrounded with 3 or 4 acres of tolerably good pasture land sufficient to maintain a cow, the milk of which together with the potatoes they grow, make a considerable part of the food of their families. How great must be the satisfaction of a humane, bene-volent landlord in seeing so many little dwelling houses of green meadows arising year after year in dismal barren spots . . . Instead of being as before, idle, careless, indolent, envious, dissatisfied and dis-affected, the fruits of their former depraved, helpless and wretched condition, they become careful and thrifty both of their money and time and soon begin to imbibe fresh notions respecting themselves and others and are happily found to be better fathers, better hus-bands and more respectable members of the community than they had ever been before.[19]

In both districts the object was to fill up the 'off core' hours of the miner, not create a mixed economy. John Harris, the Cornish miner-poet, described his father as farming seven or eight acres after following 'his daily avocation underground', in the evenings, mornings, holidays and 'leisurable opportunities'.[20] In the early-nineteenth century attempts to combine more than an acre or two with regular mining were dis-couraged, one manager declaring a preference for men with small plots as those with large ones 'do not give so much of their attention'.[21] Young noted in the north, that although rents were low, they were deliberately kept high enough to discourage miners from taking on too large plots. However he was fulsome in his praises of James Croft who managed with only four hours' sleep daily and divided the twenty hours remaining between the mine and his small farm.[22]

A full-time male manufacturing worker might be part of a family economy which was substantially mixed, since the wife and children could fill in the labour gap on the land left by the father's employment elsewhere. Autobiographies of Cornish miners record helping on family smallholdings as a regular part of childhood.[23] The clothiers of the West Riding were very much a family economy both in their manufacturing and in their farming activities, with the wife adding domestic chores to assisting at the loom and feeding the livestock.[24]

Seasonal intermixing of manufacturing with other activities was wide-spread wherever industry reached into rural districts. Cornish miners left the mines for the autumn pilchard fishing.[25] Workers of all kinds went into the fields for the harvest. Harvesting was not then accomplished in a matter of days with a combine harvester. Striking evidence survives in the letters of a west-country clothier of the time lost to manufacturing every year, as he apologised to disappointed customers for his inability to keep up supplies. By mid-June the hay harvest was underway and after it there was only a brief interlude before the corn needed gathering in mid-August. In a late and difficult year that might not end before October at which time in the West Country the apple harvest and the cider-making occupied weavers until the end of the month. The earliest dated letter from him complaining of being deserted by his employees is 15 June; the latest 26 October. For around one-third of the year he was reduced accordingly to a low level of production.[26] Other rural workers than those in the woollen trade were similarly difficult to keep to manufacturing employment at harvest-time, nail-makers for example.[27]

Clearly if the dichotomy of agriculture/manufacturing is inapplicable to eighteenth-century conditions, then that of town/industry as opposed to village/agriculture must be equally so. Eighteenth-century manufacturing had both urban and rural forms, and even these did not strictly depend upon the nature of the manufacturing occupation. There were town weavers and there were village weavers: town stockingers and village stockingers: town cutlers and village cutlers. The town cutlers of Sheffield were at least equalled in number by those working in the surrounding rural districts. To see the geography of manufacturing England through the eyes of Defoe is not to see it in terms of growing industrial towns both in number and in size, but in terms of 'populous' active districts in which sizeable towns, smaller towns, villages and hamlets were all engaged in manufacturing:

Let them view the County of Devon, and for 20 miles every way round the City of Exeter, where the trade of serges is carry'd on.
The County of Norfolk, and for as many miles every way about the

City of Norwich, where the stuff-weaving is carry'd on.

The County of Essex, for near 40 miles every way where the bay-making trade is carry'd on.

The County of Wiltshire, through that whole flourishing vale from Warminster, south to Malmsbury north, inclusive of all the great towns of Bradford, Trowbridge, Westbury, Tedbury, Frome and the Devizes etc. where the manufacture of fine Spanish and medley clothing and drugget making is carry'd on.

The Counties of Gloucester and Worcester from Cirencester and Stroudwater to the City of Worcester where the white-clothing trade, for the Turkey merchants is carry'd on.

The Counties of Warwick and Stafford, every way round the town of Birmingham, where the hard-ware manufacture and cutlery trade is carry'd on, as also about Coventry.

The Counties of Yorkshire and Lancashire, round about and every way adjacent to the great manufacturing towns of Manchester, Sheffield, Leeds and Halifax, where the known manufactures of cotton-ware, iron-ware, Yorkshire cloths, kersies etc. are carry'd on.[28]

Devonshire to Defoe was a county so full of great towns engaged in trade and manufactures that it could hardly be equalled in Europe.[29] But these 'great towns' apart from Exeter, Tiverton and possibly Honiton were small indeed by modern standards and reveal the scattered nature of the serge manufacture. The clothing districts of Essex extended for 40 to 50 miles square. The demand for yarn was always high, many spinners being needed to keep one weaver occupied, and this took employment for women into homes far removed from the centres of the manufacture. Devon needs reached into Cornwall; Norwich wove yarn spun in Cambridgeshire, Bedfordshire and Huntingdonshire. As Defoe remarked: 'some whole counties and parts of counties' were engaged in spinning even if they saw nothing of any other form of manufacturing employment. The 'whole country' around Leicester and Nottingham seemed to be employed in the stocking manufacture: 'such multitudes of people as could scarce be believed'. Somerset and Wiltshire were thickly peopled by inhabitants employed in 'the richest and most valuable manufacture in the world, the English clothing'. The great clothiers sent their wool to be spun in a 'great number of villages, hamlets and scattered houses' around.[30] Even in the very cradle of the Industrial Revolution, Yorkshire and Lancashire, a rural aspect long persisted. As late as 1811 only about one-quarter of the population of the West

Riding was urban, while the historians of the cotton trade have noted
that the growth of Lancashire was not so much an urban increase as a
'thickening of the population over the countryside'.[31]

In fact the industrial and population expansion of the eighteenth
century was almost as great proportionally in the countryside as in the
towns. In the cutlery and nail-making trades around Sheffield the villages
as well as the town expanded until mechanisation finally reduced most
of the rural craftsmen to poverty in the nineteenth century. The metal
goods produced in the villages may have been scorned as 'knock-ons'
by the town cutlers, but they had their place in the local and indeed
national economy.[32] Miners whether in the coal or metal-mining districts usually lived in villages, whose mono-occupational nature gave the
miners their solidarity and special sense of being 'communities apart'.

Samuel Bamford the child of a cotton-weaver may have been raised
to be an industrial worker, but it was through the eyes of a country
child that he first viewed Manchester:

> Next we passed over 'The Butter-style' and turned on our left, a
> vast gloom darkening before us as we advanced. Then we heard the
> rumbling of wheels, and clang of hammers, and a hubbub of con-
> fused sounds from workshops, and manufactories. As we approached
> the 'Mile-House', human shouts and cries in the streets became indis-
> tinguishable; and on the top of Red Bank, the glare of many lights,
> and faint outline of buildings in a noisy chaos below, told us we
> beheld Manchester.[33]

Midway between the manufacturing villages and the larger industrial
towns and cities were the very large number of small towns, not all as
big as Tiverton which had a population of 8,700 in 1715 even though
it had fallen to 7,000 by 1770,[34] or even Camborne, growing with the
expansion of copper mining to reach a population of 4,811 by 1801.[35]
By 1700 16 per cent of the population of England lived in towns of
5,000+ compared with 8 per cent in 1600. In 1801 perhaps one-third of
the population lived in settlements of more than 1,000 inhabitants.[36] It
is doubtful whether we can think of less than 5,000 inhabitants as offering a truly urban life experience. Even in emergent Lancashire only
Manchester/Salford and Liverpool had more than 10,000 inhabitants by
1770 while Lancaster, Wigan, Preston, Warrington and perhaps Black-
burn had 5,000. Burnley, Colne, Oldham, Bury, Ashton, Prescot and
Ormskirk all had less than 3,000.[37] Typical of the small manufacturing
towns were those of the clothing districts so proudly listed by Defoe in

the West Country, Essex and East Anglia: Frome, Pensford, Shepton Mallet, Wincanton, Malmesbury, Chippenham, Devizes, Bradford-on-Avon, Trowbridge, Warminster, Stourminster, Cirencester, Minchinhampton, Crediton, Honiton, Ashburton, Bocking, Brainbridge, Colchester, Thetford, Dis, Harleston, Windham, Dearham and Hingham. The list is illustrative not comprehensive. Defoe took much less notice of the metal-working districts, but the Black Country could have added its crop of smaller towns to the larger centres like Birmingham or Wolverhampton: towns like Dudley, Darleston, Bilston, West Bromwich and Wednesbury.

The persistence and widespread nature of village and small-town manufacturing should not be permitted to obscure the rapid growth of some large manufacturing centres even before the Industrial Revolution. Many of them had already taken on the environmental characteristics of the industrial town. To Defoe it was already 'black' Barnsley, an iron and steel town so 'black and smoky' that it was as if 'they were all smiths that lived in it'. While the narrow streets of Sheffield were 'dark and black' from the continued smoke of the forges,[38] Burslem was so smoke-filled from the potteries that even by the mid-eighteenth century, its people groped their way through the streets. By 1762 its 150 potteries were supporting 7,000 people and it continued to grow, John Wesley remarking in 1781 on how much the town had changed in twenty years with inhabitants flowing in from every side.[39] Portsmouth saw through the activities of the dockyard, the virtual creation of the 'new' town of Portsea to house the shipwrights and yard labourers. By 1801 Portsea had 4,419 houses compared with 1,134 in the old town. By this time the population of the whole borough had reached 33,226.[40]

Five of the ten largest provincial towns in 1775 owed their size primarily to manufacturing. They were Birmingham (40,000), Norwich (38,500), Manchester (30,000), Sheffield (27,000) and Leeds (24,244). Of these all but Norwich had had less than 10,000 inhabitants in 1700. Of the other five only Bath had no really significant level of manufacturing, the others, Liverpool, Bristol, Newcastle and Plymouth, having considerable manufacturing activities as well as other functions. Other centres also grew rapidly because of manufacturing between 1700 and 1775. Nottingham grew by 135.9 per cent (framework knitting), Exeter by 17.9 per cent (serge making, whose best days were already ending), Coventry by 107.1 per cent (silk-ribbon weaving), Leicester by 75 per cent (framework knitting) and Colchester by 11.1 per cent (cloth trade, like Exeter its best days were already over).[41] No town grew more spectacularly than Birmingham or Manchester. (It would be pedantic to insist on calling the latter a village though such was its eighteenth-century administrative status. Defoe rightly described it as the 'greatest mere village' in England, but overestimated its population as 50,000!)[42] William Hutton, later to become one of its leading inhabitants, first saw Birmingham in 1741 as 'large and full of inhabitants, and those inhabitants full of industry'. It was not only large, but it was growing astonishingly with its 1801 population of 73,000 *nine* times its 1700 population. Hutton thought it had increased by more than 8,000 inhabitants between 1700 and 1731, while Arthur Young thought it added 40,000 between 1768 and his visit in 1791 making it 'reckoned with justice the first manufacturing town in the world'.[43] Manchester with Salford had a population of 19,839 in 1757, having had one of around 8,000 excluding Salford in 1717. Jointly they totalled 27,246 inhabitants by 1795, by which time Manchester was becoming the world's first real factory town:

> As Manchester may bear comparison with the metropolis itself in the rapidity with which whole streets have been raised, and in its extension on every side towards the surrounding country, so it unfortunately vies with or exceeds the metropolis, in the closeness with which the poor are crowded in offensive, dark, damp, and incommodious habitations.[44]

There is too little space to describe in detail the growth of the other manufacturing towns such as Wolverhampton, specialising in locks and described in 1751 as a 'great manufacturing town'; Plymouth which with its suburb of Dock (now Devonport) was rivalling Portsmouth as a naval dockyard town by the end of the century; St Helens which grew from village to town following the erection of the British Plate Glass manufactory there in 1773 or even Kendal tucked away in the remote Lake District and according to Young in 1771 'famous for several manufacturies', including cloth-making and stocking knitting.[45]

Apart from all of these, and in a very special place of its own, stood the metropolis itself. London was important for such a range of economic activities that its manufacturing ones are not always given the attention they merit. Yet it has a claim to have been the greatest centre of manufacturing in the kingdom. From a 1700 population of 570,000 it had increased to 675,000 by 1750, equal to 11 per cent of the total population of England. Given the mobile nature of much of its population, it is not an unreasonable supposition that one-sixth of the adult

population of the country had lived there at some time.[46] Its population in 1800 was around 900,000. Best known as the great centre of the
artisan craft trades, the total number of its manufacturing tradesmen
was immense and the variety of its crafts amazing. Some groups like
tailors and shoemakers were numbered in thousands. Watchmakers
increased so that by the end of the century there were around 8,000 of
them. After such trades came ones of lesser but still considerable size:
hatters, printers, coopers, cabinet-makers, wheelwrights and coachmakers. Smaller still were groups like engravers, locksmiths, goldsmiths
and brushmakers, while after them came a very wide range of highly-
specialised craftsmen, such as the surgical-instrument makers, the
spectacle makers and the leather-shagreen-trunk makers. The building
and construction trades employed large numbers of bricklayers, masons,
house-carpenters, plumbers, painters and tilers: all with their supportive
labourers.[47]

The largest single group of manufacturing workers were the weavers.
Massie estimated in 1759 that around 14,000 families in London depended upon the textile manufacture. Although there were workers in
a variety of textiles, and even at mid-century some framework knitters
still surviving after the trade had been moving for more than a generation to the cheaper labour of the East Midlands, the large majority of
London's textile workers was made up of the silk weavers of Spitalfields.
They were the most distinctive, concentrated and proletarian of all the
city's skilled workers. Along the river worked large numbers of porters,
lightermen, coal-heavers and the shipwrights, ropemakers and caulkers
of the repair and building yards. London was the great centre then as
now of both newspaper and book printing, and there may have been as
many as 3,000 printing workers by the end of the century. All these
men worked in named trades and occupations and Massie was almost
certainly not exaggerating when he added to them 20,000 families
dependent on the earnings of unskilled 'common' labourers.[48]

There was no single all-embracing word to cover those who worked in
eighteenth-century mining and manufacturing as comprehensively as
the 'working class' was to do for the coming nineteenth century. The
'labouring poor' covered only part of the broad-band of work people, as
did the 'manufacturing poor' although that has the virtue of excluding
the purely agricultural. 'Manufacturer' to mean a person who actually
produced goods was commonly used, while 'mechanic' had a broader
meaning than it now possesses. 'Artificer' to describe some skilled
labourers was widely used and in the navy and in the dockyards has

persisted to the present day. 'Artisan' conveys some notions of independence from employers, but it was still much used to describe those groups of skilled craftsmen who through serving an apprenticeship possessed the right to view their skill as a kind of 'property'. Historians might find it useful to describe such men where they depended on working for a capitalist 'putting-out' employer as a 'dependent artisanry', but contemporaries would not have needed the qualifying adjective.[49] 'Journeyman' was the proper term for a skilled man working for wages either as an intermediate stage between completing an apprenticeship and finding the capital to set up as an employing master, or as descriptive of a permanent condition of wage working in the growing number of occupations where high capital costs put employer status beyond the reach of the trade's skilled workforce. Even 'master' was ambiguous. It could simply mean the mastering of a trade through apprenticeship and the legal right thereby to exercise it, or it could apply only to those who were, even if only on a very small scale, employers of labour. Whatever a man's position himself, if he took an apprentice, he was to him, his master. A weaver in the south-west, for example, who had served his time could be regarded as a master-weaver by his apprentice and perhaps even by a journeyman if, rarely, he employed one. He was nevertheless himself a dependent pieceworker on wool put-out by the master *clothier* and neither bought his own material nor marketed his finished product. The master framework knitter stood in a similar position to the *hosier*. 'Tradesman' still described a craft worker as frequently as it did one directly engaged in commerce with the public.[50] 'Labourer' almost always described a man with no trained skill. The Hammonds called the third volume of their famous trilogy *The Skilled Labourer*, but the eighteenth century would have seen that as a contradiction in terms. The gulf between such 'common' labourers and skilled craftsmen was often wider than that between the upper ranks of the latter and the trading middle class. It was a gulf of standing, status and income. Defoe indicates the complexity of such divisions in 1728:

> Those concerned in the meaner and first employments are called in common, working men or labourers, and the *labouring poor* such as the mere husbandman, miners, diggers, fishers and in short, all the drudges and labourers in the several productions of nature or of art. Next to them, are those who, though labouring perhaps equally with the other, have yet some art mingled with their industry, and are to be particularly instructed and taught how to perform their part, and those are called workmen or handicrafts.

Superior to these, are the guides or masters, in such works or employments, and those are called artists, mechanics or craftsmen; and in general, all are understood in this one word mechanics; such are clothiers, weavers etc. handicrafts in hardware, brass, iron, steel, copper etc.

After these was entered the world of the true middle classes, the dealers, merchants and factors.[51] In 1709 in delineating the structure of society he had placed after the great, the rich, and the 'middle sort' who lived well, 'the working trades, who labour hard but feel no want'. Fifth came the country people, farmers etc. who 'fare indifferently', but many who were primarily dependent on manufacturing employment could be realistically placed in his sixth category, 'the poor that fare hard', or even his seventh, 'the miserable, that really pinch and suffer want'.[52]

To outsiders miners were simply miners, but in the mines it mattered a lot whether a man was a 'tributer' or 'tutworkman' in the Cornish mines, or a hewer or barrowman in the Northumberland pits. Status and earnings depended upon such distinctions.[53] The bricklayer or mason jealously guarded his wage and status differential over the common labourer or quarryman.[54]

In discussing the extent of manufacturing in rural as well as in urban areas much has already been implied about the location of industry in eighteenth-century England; however the scale and extent of manufacturing employment can be more completely understood through an examination in turn of the major industries. The greatest number of manufacturing workers were employed in the various branches of the textile trade. Massie's estimate was that in 1759 114,000 families depended upon this manufacture.[55] Wool in its two main divisions of woollen and worsted cloth was by far the most important and widespread branch in the eighteenth century. It had concentrated its main centres of activity into regions with distinctive specialisations. The serges (worsteds) were associated with Devonshire in a region centred on Exeter but reaching out to several Somerset towns including Taunton. Quite distinct from this region of the south-west was the great West Country broad-cloth area in which several kinds of woollen cloth of traditional form were made. Gloucestershire, Wiltshire, parts of Somerset and the fringes of Dorsetshire were all involved in this major manufacture. In Essex there was a long-established production centred around Colchester of lighter worsted cloths: 'Those stuffs which we see the nuns and friars clothed with abroad'.[56] The manufacture of worsteds was however more important and widespread in East Anglia, around Norwich, which Defoe described as a town which seemed almost without inhabitants to the visitor they 'being all busy at their manufactures, dwell in their garrets at their looms and in their combing shops . . . twisting mills and other workhouses almost all the works they are employed in, being done within doors'.[57] In the West Riding the woollen cloth manufacture was still based on the small capitalist working-clothier producing the increasingly marketable kersies, while around Leeds a worsted manufacture organised by large capitalists was developing. Writers from Defoe onwards capture the bustling activity of this region which was carrying it forward even before the factory and coal confirmed its pre-eminence. Outside these great regional centres there were local manufactures of some importance. Banbury's coarse cloth (shag) employed several hundred weavers still by the end of the century, while in Romsey the shalloon (worsted) manufacture occupied 500 weavers at the time of Young's visit in 1768. Kendal had a thriving group of textile trades, while specialised branches included the weaving of carpets at Axminster and Wilton and of blankets at Witney.[58]

The silk manufacture was more concentrated. London's Spitalfields region with several thousand hands dominated the broader cloth production, while Coventry specialised in the ribbon trade. Further north at Derby, Sir Thomas Lombe's mill for producing silk yarn established in 1717 was perhaps the first true textile factory. By 1770 his example had been followed at Stockport, Macclesfield, Sheffield and Watford.[59]

Cotton was the growth industry of the eighteenth century, the 'leading sector' of the early industrial revolution and the true pioneer of the modern factory system. From the beginning it was concentrated in Lancashire, importing its raw material through Liverpool. By 1751 there were 4,513 looms in Manchester alone used by the town journeymen, while all around it and around other leading centres like Bolton, Preston or Oldham were thousands of country weavers. In 1788 the cotton manufacture was said to have employed 26,000 male weavers, 31,000 women and 53,000 children in spinning and to have aggregated with all its other processes 159,000 men, 90,000 women and 101,000 children.[60]

The textile manufactures all involved a number of processes and a range of specialised employments of which only the more important can be considered here. Before the advent of the mill, spinning of wool and cotton was undertaken by women working at home assisted by children, both the wives of weavers and the country wives of farmers and their labourers. The throwing process by which silk yarn was produced was also a female by-employment before the mills. A much larger number of spinners was needed to keep a given number of weavers supplied, and the search for female labour reached far into the country districts. In London part at least of the opposition to women taking to the weaving of silk was due to the fear that too few hands would be left for preparing the yarn.[61] The weaver, although women were making encroachments in the production of all three textiles by the end of the century, was the central male craftsman in textile production. The element of skill needed was often played down by contemporaries, as it has also been by subsequent historians. Apprenticeship was rapidly declining in the craft, and few would have argued that it really took seven years of training to produce a competent weaver of plain cloth. The weavers none the less thought of themselves as skilled workers, and only misunderstanding of their attitudes and actions can result if that is not kept in mind. Hardly any of them were independent in the full sense and for the most part they formed an outworking proletariat, or a permanent town journeyman class. They supplied only their labour to work on materials owned by capitalist clothiers and put-out to their cottages or town garrets. Some worked in sheds or loomshops but even in the towns these were not typical. The notable exception was in the West Riding where the independent small clothier was himself a weaver.

The worsted cloths were made with long staple wool and needed the services of a skilled male worker, the comber. Their special skills and controlled numbers made them among the best paid of the woollen workers. In the finishing processes the shearmen or croppers were another group of skilled male workers who, using heavy hand-shears, cropped the cloth after its nap had first been raised. Their special position was threatened at the end of the century by the introduction of shearing frames. In cotton a group of workers of comparable status and skill was the calico printers who patterned the cloth. Originally a London-based trade they had become concentrated in Lancashire in the 1780s and enjoyed good wages and considerable standing from their scarce skill until the development of printing machinery threatened their livelihood in the 1790s.

The framework knitters turned yarn into stockings. Sometimes known as 'stockingers' they too provided employment for spinners and, in the case of worsted stockings, combers. The lace manufacture was a specialised branch of this trade. The stocking-frame had been invented in the sixteenth century, and although not at first much encouraged, it had substantially replaced the old hand-knitting of hose by the beginning of the eighteenth century. Defoe noted the decline of the latter at Stourbridge because of 'the increase of the knitting stocking engine or frame, which has destroyed the hand-knitting trade for fine stockings through the kingdom'. Originally based in London the frame-knitting manufacture had begun its move to the East Midlands before the end of the seventeenth century, both to use cheap labour and to escape the restrictions of the Hosiers' Company. Rapidly it became the mainstay of the economies of Leicestershire, Nottinghamshire and parts of Derbyshire. By 1727 there were 4,650 frames at work in the East Midlands, and in 1811 on the eve of the famous Luddite disturbances, perhaps 29,000 frames employing in and around the hosiery trade around 50,000 workers.[62] Fewer workers clothed the hands than did the legs, and the glove manufacture was less concentrated, but several thousand workers were employed at Worcester, the main centre, in the 1770s.[63]

In the metal trades the largest group of workers was the humble nailors. By the late-eighteenth century perhaps 10,000 of them consumed half of the iron output of the Midlands.[64] As well as in the Black Country they were numerous in the villages around Sheffield. The process was a simple one. Heated rods were cut to length on an anvil and the cut lengths placed in a hole on the anvil and given a sharp tap to head them. The tap caused the headed nail to fly out and another length was straightway put in the hole: a continuous process carried out at lightning speed. It was an occupation of low esteem but one which, with women working at the anvil as well as men, was the support of a great many families. Young found the road from Birmingham to West Bromwich was for five or six miles a continuous 'village of nailors'.[65]

Much more skilled were the metal workers of Sheffield employed in the cutlery and file manufactures. More than 6,000 persons probably worked at these trades by 1800, in addition to several hundred employed in the plating trade.[66] The cutlers worked in countless small forges attached to their homes on metal put-out to them by the master cutlers manufacturing files, axes, razors and forks as well as all kinds of knife. Sheffield dominated the 'edged tool' industry, but Birmingham was the greatest centre of general hardware manufacture in the world. Like Sheffield it was for the most part characterised not by large establishments but by 'little and distinct forges for works performed by a single hand'.[67] The city manufactured through these quasi-independent craftsmen and their labourers an amazing range of products not only from iron, but from tin, brass and copper: buckles, cutlery, spurs, candlesticks, toys, guns, buttons, whip handles, coffee pots, ink stands, carriage fittings, steam-engines, snuff boxes, lead pipes, jewellery, lamps and kitchen implements, coins and medals. It was this range which made it the 'metropolis of the small master'.[68] One major aspect of the town's manufacture was, however, a pioneering factory one in every sense. The famous Soho works of Mathew Boulton was already employing 700 people in 1770, before the great days of steam-engine manufacture in partnership with James Watt, and even Soho was smaller than the establishment of Boulton's great rival John Taylor.[69] Wolverhampton manufactured in many of these lines too, but specialised in locks, as did Darleston, Bilston and Wednesbury.[70]

Following the development of coke-smelting, the Coalbrookdale region of Shropshire had become the main centre and technological leader in iron production. Abraham Darby's works there impressed Young in 1776:

> Past his new slitting mills, which are not finished, but the immense wheels 20 feet diameter of cast iron were there, and appear wonderful. Viewed the furnaces, forges etc., with the vast bellows that gave those roaring blasts, which make the whole edifice horridly sublime. These works are supposed to be the greatest in England. The whole process is here gone through from digging the ironstone to making it into cannons, pipes, cylinders, etc. etc. All the iron used is raised in the neighbouring hills, and the coal dug likewise which is char'd . . . Mr Darby in his works employs near 1000 people including colliers.[71]

There were five furnaces in the Dale, two belonging to Darby and the largest of the others to the equally famous ironmaster, Wilkinson. Young's well-known observation that: 'All the activity and industry of this kingdom is fast concentrating where there are coal pits' was certainly true so far as heavy industry was concerned. At Rotherham he found the forging of bars and castings employing, with the miners who supplied it with coal, more than 500 men. Crawley's great iron works near Newcastle he supposed to be among the largest of its kind in Europe, employing 'several hundreds of workers' sufficient to bring its annual wage bill to £12,000.[72] However, at Sheffield water-power still drove the tilting mill, a 'blacksmith's immense hammer in constant motion', with such force that a trembling motion could be felt while leaning on a gate 'at three perches distance'.[73]

Shipbuilding and repair in the eighteenth century employed craftsmen in wood not metal. Carpenters, joiners, cabinet-makers and wheelwrights were employed all over the country, but the shipyards employed the greatest concentrations of workers in wood. Largest of all were the six naval dockyards, which between them in 1772 employed more than 8,000 workers at Deptford, Woolwich, Chatham, Sheerness, Portsmouth and Plymouth. Numbers employed fluctuated a good deal according to whether the country was at peace or war. Not all of the craftsmen and labourers worked in wood. Out of an establishment of 2,704 at Portsmouth in 1803, 900 were shipwrights, 140 sawyers and 100 general carpenters. There were in addition 200 ropemakers, 140 caulkers and 350 general labourers.[74] Private yards tended to be smaller but at places like Liverpool, Bristol and the Thames yards needed large numbers of workers in similar proportions.

Craftsmen like tailors and shoemakers worked at making and mending in every town and many villages. However the large-scale manufacture of clothes and shoes was especially evident in London and there was a world of experience separating the village cobbler or tailor from the thousands of journeymen who filled two of the poorest of the larger London trades. Hatters had more status. Petitions from them in 1777 show their manufacture to have existed in several places in the provinces as well as London, but they were principally concentrated there and in Manchester and Stockport. A well-organised body of men they were among the first to form effective trade unions. There was work for printers in every sizeable town, especially with the growth through the century of the provincial newspaper, but again it was in London that the major printing works for the national press, the book and periodical trade and parliamentary bills and papers gave work for around 2,500 journeymen by 1818.[75] The bookbinders were an allied trade. London also dominated watchmaking, although before the end of the century it had become important in Coventry also.

Miners were not strictly manufacturing workers; their occupation is indisputably a special one. Coal production had been increasing since Tudor times. Production trebled between 1680 and 1780,[76] but it is difficult to estimate the total number of miners employed, which may have been between 12,000 and 15,000 by the late-seventeenth century.[77] By 1708 the mining around Newcastle was said to have been employing several thousands, and even Arthur Young, who was usually willing enough to offer a figure, on his visit to that area in 1771 wrote simply of 'many thousands' and of the miners being 'prodigiously numerous'. Old centres like the Forest of Dean employed very considerably less, there being 662 'free miners' in 1778. At the end of the seventeenth century there were only 123 colliers at Kingswood near Bristol, but their numbers must have increased significantly and rapidly for them to have become by the middle of the eighteenth century the food-rioting terrors of the district, and the first large congregations for the open-air preaching of the Methodists. Pits employing more than 100 miners were not uncommon in the Midlands, Lancashire or York-shire and with coal production in 1800 at more than 10 million tonnes compared with 2.5 million in 1700 the number of coalminers in England and Wales can hardly have numbered less than 50,000 and was most probably considerably more.[78]

More accurate figures are available for the tin and copper miners of Cornwall. A count of copper miners was made for Boulton and Watt in 1787 which lists 7,196 employees out of which 2,684 were women and child surface workers. Tin miners were not counted but probably would have added around 2,000 men. Such figures warn against the reliability of contemporary 'guesstimates' such as 20,000 (Pryce, 1778) and 40,000 (Stebbing Shaw, 1788). A 1799 figure of between 9,000 and 11,000 copper-mine employees including women seems reasonable.[79] Copper was also mined in Cumberland, but on an insignificant scale, and towards the end of the century the easily-obtained ore reserves of Anglesey were exploited in a spectacular but short-lived boom. Copper was not refined in Cornwall to any real extent, but shipped to South Wales where coal was more readily and cheaply available. The Mendip area from which the Romans had obtained so much of their lead was of no importance by the eighteenth century. The main centres by then were the Derby-shire Peaks and the Northern Pennines. In the latter region the popula-tion of the leading district Alston Moor grew from 300 in 1738 to a peak of 1,400 in 1766, falling to 612 by 1802.[80] In all, metal mining must have employed at least 13,000 miners by the end of the eighteenth century.

The industries so far outlined were the most significant employers, but others provided considerable employment between them. Not far behind the leaders was the pottery industry, rapidly concentrating its mass-production side on the 'five towns' around Burslem, where the tireless Josiah Wedgwood was rationalising its production methods. But there were other centres for the finer china and porcelain manufacture. Worcester had a reputation which it has ever since maintained, and Liverpool possessed a not inconsiderable manufacture. It also produced considerable quantities of glassware as did Bristol.[81] Sailcloth making employed 300 male weavers at Warrington and was a significant em-ployer also at Reading.[82]

Such a variety of manufactures spread over so extensive an area is bound

to make generalisation on any aspect of labour conditions or organisation difficult. One which is safe is that only a minority of the workers
was employed in large-scale production units of any kind. The factory
through the eighteenth century waited off-stage, making a few preco-
cious entries before pressing for admission to the final acts of the closing
decades. William Hutton who began work as a child in the Derby silk
mill in 1730 cursed his luck at being born in that city, implying that
anywhere else he would have escaped the factory. As we have seen,
similar silk mills had been established in a few other towns before the
end of the 1760s, but as Young noted of the one at Sheffield in 1771
their employees were chiefly women and children.[83] Since this was
also true of the early cotton-spinning mills on both the Arkwright and
Compton principles, of which there may have been around 900 by the
end of the century, factory employment can hardly be at the centre of
the concern of the historian of the adult male worker even by the 1790s.
The number of spinning mills needs placing in the perspective of aggre-
gate capacity. The 900 mills of 1797 consumed 33,000 lb of raw cotton
compared with the 1,125 mills which consumed 270,000 lb in 1833/4.
Only with the adoption of mule spinning did adult male factory employment become important, but as late as 1816 adult males accounted for
only 17.7 per cent of cotton mill employees in Lancashire and 18.4 per
cent in Nottinghamshire.[84] For the textile weaver the effect of the
spinning mills was to increase vastly the numbers of handloom weavers
to keep pace with the mass-produced yarn. Between 1795 and 1811 the
cotton handloom weavers increased from 75,000 to 225,000.[85] In wool,
a more difficult fibre for machinery to process, the pace of factory
development was even more slow. The face of Yorkshire had altered
little by 1800 and according to the industry's historian: 'half a century
had still to elapse before it could be claimed that the factory and the
power driven machinery had displaced the old hand methods'. There
were scarcely twenty factories in Yorkshire in 1800.[86]

If factories employed only an insignificant number of adult male
workers by the end of the century, what kinds of enterprise did con-
centrate large groups of workers? Probably the royal dockyards led the
field. Portsmouth had an establishment of 2,228 in 1772, Plymouth
2,033, Chatham 1,553, Deptford 939, Woolwich 868 and Sheerness
439.[87] By the end of the century several copper mines in Cornwall were
approaching such levels. In 1790 Wheal Alfred employed 1,000 men,
women and children, and Herland 300 miners besides the women and
the children on the surface. Tin Croft and Cooks Kitchen employed
similar numbers.[88] Ashton and Sykes regarded an eighteenth-century

coal mine employing 100 colliers as large, and a considerable number in Northumberland, Yorkshire, Lancashire and the Midlands qualified, although the average was around 40.[89]

Intermediate between the large establishment and the home-working out-worker with his family, an apprentice or two and perhaps a journey-man, was the 'workshop'. The 'shop' was the usual place of employment for workers in a wide range of trades. Here they experienced daily labour neither in isolation nor in large impersonal crowds, but in groups of moderate size. Woolcombers, shearmen, tailors, hatters, printers, coopers, coachmakers and some shoemakers and weavers, all worked in such 'shops'. The size of these groups, perhaps 10-20 men, provided an ideal basis for trade organisation. Most weavers, however, along with knitters, nailors, cutlers and many shoemakers were representative of the home-based out-worker.

Professor Lipson has pointed out very forcefully that the rise of a wage system as a characteristic of capitalism, stems not from the use of machinery, but from the 'divorce of the workers from the ownership of the material in which they worked'. With the loss of the right to dispose of his finished product, the manual craftsman became the labourer working for hire, even if he still worked unsupervised at home and still retained a 'property' in his craft skill. This was the basis for the 'perennial struggle between capital and labour'.[90] Adam Smith recognised that the eighteenth century was one by which the separation of labour from capital had become usual, stating that in Europe 20 workmen served under a master for every one that was independent: 'In all arts and manufactures the greater part of the workmen stand in need of a master to advance them the materials of their work, and their wages and maintenance till it be completed'. The wages of labour were to be everywhere understood to be 'what they usually are' when the labourer was one person and the owner of the stock which employed him another.[91] Even in London the great centre of the craft trades, the self-employed, according to a recent attempt at qualification, amounted to only 5 or 6 per cent of the working-class population. Master, as we have seen, if claimed as a title by many craftsmen, implied them only to be masters of their craft, not employers of labour.[92]

What had been most important in accomplishing this state of affairs had been the development of the *putting-out* system. In this mode of production a central capitalist put-out the materials to the worker to make up at a piece rate (usually called 'price') and collected and marketed the finished product. Separation was strikingly evident when the wealth of the putting-out capitalist was contrasted with the wages of

the worker. The system reached its most early and complete development in the woollen districts of the West Country where the 'gentleman
clothiers' had developed a hold on the manufacture well before the end
of the seventeenth century. Defoe was told it was not unusual for such
men to be worth from £10,000 to £40,000. They lived in the greater
towns sending out wool 'by their servants and horses' to the country
spinners and weavers. A clothier might at full trade employ a great
number of out-working weavers comparable at very least with the
factory masters of the next century.[93] Only in the West Riding did a
very different system of woollen manufacture predominate. In the
cotton, silk and hosiery trades putting-out methods were usual in the
eighteenth century, as they were in nail making, cutlery and many
branches of the hardware manufacture.

In some industries, especially framework knitting, dependence on
the capitalist was intensified by the system under which frames were
rented from the hosier as well as work taken in. An out-working weaver
or knitter might be at the same time both dependent wage earner and
himself employer if, during a brisk trade, he was encouraged to obtain
an additional loom or frame and hire a journeyman to work it. But this
in no sense affected the dependent relationship in which he stood to
the master clothier or hosier. Probably there was in both wool and
cotton weaving a rhythm to loom-owning. Setting out with one loom,
a weaver might add another when he took an apprentice, and reach a
maximum number when he had grown children to work alongside him.
As he grew older and his children set out on their own, his looms again
declined in number. Such men if they took apprentices and, for a time,
a journeyman, could at best be described as 'wage-earning small masters',
so long as they were not confused with the small clothiers of the West
Riding, who were fully independent. In the early days of the cotton
manufacture it may have been possible for some of these weavers to rise
to the ranks of 'employing manufacturers', but there is little certainty
about how easy such upward mobility was.[94] In the west and east of
England woollen districts the gap was unbridgeable. In the silk manufacture in Spitalfields small and large masters existed side by side as
late as 1823, but the trend was unmistakably towards greater capitalisation.[95]

'A journeyman', defined a writer supporting the London tailors in
their dispute of 1745, 'is understood to be one, who has by apprenticeship or other contract, served such a portion of his time to that particular business which he professes to occupy, as renders him capable to
execute every branch or part of the trade, whereby he is at full liberty,

if his ability and condition of life will permit, to set up in the world as a *master of his profession* (my italics); and is only called a Journeyman while he continues to serve under the direction of others at certain wages.'[96] We have already noted that in most of the textile areas the term 'journeyman' was applicable to very few weavers who formed a not-very-skilled part of the dependent artisanry, being technically piece-rate home-working craftsmen. But the situation was very different in several of the London craft trades. Wherever large amounts of capital were needed to set up as an employer, or even as an independent producer, and where work was carried out in 'shops' rather than at home, then the wage-earning journeyman on his master's premises was likely to be the representative workman, and his employee situation a permanent one. In some trades like calico printing it was the cost of equipment which was the impediment, while in others like tailoring or shoemaking it was the cost of renting and maintaining premises in 'respectable' areas, and of being able to allow rich customers credit, which prevented journeymen from becoming independent at other than the poor end of the trade. At the poor end independence was possible, but often so un-remunerative that journeymen's wages were preferable. For the most part the journeymen tailors of London who were 'as common as locusts' and as 'poor as rats', worked in the shops of the larger master tailors and were the representative workmen of their craft: 'It is a fact that the Journeymen, and not the masters, who are the artificers as well as labourers in that trade or calling' and they 'a multitude of poor laborious men' were 'grievously oppressed' by 'a few purse-proud idle pretenders, either to ingenuity or labour'. Given that little in the way of expensive equipment or stock was required, it was still possible for an individual like Francis Place through ambition, luck, credit and above all prodigious effort to cross the line, but such exceptions were rare. The large employers preferred to keep an available, cheap, dependent labour force and discouraged independence. There were complaints that under the law which denied journeymen tailors the right to refuse work offered at statutory wages, masters forced men to take journeywork: 'notwith-standing the journeyman may have a prospect of being a master himself, which consequently his master will endeavour to prevent'.[97]

There were many gradations in shoemaking. At the richer 'bespoke' end of the trade the labour process was subdivided with the 'clicker' cutting out the uppers, the 'closer' closing them, while the 'maker' put the sole and heel on. However, hundreds of small independent shoe-makers still worked in their traditional garrets with perhaps the assistance of an apprentice.[98] So poor were some of the independent shoemakers that a new trade of leather-cutting had grown up in which 'decayed' shoemakers were employed at low wages cutting large pieces of leather into pieces small enough to be purchased by the 'garret-maker' who was often unable to lay out more than enough to buy materials for one pair of boots or shoes at a time. These 'cutters' had survived despite the efforts of the larger employers to prevent the increase of independent makers creating a shortage of journeyman labour for their shops. In 1738 they attempted to persuade Parliament into a prohibition of selling less than whole hides at a time. At the Leadenhall Market these would have cost at least £10 each. A committee heard evidence from several shoemakers on the issue. One claimed that for 2s a man could buy enough leather to maintain his family for the week when made up. Another that 5s worth of leather could be turned into a product worth 10s in two days' work. There were probably only 500 shoemakers in the whole of London who could afford to buy whole hides, and their object was to reduce the independent makers to journeywork: 'the master shoemakers do not care that journeymen should work for themselves'.[99]

By 1777 only 50 master hatters in London worked up their own materials and took apprentices. For the most part hatters when out of their time worked in shops under the supervision of foremen. Some paid a 'waiting' rent to another person to work in his shop when their employer had not room enough in his own premises. But there was also in the trade another type of master, the 'little master' who worked at home on delivered-out materials for the larger masters, but who was a sub-contractor rather than a piece-worker. These men were not highly regarded and were not allowed by the powerful journeymen's union to take apprentices.[100] The journeymen hatters may have had little prospect of becoming masters, but they were a confident, well-organised, powerful body of men who through their control of apprenticeship preserved good weekly wages of around 15s a week.[101] Journeymen printers were similarly situated, enjoying if they worked regularly, the comfort of £1 a week or more, even though they complained in 1809 that the capital cost of setting-up independently was too great to offer them hope of emerging from a journeyman condition, and, with great exaggeration, claimed that the possibility still remained in 'most working businesses' which offered 'almost a moral certainty' to their employees that by 'industry, economy, and prudence, they may sooner or later emerge from the condition of journeymen'. In contrast the compositors drudged on to the end of their lives with prospects blackening as years advanced.[102] In fact they were a well-organised body of men with wages for the most part superior to the shaky incomes of many 'garret-masters' for all the independence of the latter. No ordinary journeyman could hope to raise the capital to set up independently as a coachmaker, but Campbell thought that the business was 'genteel and profitable enough' both to the master and the journeymen, whose 5s a day were good wages in a trade not overstocked with hands.[103]

In many trades distinctions in status could only be drawn with difficulty. Journeymen not only took work by the piece, but even sometimes employed other journeymen.[104] Large masters might dominate the richer end of a trade, while still leaving the unprofitable end to small men, whose standards were lower than those of many a group of permanent journeymen; especially those of the latter whose recognition of the separation of interest implied by their lifelong employee status had led them to organise effectively to control entry into their trades. In the watchmaking trade 'putting-out' had developed to an extent comparable with cloth manufacture. By mid-century in London the division of labour was such that hardly any journeyman could have produced a whole watch and the watchmaker whose name appeared on the article was that of the shopman retailing it: 'though he has not made in his shop the smallest wheel belonging to it'.[105] Half the population of Clerkenwell was dependent on the manufacture, perhaps to the extent by the end of the century of 8,000 hands. One 'maker' made between 3-4,000 watches in 1795/6 employing over 100 men in making the separate components in their Clerkenwell garrets. Although most of these workmen would have considered themselves outworkers on piece rates, others might be regarded as 'chamber' or garret masters making parts and offering them for sale.[106]

Few were so humble as the pinmakers who could expect to earn no more than a common labourer in a manufacture where the making was so sub-divided that it supplied Adam Smith with his famous illustration of the division of labour. But at the beginning of the century, pinmakers were not journeymen but home workers who purchased their own wire. Being poor they could do so only in small parcels from 'second and third buyers' as they needed it. Desperation forced them to sell their pins from week to week as soon as they were made at beaten-down prices for ready money to feed their families and buy their next 'small parcel of wire'.[107]

There were still some trades offering a decent possibility of the traditional apprentice-through-journeyman-to-master mobility. Trades where the costs of setting-up were not low, but within the reach of a journeyman saving from sound earnings at constant employment, included cabinet-making, saddle-making, lock-making and engraving.[108] Within trades there was often an internal hierarchy of status from 'genteel' through the ordinary to the 'mean', 'nasty', 'stinking' or 'starving'. A cabinet-maker at one end of the market might own a palace of a shop, at the other little more than a set of tools. Any trade where the apprenticeship premium was as low as £5 was likely to offer poor prospects, and where a trade was especially disagreeable there might be no premium at all, and employers like the chimneysweeps relied on the parish for a supply of exploitable young labour. Tailoring was a low-premium trade and much overstocked, but even within it there was a division in status among the journeymen, between the 'flints' who worked on day wages, and the less-skilled 'dungs' who were prepared to take under-cutting piece rates.[109] Among the independent, the quality of the customer was a fair indication of the standing of the master. There was a world of difference between a master shoemaker with a shop full of journeymen sewing slippers for genteel ladies, and the poor cobbler at the other end of town toiling with a parish apprentice, and spending more time repairing and remaking boots than crafting fine footwear.

In the metal working trades of Birmingham and Sheffield, the artisans were for the most part dependent upon materials put-out to them and did not in general market their own product. However, the small scale of operations gave them a special kind of independence, which lay behind the distinctive 'artisan culture' which historians have found in these towns. Birmingham was a 'matrix of small workshops'. There were employers in brass founding with a capital of £20,000, but there were hundreds with a very small capital concentrating on the production of a particular article of hardware: 'for one man makes a drawer knob, another a commode handle, another a bell-pull etc. etc.' If the masters tried to pay less than fair journeyman rates then: 'the man has nothing to do but go and manufacture the article himself'.[110] So little capital was needed to set up the small forges characteristic of Sheffield that: 'a man with a very small sum of money can employ two, three, or four men'.[111] In such towns the small investment needed blurred the line between dependent artisan working at piece rates on put-out material, and small master producing on a sub-contract basis perhaps even for the very same merchant capitalist who put-out materials to other men.

The most heralded of all the 'independent' craftsmen surviving and flourishing until the very end of the century were the woollen clothiers of the West Riding. Something has already been described of their houses surrounded by a few fields giving a characteristic aspect to the area. Defoe's description of the manufacture around Halifax has become something of a classic:

> Among the manufacturers' houses are likewise scattered an infinite
> number of cottages or small dwellings in which dwell the workmen
> which are employed, the women and children of whom are always
> busy carding, spinning etc. so that no hands are . . . unemployed . . .
> If we knocked at the door of any of the master manufacturers we
> presently saw a house full of lusty fellows, some at the dye-fat, some
> dressing the cloths, some in the loom, some one thing, some another,
> all hard at work, and full employed upon the manufacture, and all
> seeming to have sufficient business.[112]

Defoe did not employ the term 'manufacturer' unless he was describing
someone who was actually engaged in the production process: the
organising non-working entrepreneurs of the West Country he termed
'master clothiers'. The houses described are then clearly those of the
working small masters, carrying on the cloth manufacture in the 'domestic' manner. A late-eighteenth-century estimate gives around 3,240
master broadcloth makers in the West Riding.[113] A witness contrasted
the area with the West Country for the benefit of a parliamentary committee in 1806. In that region there was:

> No such thing as what we in Yorkshire call the domestic system;
> what I mean by the domestic system is the little clothiers living in
> villages, or in detached places, with all their comforts, carrying on
> business with their own capital . . . I understand that in the west of
> England it is quite the reverse of that, the manufacturer there is the
> same as our common workman in a factory in Yorkshire, except
> living in a detached house; in the west the wool is delivered out to
> them to weave, in Yorkshire it is the man's own property.[114]

They bought the wool from the dealers and assisted by their wives,
children, apprentices and perhaps from two to six journeymen, took
it through all its stages to undressed cloth. Perhaps the system was in
decline by the last years of the eighteenth century, with the putting-
out system which had in any case always predominated in the worsted
manufacture around Leeds making encroachments, but it was nevertheless the characteristic form of woollen cloth manufacture in the West
Riding in the eighteenth century.[115] Contemporary approval rested not
so much on a presumed economic efficiency as on a paternalistic moral
superiority: 'The dispersed state of the manufacturers in villages and

single houses over the whole face of the country is highly favourable to their morals and happiness,' wrote John Aiken in 1795. A model was idealised in which there was no wide gulf between the small clothier and his journeyman, for not only did they work side-by-side at the dye-vat or loom, but given small capital needs the journeyman could still expect to become himself a master clothier. Such a system was thought to have been 'highly favourable to the paternal, filial, and fraternal happiness — and to the cultivation of good moral and civil habits — the sources of public tranquillity'.[116] The 'family' atmosphere with the work involving not just the loom, but fetching and carrying from market and the tasks around the small farm is caught in a somewhat idealised manner in a poem of 1730, which describes the 'master' and 'dame' seated around a common table with the weavers, Tom, Will, Jack and Joe, who may have been sons, apprentices or journeymen, or perhaps a mixture of all three. After breakfasting on a leg of mutton brought by 'prentice Bess, they get to work weaving from 'five at morn till eight at neet'. At the end of the day they sit down together for supper and the master sets out the tasks ahead for the morrow:

> Quoth Maister — 'Lads, work hard, I pray,
> Cloth mun be peark'd next market-day,
> And Tom mun go tomorn to t'spinners,
> And Will mun seek about for t'swingers;
> And Jack tomorn, by time be rising,
> And go to t'sizing mill for sizing,
> And get your web and warping done
> That ye may get it into t'loom.
> Joe — go give my horse some corn
> For I design for t'Wolds tomorn;
> So mind and clean my boots and shoon,
> For I'll be up i' t'morn right soon!
> Mary — there's wool — tak thee and dye it
> Its that 'at ligs in th' clouted sheet!

But Mary, the mistress of the house, has something to say about being allotted a special task:

> So thou's setting me my work,
> I think I'd more need mend thy sark,
> 'Prithie, who mun sit at bobbin weel?
> And ne'er a cake at top o' th' creel!

And we to bake; and swing and blend,
And milk, and bairns to school to send,
And dumplings for the lads to mak,
And yeast to seek, and syk as that!
And washing up, morn, noon, and neet,
And bowls to scald, and milk to fleet,
And bairns to fetch again at neet!

Her husband fully appreciates all that must be done, but she and Bessy, the servant lass, must get up 'soon and stir about and get all done' for the manufacture must take clear priority:

For all things mun aside be laid —
When we want help about our trade.

The master and dame go off to spend the rest of the evening with a neighbour, while the young men joined by a lad and lass from a neighbouring household sit happily around a good coal fire: 'More free from care than knight or squire'.[117]

It is of course an idealised picture, but its contrast with the west-country weavers' poem *The Clothiers' Delight* is striking and can be used to make the point about the difference in relationship between master and men in the domestic system of the West Riding and the capitalist controlled putting-out system in the West Country in an 'ideal' way. That second poem is sub-titled 'The Rich Men's Joy and the Poor Men's Sorrow', and the first verse concludes:

We live at our pleasure, and take out delight;
We heapeth up riches and treasure great store,
Which we get by griping and grinding the poor.
(*refrain*) And this is a way for to fill up our purse,
        Although we do get it with many a curse.

A concluding verse repeats the contrast:

Then hay for the Clothing Trade, it goes on brave;
We scorn for to toyl and moyl, nor yet to starve.
Our workmen do work hard, but we live at ease;
We go when we will, and come when we please;
We hoard up our bags of silver and gold;
But conscience and charity with us are cold.[118]

The two poems present an obvious polarisation. There were times when relations between masters and men could be friendly and mutually regarding even under the putting-out system. In a well-known passage Samuel Bamford contrasted in a 'conversation' between a weaver and his putting-out employer in the cotton trade, the caring attitude of the 'old' masters with the uncaring, exploitative ones of the new race of capitalists.[119]

Simple day-wage labourers were not the representative type in eighteenth-century manufacturing as a whole, but in some industries they had become so, working often under foremen. Such was the case in the brewing, distilling and sugar-boiling trades with high capital costs and large-scale operations. In the paint trade, the mixing of the colours, the real element of skill in the traditional craft of the house-painter, was by mid-century taking place in paint shops employing unskilled labour. Similar trends had taken place in the manufacture of white and red lead, printers' ink and glue. The master dyers were anxious to follow suit and sought in 1777 a parliamentary dispensation from statutory apprenticeship requirements. The portering and carrying trades of various kinds employed large numbers of labourers, but some branches like the keelmen of the Tyne and Wear and the lighter men and coal-heavers of the Thames, preserved their status and income by exercising a control over entry to their trade as effective as that of many craft workers, confining their recruitment to a circle of relatives and friends.[120]

Miners were rarely recruited or paid as common day labourers. They followed an occupation in which physical strength needed to be combined with skilled operation of tools and a selectivity in the quality of coal or ore sent to the surface. In metal mines there was usually a division between the men who raised the actual ore, and the men who worked the 'dead' ground driving levels and sinking shafts. Both usually worked on a form of sub-contract measured by the task, but with the precise form often very sophisticated in relating to the precise productivity emphasis needed. In the north-east coalfields the pitmen were hired by the year under the 'bond' system, which if it prevented men from moving freely from one employer to another, at least gave them a powerful collective renegotiating position when all the bonds came up collectively for renewal. In the coalmines outside the north-east the bond system was not in use, and the hated 'butty' system of gang sub-contracting through middle men had not yet come into being. Colliers could view themselves as equal members of contracting gangs working for piece rates. Coal mining requires the shifting of a much larger amount of material than does selective metal mining, and the division of labour between the 'hewers' and the 'barrowmen' was the basic one in the north-east. The removal of the excavated coal in trucks pulled by women or small children was not unknown in the eighteenth century but it was undoubtedly increased and intensified in the nineteenth.[121]

The subject matter of this book is the labouring life of adult males. The part played by women and children was a significant, and in the view of contemporaries, an essential one. Women workers have already their historian, and here no more than a brief description of their place in manufacturing can be given. There were three main ways in which female labour was used. There were some, but not many, female craft trades; women as well as children formed the cheap labour force of the early factories and they were an essential part of the functioning of the household unit of production which was the basis of the putting-out and domestic systems of manufacture. The male weaver took the name of the trade and for the most part did perform the core craft operation, but the family was necessary to perform the many subsidiary but essential operations in the making of cloth.[122]

There is little to be said of the specifically female craft trades. Campbell in his survey of 1747 thought the pay of such as milliners, mantua-makers and stay and bodice-makers so low compared even with that of male labourers, that prostitution was an almost inevitable accompaniment, and regarded many milliners' premises as little more than brothels: 'Take a survey of all the common women of the town, who take their walks between Charing Cross and Fleet Ditch, and I am persuaded more than half of them have been bred milliners'.[123]

Women were essential to all branches of the textile manufacture as spinners, with the wives and daughters of country people working in extensive areas all around the main wool and cotton districts. They received low wages, but lifted the family income of the rural labourer's household.[124] The stocking manufacture as well as the cloth needed its army of female spinners, around Derby 300 women employed in spinning jersey brought forth Hutton's comment on 'humble beauty' toiling for 2s 6d a week. Until the coming of mule spinning the production of the yarn continued to be the work of women and children in the early factory era. The sad aspect of the cotton mills of Lancashire had already been anticipated in the silk mills of Derby and other places, such as Sheffield where Young in 1771 saw 152 women and children working for 5-6s a week in the case of the former, and 1s or 1s 2d in the case of the latter.[125] Women were employed around metal mines picking and sorting ores, especially in copper and lead. Defoe's cave-dwelling Peak miner's wife earned 3d a day washing ores whenever her domestic commitment to her children and smallholding allowed her.[126]

Most important, however, was the role of women and children within a family unit of production. The common structural foundation of rural industry under the putting-out system — whether one insists on employing such marginally useful and partially applicable terms as the now fashionable 'proto-industrialisation', or not — was the close association between household production based on the family economy on the one hand and the capitalist organisation of trade, putting-out and marketing of the products on the other.[127] Historians have recently insisted that it is the links between demography, economic production and the family which constitute the basic structural-functional aspect of rural manufacturing before the machine age. The opportunity for manufacturing employment undermined the demographic basis of agrarian society. In so far as independence had been a necessary condition for marriage, the age at marriage was kept high as the retirement or death of a parent was needed to bring control of farm or workshop. A prudent lifestyle in such a society depended upon late marriage. The industrial worker able to enter earning independence at an earlier age had a positive as well as a permissive incentive to marry younger, for the labour of a wife and children was essential to his occupation. Hence not only earlier marriage, but also larger families were encouraged by the spread of rural manufacturing.

It can be argued that the prosperity of a weaving household was tied to the family cycle: with the birth of children the parents came under strain, but with their growing up the earning potential of the family reached its height, while with their leaving to marry, poverty descended once more.[128] The role of the wife as industrial 'helpmate' was not confined to the rural clothing trade. A London hatter reckoned that the services of his wife in picking the coarse hairs out of his material saved him anything from 6s to 9s 4d a week, out of his wage in 1824 of between £2-3.[129]

The great merit of manufacturing to observers like Defoe lay precisely in its employment of the whole family, including children. There was not, he remarked, in the clothing districts of Norfolk: 'any hand unemployed, if they would work; and that the very children after four or five years of age, could everyone earn their own bread'. In the West Riding he saw 'hardly anything above a few years old, but its hands are sufficient to itself'. He made similar comments at Taunton and in Essex.[130] Arthur Young a generation later was similarly moved to remark

of Manchester: 'large families in this place are no incumbrance; all are
set to work'. William Temple, the best known of the west-country
clothiers' polemicists, stressed that it was the *family* earnings of the
weaver which lifted him above the condition of the farm worker.[131] Child
labour not only existed but was lauded and widespread in eighteenth-
century manufacturing. This does not in itself make 'sentimentalists'
of those who present a dark picture of the 'Satanic mills' of the early
industrial revolution. No one supposes child labour to have been a creation of the factory system, but it must take on a qualitatively different
nature when removed from the home and even the locality of upbring-
ing. Claims for a continuation of the parental supervision role into the
early cotton mills do not really modify this substantial differentiation
and in any event have been effectively challenged since they were first
put forward. In fact by removing pauper contract labour from southern
districts to provide the factory apprentices of the cotton mills, the
northern masters not only systematised child labour, but brutalised it.
It may have been only a 'stage' in the evolution of the factory labour
force, and a fairly short-lived one, but no amount of special pleading
can hide the fact that it happened.[132]

Child labour in the family cottage was no bed of roses. Samuel Bamford recalled that bobbin winding with his aunt for his weaver uncle
was work of a 'cramping, confining and boring nature'. He often was
led by boredom to acts of teasing mischief to the exasperation of his
aunt who dealt him many a quick rap with her rod, but the atmosphere
was a relaxed one in which his uncle could laugh when his nephew's
pranks were related to him. William Hutton had very different memories
of his childhood in Derby's silk mill. He began at 5 am from the age of
eight, and bore the scars of corporal punishment for the rest of his life.
He was so small at first that special pattens had to be made to give him
the inches to reach the machinery. One does not have to go so far as
Mr Laslett's 'extra sons and daughters' working in a 'circle of affection',
to see that under domestic production conditions, apprentices must be
counted as part of a 'family' unit even if conditions were very often less
'homely' that those portrayed in the poem on the clothiers of the West
Riding given above.[133] Cruelty to apprentices was common enough in
eighteenth-century manufacturing, but it is absurd to play down the
very real differences between the factory and the household, both in
terms of environment and in terms of the social relations characteristic
of each.

The family was the main determinant of the occupation its progeny
would follow. For the most part sons followed naturally into the trades

of their fathers. Often there was little or no alternative. But there were a good many exceptions. Indeed there had to be, for in some skilled crafts deliberate attempts to prevent overstocking produced prohibitions by trade unions on all but one son following his father's trade.[134] Even where this did not apply, over several generations a variety of trades might be followed within an artisan's family. William Hutton's great-great-grandfather had been a hatter; his great-grandfather a shearman; his grandfather a flaxdresser and his father a woolcomber. His case illustrates the importance of the wider family, for like many others, he was apprenticed to his uncle, a framework knitter. Marriage could increase opportunities for in-laws. Francis Place might not have become the 'radical tailor' at all if he had not quarrelled with his brother-in-law who had begun to teach him the fairly good trade of chair-carving.[135]

Notes

1. Daniel Defoe, *A Plan of the English Commerce* (1728, reprinted Oxford, 1928), p. 67.

2. B.A. Holderness, *Pre-industrial England. Economy and Society from 1500 to 1750* (London, 1976), p. 83.

3. H. Perkin, *The Origins of Modern English Society 1780-1880* (London, 1969), p. 31; P. Deane, *The First Industrial Revolution* (Cambridge, 1965), p. 16.

4. P. Deane and W.A. Cole, *British Economic Growth 1688-1959*, 2nd edn (Cambridge, 1969), p. 142, Table 30.

5. P. Mathias, 'The Social Structure in the Eighteenth Century: A Calculation by Joseph Massie', reprinted in *The Transformation of England* (London, 1979), pp. 180-1.

6. See J.G. Rule, 'Some Social Aspects of the Industrial Revolution in Cornwall' in R. Burt (ed.), *Industry and Society in the South West* (Exeter, 1970), pp. 72-3.

7. J.G. Rule, 'The Labouring Miner in Cornwall c. 1740-1870: A Study in Social History', unpublished PhD thesis, University of Warwick, 1971, p. 99.

8. Arthur Young, *A Six Months Tour Through the North of England*, 2nd edn (London, 1771), Vol. II, pp. 218-19, 261-3.

9. A.P. Wadsworth and J. de L. Mann, *The Cotton Trade and Industrial Lancashire 1600-1780* (Manchester, 1931), pp. 102, 316-17, footnote to p. 311, pp. 325-6.

10. H. Heaton, *The Yorkshire Woollen and Worsted Industries* (Oxford, 1920), p. 292.

11. Daniel Defoe, *A Tour Through the Whole Island of Great Britain* (Everyman edition, two volumes, reprinted London, 1962), Vol. II, p. 195.

12. Ibid., p. 193.

13. J. Aikin, *A Description of the Country from Thirty to Forty Miles round Manchester* (London, 1795; reprinted New York, 1968), pp. 93, 573.

14. Ibid., p. 312.

15. Arthur Young, *Tours in England and Wales selected from The Annals of Agriculture* (London, 1932), pp. 140, 142, 259 (footnote).

16. E.P. Thompson, *The Making of the English Working Class* (Harmondsworth, 1968 edn), p. 157.

17. Wadsworth and Mann, *Cotton Trade*, p. 317; Rule, 'Labouring Miner', p. 81.

18. Young, *Northern Tour*, Vol. II, p. 263.

19. Rule, 'Labouring Miner', p. 98.

20. Ibid., p. 95.

21. Rule, 'Industrial Revolution in Cornwall', p. 73 (footnote).

22. Young, *Northern Tour*, Vol. II, pp. 264-70.

23. J.H. Drew, *Samuel Drew, M.A. – The Self-taught Cornishman* (1861), pp. 17, 22; J.B. Cornish (ed.), *The Autobiography of a Cornish Smuggler* (1894, reprinted Truro, 1971), p. 2; J.H. Harris, *John Harris, the Cornish Poet. The Story of his Life* (n.d.), p. 10.

24. See especially the poem 'Descriptive of the Manners of the Clothiers' written about 1730 and reprinted in Heaton, *Woollen and Worsted Industries*, pp. 344-6.

25. W. Pryce, *Mineralogia Cornubiensis* (Oxford, 1778), p. 35.

26. Letter book of Henry Hindley, reprinted in J. de L. Mann (ed.), *Documents Illustrating the Wiltshire Textile Trades in the Eighteenth Century* (Devizes, 1964), doc. nos. 262, 275, 398, 406, 413, 592.

27. D. Hey, *The Rural Metalworkers of the Sheffield Region* (Leicester, 1972), p. 34.

28. Defoe, *Plan of Commerce*, p. 65.

29. Defoe, *Tour*, Vol. I, p. 221.

30. Ibid., Vol. I, pp. 218, 221, 233, 280; Vol. II, pp. 88-9, 189-90.

31. Heaton, *Woollen and Worsted Industries*, p. 289; Wadsworth & Mann, *Cotton Trade*, p. 312.

32. Hey, *Rural Metalworkers*, p. 6.

33. Samuel Bamford, *Early Days* (1848-9, reprinted London, 1967), p. 54.

34. M. Dunsford, *Historical Memoirs of Tiverton*, 2nd edn (Exeter, 1790), pp. 54, 56.

35. Rule, 'Labouring Miner', p. 194.

36. P. Corfield, 'The Industrial Towns before the Factory' in *The Rise of the New Urban Society* (Milton Keynes, 1977), pp. 114-16.

37. Wadsworth & Mann, *Cotton Trade*, p. 311.

38. Defoe, *Tour*, Vol. II, p. 183.

39. J.L. and Barbara Hammond, 'The new town' in J. Lovell (ed.), *The Town Labourer* (London, 1978), p. 31; A. Finer and G. Savage (eds.), *The Selected Letters of Josiah Wedgwood* (London, 1965), p. 24; John Wesley, *Journal* (Everyman edition, 4 volumes, London, 1906), Vol. IV, p. 202, 28 March 1781.

40. D. Wilson, 'Government Dockyard Workers in Portsmouth 1793-1815', unpublished PhD thesis, University of Warwick, 1975, pp. 18, Table 1.1; 36, Table 1.4.

41. Corfield, 'Industrial Towns', pp. 79-80.

42. Defoe, *Tour*, Vol. II, p. 261.

43. William Hutton, *Life of William Hutton F.A.S.S.* (1817 edn), p. 110; Corfield, 'Industrial Towns', p. 72; William Hutton, *A History of Birmingham* (Birmingham, 1781), p. 44; Young, *Tours in England and Wales*, p. 257.

44. Aikin, *Description*, p. 192.

45. R. Pococke, *Travels through England* (1751, edited by J.J. Cartwright for Camden Society, 1888), Vol. II, p. 285; Aikin, *Description*, p. 312; Young, *Northern Tour*, Vol. III, pp. 133-5.

46. E.A. Wrigley, 'A Simple Model of London's Importance in Changing English Society and Economy', *Past & Present*, no. 37 (1967), pp. 44-5, 49.

47. J. Stevenson, 'London, 1660-1780' in *The Rise of the New Urban Society* (Milton Keynes, 1977), pp. 18-19. An idea of the great range of trades can be gathered from directories such as R. Campbell, *The London Tradesman* (1747, reprinted Newton Abbot, 1969).

48. Mathias, 'Joseph Massie', pp. 186-7, Table 9.1.

49. 'Dependent artisanry' is for example applied to Sheffield cutlers by F.K. Donnelly and J.L. Baxter, 'Sheffield and the English Revolutionary Tradition 1791-1820', *International Review of Social History*, XX, 3 (1975), pp. 398-423.

50. This is the main meaning of tradesman to Campbell in his *London Tradesman* of 1747.

51. Defoe, *Plan of Commerce*, p. 3.

52. P. Earle, *The World of Daniel Defoe* (London, 1976), p. 164.

53. See Rule, 'Labouring Miner', p. 54.

54. Alexander Somerville has described the 'right' of the masons in Scottish quarries in the early-nineteenth century to inflict physical chastisement on labourers who offended them or questioned their privileges (*The Autobiography of a Working Man* (1848, reprinted London, 1967), pp. 96-9).

55. Mathias, 'Joseph Massie', pp. 186-7, Table 9.1.

56. P. Mantoux, *The Industrial Revolution in the Eighteenth Century* (revised edn, London, 1961), p. 50.

57. Defoe, *Tour*, Vol. I, p. 63.

58. Arthur Young, *A Six Weeks Tour through the Southern Counties of England and Wales* (London, 1768), pp. 100, 171.

59. S.D. Chapman, *The Cotton Industry in the Industrial Revolution* (London, 1972), p. 15.

60. Wadsworth & Mann, *Cotton Trade*, pp. 326, 313; Aikin, *Description*, p. 179.

61. M.D. George, *London Life in the Eighteenth Century* (Harmondsworth, 1966 edn), p. 183.

62. Defoe, *Tour*, Vol. I, p. 213; E.A. Wells, *The British Hosiery and Knitwear Industry: Its History and Organisation* (Newton Abbot, 1972), pp. 48-9; Thompson, *Making of the English Working Class*, p. 580.

63. Young, *Northern Tour*, Vol. III, p. 306.

64. C. Wilson, *England's Apprenticeship 1603-1763* (London, 1965), p. 300.

65. Hey, *Rural Metalworkers*, pp. 34-6; Young, *Tours in England and Wales*, p. 140; Hutton, *Life*, p. 110.

66. G.I.H. Lloyd, *The Cutlery Trades* (London, 1913), p. 154; Young, *Northern Tour*, I, p. 123.

67. Young, *Tours in England and Wales*, p. 254.

68. Thompson, *Making of the English Working Class*, p. 265.

69. Wilson, *England's Apprenticeship*, p. 302.

70. Young, *Tours in England and Wales*, p. 142.

71. Ibid., p. 151.

72. Young, *Tours in England and Wales*, p. 275; *Northern Tour*, Vol. I, pp. 115, 122; III, p. 9.

73. Young, *Northern Tour*, Vol. I, p. 122.

74. M. Oppenheim, 'The Royal Dockyards' in *Victoria County History of Kent*, Vol. II (London, 1926), p. 378; Wilson, 'Government Dockyard Workers', p. 148.

75. E. Howe (ed.), *The London Compositor: Documents relating to Wages, Working Conditions and Customs of the London Printing Trade* (London, 1947), p. 133.

76. Wilson, *England's Apprenticeship*, p. 301.

77. L.A. Clarkson, *The Pre-industrial Economy in England 1500-1750*

(London, 1971), p. 84.

78. J.C., *The Compleat Collier* (1708, reprinted Newcastle, 1968), p. 9; Young, *Northern Tour*, Vol. III, p. 8; T.S. Ashton and J. Sykes, *The Coal Industry of the Eighteenth Century*, revised edn (Manchester, 1964), p. 7. For the Kingswood colliers see R.W. Malcolmson, 'A set of Ungovernable People: The Kingswood Colliers in the Eighteenth Century' in J. Brewer and J. Styles (eds.), *An Ungovernable People. The English and their Law in the Seventeenth and Eighteenth Centuries* (London, 1980), pp. 85-127.

79. Rule, 'Labouring Miner', p. 9.

80. C.J. Hunt, *The Lead Miners of the Northern Pennines in the Eighteenth and Nineteenth Centuries* (Manchester, 1970), pp. 188-9.

81. Young, *Northern Tour*, Vol. III, p. 252; Vol. I, p. 116.

82. Ibid., Vol. III, pp. 163-4.

83. W. Hutton, *The History of Derby*, 2nd edn (London, 1817), p. 158; Young, *Northern Tour*, Vol. I, p. 123.

84. Chapman, *Cotton Industry*, p. 70; N.J. Smelser, *Social Change in the Industrial Revolution. An Application of Theory to the Lancashire Cotton Industry 1770-1840* (London, 1959), pp. 185, 188.

85. Chapman, *Cotton Industry*, p. 60.

86. Heaton, *Woollen and Worsted Industries*, pp. 283-4.

87. Oppenheim, 'Royal Dockyards', p. 378.

88. Rule, 'Labouring Miner', p. 13.

89. Ashton & Sykes, *Coal Industry*, pp. 8-10.

90. E. Lipson, *The Economic History of England Vol. III. The Age of Mercantilism* (revised edn, London, 1943), pp. 248-9.

91. Adam Smith, *The Wealth of Nations* (1776, edited by E. Cannan, 1904, paperback edition, London, 1961), Vol. I, pp. 73-4.

92. L.D. Schwarz, 'Income Distribution and Social Structure in London in the Late Eighteenth Century', *Economic History Review*, XXXII, no. 2 (1979), pp. 256-7.

93. Defoe, *Tour*, Vol. I, p. 281.

94. Wadsworth & Mann, *Cotton Trade*, pp. 326-7.

95. George, *London Life*, pp. 179-80.

96. F.W. Galton (ed.), *Select Documents Illustrating the History of Trade Unionism. The Tailoring Trade* (London, 1896), p. 30.

97. Ibid., pp. 24, 7.

98. George, *London Life*, p. 196.

99. Campbell, *London Tradesman*, pp. 217-18; *Commons Journals*, XXIII, 12 April 1738, pp. 176-7.

100. *Commons Journals*, XXXVI, 18 February 1777, p. 193.

101. Campbell, *London Tradesman*, p. 221.

102. Howe, *London Compositor*, doc. XLII, p. 143.

103. Campbell, *London Tradesman*, p. 229.

104. George, *London Life*, p. 160.

105. Campbell, *London Tradesman*, pp. 250-1.

106. George, *London Life*, p. 174.

107. Campbell, *London Tradesman*, p. 256; S. and B. Webb, *The History of Trade Unionism* (London, 1911 edn), pp. 35-6.

108. Campbell, *London Tradesman*, pp. 234, 162, 114.

109. George, *London Life*, p. 165; *Second Report from the Select Committee on Artisans and Machinery*, P.P. 1824 (51), V, p. 46.

110. D.A. Reid, 'The Decline of Saint Monday 1766-1876', *Past & Present*, no. 71 (1976), p. 77; *Fourth Report from the Select Committee on Artisans and Machinery*, P.P. 1824 (51), V, pp. 319-20.

111. A. Aspinall (ed.), *The Early English Trade Unions* (London, 1949), doc. 6, p. 4.

112. Defoe, *Tour*, Vol. II, p. 195.

113. Aikin, *Description*, p. 573.

114. Thompson, *Making of the English Working Class*, pp. 299-300. 'Domestic system' has not been used in this sense by historians, who usually reserve it for the situation in which the worker himself worked at home.

115. Lloyd, *Cutlery Trades*, p. 16; Thompson, *Making of the English Working Class*, p. 310.

116. Aikin, *Description*, p. 573; Heaton, *Woollen and Worsted Industries*, p. 313; Lloyd, *Cutlery Trades*, p. 18.

117. 'A Poem descriptive of the manners of the clothiers', several works cite large portions of the poem, sometimes with minor variations, but the best text is in *Publications of Thoresby Society*, XLI, part 3, no. 95 (1947), pp. 275-9.

118. Printed in Mantoux, *Industrial Revolution in the Eighteenth Century*, pp. 75-7.

119. Bamford, *Early Days*, pp. 119-25.

120. George, *London Life*, p. 160; *Commons Journals*, XXXVI, 18 February 1777, p. 193.

121. Rule, 'Labouring Miner', pp. 34-5, 63-70; E. Welbourne, *The Miners' Unions of Northumberland and Durham* (Cambridge, 1923), p. 11.

122. The standard account is I. Pinchbeck, *Women Workers and the Industrial Revolution 1750-1850* (reprinted London, 1977).

123. Campbell, *London Tradesman*, pp. 206-9, 225-8.

124. See *An Impartial Representation of the Case of the Poor Cotton Spinners in Lancashire etc.* in K. Carpenter (ed.), *Labour Disputes in the Early Days of the Industrial Revolution* (New York, 1972), pp. 2-5.

125. Hutton, *Derby*, p. 158; Young, *Northern Tour*, Vol. I, p. 123.

126. Defoe, *Tour*, Vol. II, p. 162.

127. H. Medick, 'The Proto-industrial Family Economy: The Structural Function of Household and Family during the Transition from Peasant Society to Industrial Capitalism', *Social History*, 3 (1976), p. 296.

128. Ibid., p. 306.

129. *Third Report from the Select Committee on Artisans and Machinery*, P.P. 1824 (51), V, p. 97.

130. Defoe, *Tour*, Vol. I, p. 62; Vol. II, p. 193; Vol. I, p. 266; p. 17.

131. Young, *Northern Tour*, Vol. III, p. 194; William Temple, *The Case as It Now Stands* (1739) reprinted in K. Carpenter, *Labour Problems before the Industrial Revolution* (New York, 1972), p. 16.

132. See M. Anderson, 'Sociological History and the Working-class Family: Smelser Revisited', *Social History*, 3 (1976), pp. 317-32.

133. Bamford, *Early Days*, pp. 111-12; Hutton, *Life*, p. 82, *Derby*, pp. 159-60; P. Laslett, *The World We Have Lost*, 2nd edn (London, 1971), pp. 3, 5.

134. See below p. 98.

135. Hutton, *Life*, pp. 9-19, 51; Francis Place, *Autobiography* (edited by M. Thale, Cambridge, 1972), p. 93.

2 UNCERTAINTY, IRREGULARITY, HOURS AND WAGES

One of the features of employment in eighteenth-century manufacturing was its fluctuating nature. Uncertain and irregular employment was to be found in almost every trade. The putting-out system was by its nature likely to bring into existence a pool of labour equal to the employers' needs at brisk times, and hence produce a 'natural' redundancy whenever trade turned down. Defoe clearly perceived this rhythm:

> Upon some sudden accident in trade there comes a great unusual demand for goods . . . The country manufacturer looks out sharp, hires more looms, gets more spinners, gives more wages, and animated by the advanced price, is not content to answer his new orders only, but he continues [and] gluts the market with the goods. The accident of trade which from abroad filled the merchants' commissions and the factor's orders being over, those demands are also over, and the trade returns to its usual channel, but the manufacturer in the country who had run out to an unusual excess in his business, without regard to the circumstances of it, having not stopped his hand as his orders stopped, falls into the mire, his goods lie on hand, the poor which he called from the plough and the dairy to spin and weave are cast off again, and not finding their way back to their old drudgery lie and starve for want of work, and then they cry out trade is decayed, the manufactures are lost, foreigners encroach upon us, the poor are starved.[1]

The smallware weavers of Lancashire complained in 1756 of the 'bad conduct' of those who when trade was brisk took more apprentices than was good for the trade, with the result that when normal times returned the trade was oversupplied with labour, and many 'new' weavers returning to agricultural work in the summer, came back in the winter to work at the looms upon any terms they could get.[2]

Redundancy was probably more unusual than underemployment. In order to keep contact with their weavers so as to be ready to expand production quickly when the market changed, masters preferred to spread what work was available rather than keep a smaller number fully employed. Professor Ashton in a well-known study has identified the periods of depression characterised by redundancy and severe under-employment. The war with Spain in 1718 affected the Mediterranean and the Baltic trades. In the bad years of 1740-2 wars in Europe closed west-country cloth markets, as they did again in 1744-6. In October 1740 a Tiverton serge dealer received a threat to burn his house down and murder him if he did not increase his trade, while at Frome some clothiers had turned off 1,000 hands each, and others more than 500.[3] Trade was bad in 1756 when one west-country clothier recorded in his diary: 'a stop is put to trade and payments, our poor are in a miserable condition'.[4] War with Spain caused difficulties again in 1762, and the tension with America dulled trade between 1766 and 1770, as did war in Europe from 1772 to 1774. During which period John Wesley saw at Norwich 'such a decay of trade', as had 'hardly been known in the memory of man'.[5] The war with the American colonies came in 1776 closing the markets of nailors as well as cloth workers and hardware manufacturers. Official export figures in 1779 were the lowest since 1745, with no real recovery until 1782-4. The first year of the war with France in 1793 closed all overseas markets except the Far East, and although there was a revival in 1794, a decline in exports which began in 1797 lasted until the end of the century. The effects of the famous 'orders in council' in precipitating the Luddite disturbances of 1811-12 in the East Midlands are well-known.[6] The irony of war was that by closing markets it helped supply its own needs for soldiers. 'But let them come when Trade is dead', remarked Defoe, 'and the people want work, and they may get soldiers enough'. Henry Fielding's recruiting sergeant in *Joseph Andrews* furnished the army with 'a great number of recruits' on a march from Bristol to Frome in a year when the *Sherborne Mercury* was reporting the enlisting of 1,000 young men in a 14-week period.[7]

General trade depressions reduced the consuming power of normally comfortable artisans, and thereby passed the depression on to home market producers. The watchmakers of Clerkenwell blamed not only foreign competition, but also a general trade depression for their misery in 1817 when the poorhouse was full and the pawnbrokers holding hundreds of pounds worth of tools. Home demand for watches collapsed at a time when the middling and lower classes were pawning whatever they possessed down to their wedding rings.[8] If most artisans prayed for peace, others might be suspected of praying for the continuation of war. The shipyard men at Portsmouth and the other naval yards dreaded the lay-offs which accompanied the return of peace.

More than 1,000 were discharged from Portsmouth during the short peace of 1802/3, while in the 1780s short-time was general with men working for a day-and-a-half rather than the full week.[9]

The natural forces of the elements and seasons were no less disruptive of constant employment than were wars. 'A flush and ebb is common to almost all trades', wrote a pamphleteer in 1719 complaining that the poor lacked the foresight to put by in good times for their support in bad.[10] Severe and especially frosty weather brought unemployment in winter to many trades. Calico printers could not wash their fabric, weavers could not size their cloth, shoemakers could not use frozen waxed-threads, and outside building workers might lose as much as three months' work in a long winter. In 1740 a sad procession of bricklayers and their labourers marched begging through the streets of London with their hods in sable, when severe weather had reduced them to destitution.[11] Adam Smith used the bricklayer and the mason as examples of those who 'could work neither in frost nor in foul weather', and thought they needed wages half as much again as those of common labour to compensate, whereas in the summer so much building activity went on, that large amounts of casual labour were drawn into the trade.[12] House painters too lost many weeks' work in a year.[13] Adverse winter winds kept the east-coast colliers from plying their trade from the Tyne and Wear ports to London, and forced a month-long winter's holiday on the pitmen around Christmas.[14]

Summer was a period of good earnings for most with the long candle-saving hours, but for some trades, like papermaking, dependent on a constant and steady flow of water, it was often a slack time.[15] Spring brought an increase in activity in the clothing manufacture – the 'flush' of work so often commented on – while hatters relied on heavy spring orders to compensate for three or four winter months when 'the men have very little to do'.[16] However the 'season' in such trades in London had a less natural meaning. The city's hatters, quality shoemakers, milliners, dressmakers and tailors were at the mercy of the annual retreat when the 'quality' returned to their country estates. To tailors this period of enforced summer inactivity was known as 'cucumber time', when the journeymen could afford to live on little else.[17] London tailors in fact complained that they were not employed for 'above half-the-year', while Campbell conceded that they could annually expect three or four months out of work. Occasionally an unusual demand resulting from the celebrations or mournings of the well-to-do produced a brisk improvement in prospects. *The Times* commenting in 1789 that the approach of the Queen's Birthday celebrations had brought about a demand for silk and velvet suits so that there had not been for three months past an idle hand in Spitalfields, remarked: 'When the great are thus patriotic the poor will get bread'.[18] Statutory regulation of tailors' wages allowed for an increase in time of general mourning. But if the quality wanted their bright new clothes for the London 'season', they did not want their city mansions cluttered with tradesmen and their messy paraphenalia, so house painters and moulders found themselves out of employ when the season was on.[19]

If uncertainty of employment was of major concern to the worker, then irregularity of labour was equally so for his employer. Historians, sociologists and economists have provided an extensive literature on the irregular responses of labour before the internalisation of the work values of modern industrial society. 'Leisure preference' from the point of view of the sociologist or 'backward sloping supply curve for labour' from that of the economist are useful concepts in that they remind us that there is more than one facet to the problem. Two main ones are clearly related, but essentially distinct. They are the tendency of labourers to decrease their weekly amount of work in times when higher wages or lower food prices meant that the usual expectation of comfort could be obtained from fewer hours' labour and, secondly, the ability of the home-based unsupervised worker to control the spread and pace of the hours he worked, compensating with late bursts of intense activity for early week slackness. The first of these two is the more important from the perspective of the pre-factory capitalist. The economists' backward sloping supply curve may seem an inappropriate way of viewing an essentially sociological phenomenon, but it does remind us that the normal expectation of the working of the market was being contradicted for an increase in demand expressed in higher prices (wages) was being met by a decrease in the supply of labour. Max Weber layed great stress on the need for 'rational' capitalism to overcome the 'traditionalism' of workers by which the opportunity of earning more was less attractive than that of working less:

> He did not ask: how much can I earn in a day if I do as much work as possible? but: how much must I work in order to earn the wage which I earned before and which takes care of my traditional needs? ... A man does not by nature wish to earn more and more money, but simply to live as he is accustomed to live and to earn as much as is necessary for that purpose.[20]

Recently historians have stressed this kind of response as a characteristic of the 'proto-industrial' stage of economic development: that stage characterised by the spread of manufacturing activity to rural peasant households which 'preceded and prepared modern industrialisation proper'.[21] They emphasise that the manufacturing household, not being governed by the objective of accumulating a monetary surplus − 'it could not maximise what it could not measure' − brought into equilibrium a labour-consumer balance between its basic economic, social and cultural necessities on the one side and the output of labour by the family on the other. If the returns of the family fell it increased its labour output; if they rose it felt no need to make such a response and converted labour into leisure time.[22] There are some difficulties about applying the concept of 'proto-industrialisation' to eighteenth-century England, which had long since lost its peasantry and in whose industrialisation the role of towns was evident, but contemporary comment shows a great concern with the 'leisure preference' of the labouring classes.

The only way to make the poor 'sober, industrious and obedient' proclaimed William Temple in 1739, was to remove the means of 'idleness and intemperance, such as high wages'. The best goods were made when subsistence was most difficult and the workers were 'obliged to work more and debauch less'. When wages were high they were 'loose, debauched, insolent, idle and luxurious'.[23] William Hutton was a more moderate commentator and had himself worked as a framework knitter before becoming a successful businessman, but even he wrote in 1781, that manufactures tended to decay when 'plenty preponderates'. A man who could support his family with three days' labour would not work six. The generality of men would perform no more than could produce maintenance. A commercial people therefore would endeavour to keep provisions at a superior rate, yet within reach of the poor.[24] Arthur Young was a major propagator of the view. 'Great earnings' had the effect of causing all those the 'least inclined to idleness or other ill-courses' to work only four or five days: 'This is a fact so well-known in every manufacturing town, that it would be idle to think of proving it by argument'. In an even better known passage he emphasised the point:

The master manufacturers of Manchester wish that prices might always be high enough to enforce a general industry; to keep the hands employed six days for a week's work; as they find that even one idle day, in the chance of its being a drunken one, damages all the other five, or rather the work of them.[25]

Some complained that the earnings foregone for extra leisure were substantial. In 1794 woolcombers were accused of working only 'half their time' and contenting themselves with 10s a week when 25s or even 28s was within their grasp. The complaint was made by the inventor of a machine aimed at replacing them! It is difficult to accept that a crafts-man would have contented himself with 10s a week in the inflationary nineties, although a single man might have done so.[26]

Since the evidence comes from employer polemicists and propa-gandists of high food prices like Arthur Young, it does, as Professor Mathias has pointed out, raise the question of whether it should be viewed as description (objective truth) or as opinion revealing employer attitudes.[27] Perhaps it comes between the two. As normative reporting it justified the 'utility of poverty' theory of low wages associated with the mercantilist obsession with low export prices. As such it was to a degree independent of its truth. Certainly in the writings of clothier employers like Temple it is closely linked with theories of the low wage need of exporting economies. But it can also be found in the writings of those, like Defoe, who were not low wage advocates and argued for the importance of a broad-based home demand and in unpublished sources where no propaganda motive can have been intended. It was in his personal diary that a west-country clothier wrote that high wages had made his workfolk 'scarce, saucy and bad', and in a private letter that a Cornish mine agent complained to his employer in 1793:

> The common tinners continue to be very refractory and insolent: many of them refuse to work, and have not gone underground for three weeks past − They have no just cause for it; for their wages have been rather too high lately than otherwise; the consequence has been too much brandy drinking, and other bad practices.[28]

The last sentence reveals a paradox at the heart of the employers' reac-tion. If workers were spending their time in brandy shops, gin shops or ale-houses to a greater extent than usual, then they were exercising not only a leisure preference, but also increasing their consumption of non-essentials. There is conflict between the complaints of a leisure preference coming into play *as soon as* wages moved above subsistence level and the accompanying complaints on the increasing 'luxury' expec-tations of the labouring poor, which were equally used to justify a cut in wage rates. Tea, tobacco, sugar, dress styles which 'aped their betters', as well as spirit drinking were all roundly condemned by those seeking to establish that the poor lived above their station. More soberly, Adam

Smith and others drew attention to the increasing range of working-class consumption, while economic historians have stressed the importance of the home market in sustaining the industrial revolution.[29]

Professor Mathias has pointed out that in fact whatever their protestations, employers did not reduce wages when they wanted an increase in labour supply.[30] In some situations high earning possibilities may have had a compensating effect, for although they increased the 'idleness' of those already employed, they also drew fresh hands into the trade, as happened during the 'golden age' of handloom weaving in cotton. This effect had often the later consequence of lowering wages from the height which had proved the initial attraction through an over-stocking of the labour force.[31] If these qualifications are kept in mind we can probably conclude that the situation conveyed by such ideas as 'leisure preference' or 'backward sloping supply curve for labour' remained very important in the eighteenth-century economy, but were almost certainly less *generally* characteristic of it than they had been in the seventeenth century, or than they still were in the more peasant-dominated rural manufactures of some continental economies.[32]

The essence of the second facet of labour irregularity lies in the contrast between traditional work rhythms and those of the modern factory economy. Edward Thompson has written of a 'deep-rooted folk memory' resting for a long time on 'nostalgia for the pattern of work and leisure which obtained before the outer and inner discipline of industrialism settled upon the working man'.[33] In an article which has become the starting point for any discussion of the problem, he writes of the 'characteristic irregularity of labour patterns before the coming of large-scale machine powered industry'. This pattern was one of 'alternate bouts of intense labour and of idleness wherever men were in control of their own working lives'.[34] That a man could control his own pace when working in his cottage is evident, but the pattern was also characteristic of the small workshops, where men paid by the piece came and went with an irregularity which did not pose too many problems for employers with little investment in fixed capital. It has been noted that an irregular working pattern was common in Birmingham where the 'matrix of small workshops' formed a 'conducive environment for the survival of immemorial work rhythms'. A hatter's day was said to be long, 'a man goes early and works late', but there were no fixed hours.[35] Nowhere is the customary rhythm better conveyed than in Joseph Mather's best known song *The Jovial Cutlers*. So perfectly and succinctly does it convey the pace of the cutler's week that it has been quoted in almost every work on the subject! The song was written

in 1793 and portrays the cutler sitting before the fire in his small forge
on a Monday:

> Brother workmen cease your labour,
> Lay your files and hammers by,
> Listen while a brother neighbour
> Sings a cutler's destiny;
> How upon a good Saint Monday,
> Sitting by the smithy fire
> Telling what's been done o' t' Sunday
> And in cheerful mirth conspire.

The cutler's wife enters the scene indicating by reference to her ragged
and outmoded attire, that she, at least, would welcome a little less
leisure preference and a little more response to monetary incentives.
As she nags her husband he complains that her tongue is moving faster
than his 'boring stick at a Friday's pace'.[36] Here is the rhythm of the
outworker controlling his own pace. Monday was a holiday, Tuesday
a slow day, while Friday demanded a furious pace to complete the
number of cutlery items needed to secure a reasonable income. Obviously such a rhythm was much affected by piece rates and by food
price levels. Adverse movement in either would lessen the number of
hours which could be taken as play, but it still would not dictate just
which hours had to be worked. In other words the response was as
typical of normal wage conditions as it was of high wage ones. There is
more than one way, as every student knows, of putting a given number
of necessary hours of work together in a week.

'Saint Monday' was honoured almost universally in the trades and
in the mines (in Cornwall it was known as 'Mazed Monday'). Weavers,
woolcombers, shearmen, cobblers and printers were among the many
who drew comment for their Monday holidays. Benjamin Franklin may
have made himself popular with his employer by his 'not keeping Saint
Monday' but certainly did not make himself so with his fellow journeymen printers.[37]

The year as well as the week was punctuated with holidays. Even
Josiah Wedgwood, who boasted that he could make 'such machines of
men as cannot err', could not prevent his workmen absenting themselves
for the local wakes.[38] Because of their 'numerous holidays, holiday
eves, feats, account days (once a month) Yeuwhiddens or one way or
another they invent to loiter away their time, they do not work one
half of their month for the owners and employers', complained a writer

on Cornish miners in the early-eighteenth century. The attempts of 'several gentlemen' to end these customs had been to little purpose, and in 1802 similar complaints were still being made of 'paydays, taking days and those so-called holidays' costing the shareholders £100 a day.[39] Northern colliers observed a long Christmas break and also from time to time proclaimed 'Gaudy days' on such occasions as hearing the first cuckoo. Every trade took a holiday on the day of its own patron saint.[40]

Adam Smith took a rather different view of irregular working, suggesting that drunken dissipation was the *result* of previous intensity of labour producing a compulsion for leisure. Even Francis Place recognised this desire for leisure from which even the most painstaking and industrious were not free, as the 'sickening aversion' which followed a period of intense labour stole over working men and 'utterly disabled' them from following their occupations for a time, and compelled them 'to indulge in idleness'.[41] Such behaviour strikes a chord with any student who has gone on a drinking bout after finishing his examinations following a period of heavy revision, just as it does with any worker who had put in double and extra shifts to save for marriage, a holiday or a home. It is a familiar enough pattern of human behaviour. However it is a different phenomenon from that characteristic irregular pattern of work followed by eighteenth-century workers in home- or small workshop-based occupations. Joseph Mather was himself a working cutler: he wrote *The Jovial Cutlers* to be read and appreciated by his fellows. What he describes was a usual aspect of working-class life: what Smith describes was an occasional one.

Fluctuating employment and irregular working make it difficult to measure the number of hours that represented the average 'working day' of the eighteenth-century industrial worker. We can be most certain about the hours of those who worked away from home on their employer's premises. For this group the journeymen tailors of London offer a convenient starting point because of the regulation of their hours by the statute of 1721.[42] This act required them to work from 6 am to 8 pm with an hour for dinner. How typical of the urban artisan were these hours? The tailors themselves complained in 1752 that the hours in most 'handicraft trades' were in fact from 6 am to 6 pm saving them from the sight-impairing effects of prolonged winter candle-lit hours.[43] In fact a 14-hour day seems to have been usual in comparable trades in 1747. Campbell thought it so for breeches-makers, carpet weavers, harness makers, coopers, engravers, saddlers, stocking knitters, woolcombers and shoemakers. There were exceptions – some trades seemed to have worked an extra hour until 9 pm. These included book-binders, broom makers, buckle makers, calico printers, glovers, knife grinders and pin makers. A shorter 12-hour day usually from 6 am to 6 pm was worked in the daylight-dependent trades, presumably in the middle of winter it might have had to have been even shorter. Workmen like bricklayers, masons, house carpenters and painters or shipwrights clearly had to adjust their working day to the season.[44] In 1768 the statutory hours of the tailors were cut to 13, but whether this was in line or not with a general trend across comparable trades is not known.[45]

Such hours can only be regarded as a general guide, for in many workshop trades, piece rather than day rates were paid, even in trades as close to tailoring as leather breeches-making. Here, as commonly in printing, a day represented a quota of work rather than a uniform period of hours. A hatter thought that although there were no fixed hours for the journeymen, the making of eight hats was considered a fair day's labour.[46] In the royal dockyards the basic day was a 12-hour one beginning at six in the morning with one-and-a-half hours for dinner. But there were many variations. In winter daylight hours were shorter, and in summer workers often worked overtime measures in units of one-and-a-half hours known as 'tides'. Workers in paper mills had their wages calculated on a quota of output judged to occupy eight hours, but normally added four hours' overtime.[47] Fellmongers' hours varied with the available daylight from 10 to as much as 16 hours. Wages of £4 a week were being received at some points in the year, but only by those who by 'working late and early' put in 15 or 16 hours a day. Exeter woolsorters worked in their masters' houses: 'from the time of being able to discern the quality of wool until the evening' which amounted to about 8½ hours in winter and 12 in summer.[48]

The long colliery shifts of the nineteenth century were not usual in the eighteenth. Miners worked the fewest hours of all eighteenth-century workers. Young commented that the lead miners of the Dales had finished their day's work by noon or 1 o'clock. Yorkshire pitmen worked usually no more than eight hours and sometimes only six. In the lead mines of the northern Pennines men driving shafts and sinking shafts seem to have worked on a two-shift system of five eight-hour days, and in the Yorkshire lead mines sometimes instead a six-day week of six-hour shifts. Pitmen in Northumberland and Durham were work-ing six or seven hours in 1765, but perhaps eight or ten by the end of the century, which latter hours the miners of Whitehaven had already been working in 1765. In Derbyshire in 1776 eight hours was usual with six being worked when the labour was especially hard and difficult. Around Leeds in 1787 the eight-hour day was still usual instead of the 12-hour one which was common by 1842. Boys filling the baskets and trucks worked considerably longer days, commonly 14 and, at especially busy times, as many as 18.[49]

In the tin and copper mines of Cornwall the tutworkers who worked in the dead ground, driving and sinking, usually worked eight-hour shifts, with three through the twenty-four hours being known by mid-century. Tributers who raised the ore on agreed rates came and went with greater freedom. Carew writing at the beginning of the seventeenth century thought that four hours underground was as much as a tinner could take, but shifts of six or eight hours (locally known as 'cores') were normal in the eighteenth century. Longer shifts may have been tried but were found to be less productive. Pryce in 1778 describes an attempt to introduce a 12-hour shift:

> they were nothing but an excuse for idleness; twelve hours being too many for a man to work underground without intermission. Accordingly when a pair of men went underground formerly, they made it a rule, to sleep out a candle, before they set about their work; that is, if their place of work was dry, they would lay themselves down and sleep, as long as a whole candle would continue burning; then rise up and work for two or three hours pretty briskly; after that, have a touch pipe, that is rest themselves half-an-hour to smoke a pipe of tobacco, and so play and sleep away half their working time: but mining being more expensive than it formerly was, those idle customs are superseded by more labour and industry.[50]

The demands of a capitalising industry were progressively intensifying and before the end of the century conflicting with slacker customary work practices. Pryce assumed that tutworkers relieved each other in place, in fact this was still a matter of dispute in some mines as late as 1795:

> A bad custom has prevailed lately in our mines in general, which is that the men work only 6 hours whereas they used to work 8 hours, and they expect to get more than they used to when they worked longer.
>
> We took up the subject very seriously this day week at Prince George Account, where we found the last two months cost to exceed £1,300. And we entered into a resolution to insist on the men working 8 hours in future, instead of 6 and relieve in place.

It was not a matter easily resolved, for seven years later the same mine steward was reporting that six hours was the time 'generally allotted' for underground labour, and at certain very hot mines it was still usual in the 1840s. Tributors did not work a shift system like tutworkers. They had discretion, but as Pryce records, the expectation of their contract was that they would mine the ore 'at all working times, in a regular manner'.[51] A tributor who got a reputation for doing otherwise was not likely to find himself regularly offered employment.

We can only suggest at the likely number of hours worked in normal times by home-based workers. It was not the length of the factory day, but its regularity which contrasted with the cottage labour rhythm. Indeed one weaver in 1802 complained that the trouble with factory weaving was that: 'In the factory we can never work the hours we can at home, nor make the best of our time. We cannot work above 7½ hours in winter and about 12 in summer'. At home even in winter with candlelight he could work 14 or 15 hours a day: 'I have worked from five to seven at night in winter, and from four to nine in summer'. Asked how long he could keep that up, he replied, 'As long as God Almighty gives me strength. I have done it for years. I hardly know anybody but what does; the greatest part of the inhabitants do'. A Huddersfield clothier supported the view. He preferred to put work out to weavers at home: 'In a factory you confine them to the hours the master pleases, in the cottage they work very often 15 or 16 hours'.[52] Two broadcloth weavers giving evidence in 1757 in support of their masters' petition, testified to good wages, but did so on the assumption that 14, 15 or 16 hours at the loom was put in. Many framework knitters were said in 1778 to have been working from 5 am to 10 pm but it was more usual to begin at 6 am and work until 10 pm in summer, and in winter until dark.[53]

Given what has already been observed about the rhythms of the working week and the keeping of Saint Monday, it is highly unlikely that home-based workers *averaged* such hours daily for the week, although not at all that they worked them on two or three days of the week. Only at times when rates were very low, as for example, during the long decline of the handloom weavers, would such hours be worked on a more or less daily basis. In cotton weaving by 1808 rates had fallen so low that weavers were reported to be working 15-, 16-, or even 20-hour days, but as an employer remarked that was an impossible situation for a man would not work 18 hours by choice, if he could live from the labour of 12.[54]

Twelve hours as an average in normal times over the week as a whole seems a fair measure of working time. It was what the shearmen regarded as a usual day's work.[55] However, in times of cheap food and high rates, as we have seen, large numbers of workers might opt for working fewer hours. On the other hand in times of slack trade although rates were low, workers might very well not be able to get enough work from employers contracting their operations to compensate for lower rates. In such periods they would not be enjoying extra freely chosen leisure, but enduring enforced idleness with hungry stomachs.[56]

The regular hours of the early cotton mills varied. Mantoux on the basis of the enquiry of 1816 instances 14, 16 and even 18 hours with a dinner break of 40 minutes for the largely female and juvenile work-force. Around Manchester 14 hours or a shift system with 16 hours on and 8 off relieving in thirds was common. Even Samuel Oldknow, generally regarded as a humane employer, expected his apprentices to work 13 hours from 6 am.[57]

Even in workshops, work was not always available for journeymen on piece rates even when they stood by waiting for it. Francis Place claimed that although a breeches-maker could get a guinea a week if fully employed, masters were not so well organised as to have work always ready, and even in the best shops the journeymen could not make more than 18s and much less in the poorer ones. He himself worked for one master who was so poorly organised that he could not get work enough to earn more than 14s a week.[58]

Such circumstances emphasise the connection between irregularity of work and uncertainty of earnings. Precision about wages is made even more difficult by the wide variety of methods of payment and calculation. What is strikingly evident is that before the closing decade of the century, piece rates were as much a matter of custom as of market determination, and hence exhibited in most trades an amazing stability. A west-country weaver informed a committee of enquiry in 1802 that during the 26 years he had been weaving Spanish cloth the rate of 1s 3d a yard had never altered: 'nor yet in my father's memory'. The 2s 1d day rate paid to Portsmouth shipwrights in 1784 had persisted since early in the century, while London masons complained in 1775 that their weekly 15s had been fixed 70 years previously. A hewer's pay in the north-east rose in 1740 from 1s 2d a day to 1s 8d but it stayed at that level until 1790. The fellmongers during a strike in 1800 were asking for an advance on one rate which had been unchanged for 40 years, while the Taunton weavers in 1764 were said to have accepted 9s as the rate for a 42 yard piece of plain cloth for 30 years previously.[59]

Joseph Massie's survey of 1759 emphasised two basic differentials:

(i) craftsmen's wages were higher than those of common labourers, (ii) in both categories London wages were higher than provincial ones. Labourers in London earned 9s a week, while those in the country earned 5s. Textile workers earned 10s 1d in London and 7s 6d elsewhere, while craftsmen in wood or metal earned 12s in London and 9s in the country.[60] As generalisations these do not seem too wide of the mark. His workmen are placed in far too broad categories, and he clearly fails to indicate the significantly higher wages of several kinds of skilled workers, but when fluctuations in employment are taken into account, they can be considered a useful working basis for an examination of wage levels. Adam Smith's 18d a day for the 'common price of labour in London' agrees well with Massie, although his 8d a day for country labour sharpens the differential somewhat. Smith reckoned the earnings of masons and bricklayers to be from 50-100 per cent better than those of common labourers being 7-8s compared with 4-5s in the provinces and 15-18s compared with 9-10s in London.[61] Dorothy George believed the wages of ordinary labourers in London in the building trades to have been about two-thirds of those of the craftsmen.[62]

The height of London wages was often assumed to be the reason for the movement of many trades out to the cheaper labour of the provinces; framework knitting and shoemaking for example. Early in the century Defoe's 'topping workmen' who, although only journeymen, could earn from 15s to as much as 50s a week and live better than masters and employers in foreign countries, were 'very substantial fellows' indeed, but more to be found in London than in the country areas, despite Defoe's suggestion of a more widespread applicability.[63] The earnings of London craftsmen, independent masters or journeymen, clearly depended upon the level of skill required and the related question of the ratio of hands to the work available. The over-stocking of the easier, low-premium entry trades made them much less well-paid, in many instances little above the rates of common labour. Adam Smith thought that trades like weaving were so relatively unskilled and cheap to learn that their wages in most places were little above labouring rates, their advantage being in less casual employment. That he was right in placing tailors among the 'lowest order of artificers' is suggested by their own reluctantly expressed view that statutory wages of 1s 8d a day would have been all right if employment had been constant, for on a six-day assumption this would have produced only 10s weekly. Around the level of common labour in London it confirms the view that they were 'as poor as rats' on account of being 'as common as locusts'.[64]

A basic literacy need controlled the supply of compositors: even so

Dr Johnson thought a guinea a week made their trade a very desirable one when it was considered how little 'mental powers and corporal labour' was expended by them. The saddlers were justified in their complaint in 1777 that 12-15s a week received by them was lower than the normal for handicraft trades to which considerable apprenticeship premiums had been paid.[65] The 15s which was for 70 years the masons' usual weekly earnings can be taken as representing a middle line of satisfactory remuneration on the assumption of reasonably constant employment, but as Table 2.1 constructed from Campbell's figures of 1747 shows, there were many instances of both greater and smaller earnings.

Skilled workers' earnings outside London are even more difficult to generalise about with any degree of confidence. It has been recently pointed out that in order to make full sense of earnings in just one occupation, the shipwrights of the royal dockyards, the historian has to understand the meaning of: treble days, double days, day-and-a-half, two for one, task, job, common hours, nights and 'tides'. Nor do all of these terms mean exactly what they appear to mean.[66] The paper makers of southern England were paid in a hardly less complicated way. It was the custom to pay so much for a day's work taking about eight hours, when in fact the men worked usually 12 hours at an overtime rate. Thus, complained an employer in 1796, their demand for another 3-4s on the weekly wage was in fact a demand for an extra 7s 6d. The earnings of miners were complicated enough to merit a book to themselves.[67]

Weavers were the most widespread of rural manufacturing workers, and the suggestion of Massie that a mid-century level of 7s 6d was normal is far from misleading. The recent historian of the west-country branch of the woollen manufacture thinks a weaver early in the century might have earned around £20 a year, but only on the assumption of constant employment. Two weavers giving evidence to an enquiry in 1757 claimed fairly constant earnings of 13-18s a week, but were assuming a 14-16-hour day for a family unit. A living-in journeyman received 6s a week in addition to his keep, which had been constant for 20 years.[68] These witnesses had been deliberately produced by the clothiers to support their case against a legal regulation of wages. They can hardly have been typical of the manufacture at a time when a massively supported weavers' petition for regulation was claiming that wages for some kinds of work were down to 4d a day.[69] Both claims may be regarded as polemical extremes, but where did the truth lie? Probably not far from Massie's 7s 6d. Hoskins accepts 9s as usual for an Exeter

Table 2.1: Journeymen's Wages in London in 1747

Trade	Wage	Comment
Bookbinder	10s	As many set up for themselves as remain journeymen.
Shoemaker	9-10s	Overstocked, out of business for three or four months a year.
Tailor	10s (winter) 15s (summer)	Overstocked, out of business for four or five months a year.
House painter	15s (long days) 12s (short days)	Out of business for five or six months a year.
Bricklayer	15s	Out of business for four months a year.
Stone mason	15-18s	High risk of lead poisoning.
Glazier	12s	
House carpenter	12s-15s	
Locksmith	14-15s (9s when first out of time)	Constantly employed.
Joiner	15s	Sometimes earn more on piecework.
Leather-dresser	15s to £1	Nauseous dirty business.
Hatter	15s	Constantly employed.
Cooper	15-16s	
Rope maker	15s-£1	
Silk weaver	18s-£1 1s	If fully employed.
Plumber	15s-£1 1s	High risk of lead poisoning.
Compositor	£1 1s	Constant employment available, but many 'play' great part of time.
Cabinet-maker	£1 1s	Sometimes earn more on piecework.
Engraver of dies and seals	£1 1s-£1 10s	Not overstocked, employed constantly.
Engraver of copper plates	£1 10s	Not overstocked, employed constantly.
Coachmaker	£1 10s	Not overstocked with good hands.
Enameller	£1 10s-£2	
Sadler	£20 per annum plus bed and board	A profitable enough trade, not overstocked.

Source: R. Campbell, *The London Tradesman* (1747).

weaver in 1750, while 7-8s was estimated in 1763, and 9s for Taunton in 1764.[70]

Arthur Young provides several examples of weavers' wages from various parts of the country in his tours of the 1770s:

Sudbury 7s usual up to 9s	Norfolk 5s
Salisbury 7-9s	Leeds (broadcloth) 8-10s 6d
Wilton (carpets) 10-12s	Leeds (stuff, worsted) av. 7s
Romsey 9s	Warrington (sailcloth) 9s
Witney (blankets) 10-12s	Kendal 9-10s
Bocking and Braintree 9s	

Combers in the worsted manufacture earned more than weavers, and probably since they were notorious for their 'leisure preference' could have earned even more than they contented themselves with: Young gives 6-12s in Leeds, 12s in Essex and 10s in Kendal. Shearmen too could command higher wages perhaps in general 2-3s a week above weavers. For Manchester cotton weavers Young gives rates for about 30 different kinds of cloth. These range from as low as 4s or 5s to 12s, with around 7s being both the average and the usual. Dyers and finishers earned 7s 6d and bleachers 6s 6d. Manchester also employed large numbers of hatters who earned from 7s 6d for basic work to 12s for finishing.[71]

By provincial standards coal miners' earnings were generally high. Adam Smith thought this was compensation for the dangers of their occupation, and explained why as 'unskilled' labourers they earned more than many artificers.[72] Up to 1740 hewers around Newcastle earned 7s a week, and between then and 1790 around 10s, although some evidence suggests that 12s or even 14s was not unusual. Professor Ashton suggests around 9s was about right. In other coalfields wages around Wigan were 10s 10d in 1752 and 1s 6d a day around 1764-76. Wages improved in the last quarter with Lancashire colliers earning 1s 9d a day in 1786 while around Leeds the rate was 2-3s. Staffordshire colliers were on strike at that time for 3s a day. In the 1790s around Newcastle the leading rate rose by one-third from 1s 6d to 2s a day. In many areas a coal allowance significantly improved the real value of colliers' wages.[73]

Miners in coal paid by the day or by the amount raised are at least more easy to generalise about than were most metal miners whose peculiar and often local methods of paying wages allowed an extreme range of fluctuations. Special methods were more evident and widespread in the Cornish mines than elsewhere, although lead mining districts too had their peculiar systems.[74] Average monthly wages for Cornish tin and copper miners were 20-27s in 1730, 30s in 1778 and £2 by 1797. Much of the late improvement had taken place in the 1790s, a witness before a select committee in 1799 stating that wages had increased in copper mining from a range of £1 10s-£2 2s in 1791 to one of £2 5s-£3 3s in 1798.[75] Such averages probably conceal greater fluctuations in Cornish mining than in any other industry. Of the two main classes of workers, the tutworkers were employed to sink shafts and drive levels and were paid by the cubic fathom. They agreed a rate after calculating the hardness of the ground to be driven. There was a certain limited gamble in agreeing the rate but on the whole tutworkers made constant wages. The men who excavated the actual tin or copper ore were the tributers, they enjoyed higher status and, on average, higher earnings but their gamble was a real one. They undertook to work in a defined part of the mine, a 'pitch', for an agreed rate in the pound of the value of the ore raised by them when sold by the mine. The pitches were offered to the tributers on 'setting' days in a form of Dutch auction. The team, known as the 'pare', who offered to take the pitch at the lowest rate securing the 'bargain'. The mine captain acted as the agent of the owners — in Cornwall usually a large number of shareholders known as 'adventurers' — and in the majority of cases both he and the experienced tributers could judge the potential of a pitch so that it was set at a rate which would likely produce normal earnings. But the geology of a tin or copper mine is more complicated than that of a coal mine. The mineral vein could narrow or even disappear. It could promise high-grade but return low-grade ore. On the other hand, it could suddenly widen or significantly improve in quality. There was accordingly a substantial element of uncertainty — part of which at least was the exciting prospect of a real windfall, or 'start' as the tributers called it. Outstanding luck might come to a tributer only once or twice in a working life, but it came frequently enough to someone to make substantial gain a definite prospect. Tributers would endure long periods of low earnings as long as the hope of a 'start' remained. In 1802 four tributers working in a part of a mine supposed to be poor were doing so badly that they tried to abandon their contract, but suddenly they broke into ore of such unexpected quantity and quality that they made £50 each for their two-month contract. In 1804 two tributors working at the rather high tribute rate of 12s in the pound in a part of the mine with modest potential broke into ore from the sale of which they expected £100 each. On the other hand a good pitch was so sought after that it was eventually taken at only 5d in the pound, although the captain's own estimate was that at least 1s would have been needed to make ordinary wages. In 1798 a rich lode of such potential was discovered that a pitch was taken for 6d: 'rich as it is', remarked a mine steward, 'I fear the men will not get wages in that price. They ought to have 1s instead of 6d, but 'twas their own fault in cutting it so low.'[76]

It has been suggested that this form of direct contracting by the miners made them the descendants of the 'free' miners of the middle ages. In fact a period of working mines by contracting entrepreneurs employing wage labour intervened between the middle ages and the capitalisation of the eighteenth century, and during this period contractors took whole mines on tribute. The tributers of the eighteenth century had rather emerged from wage status as a result of the needs of the capitalised industry to develop a sophisticated method of payment which, while it would ensure the largest degree of application possible from unsupervised labour, would also encourage selectivity and the prospecting streak in the miners for the ultimate benefit of the shareholders, and at the same time associate the labourers with the capitalist in sharing the risks of exploration. Since the system could not offer final settlement at less than two-month, or at best one-month intervals, a method of wage advancement known as 'subsist' developed under which up to £2 a man a month was advanced against the anticipated earnings. Frequently if tributers had been unlucky they had nothing at all to receive at the end of the month. Subsist had something of the nature of a minimum wage, but it was a discretionary payment, and although usual, could be refused.[77] Similar systems were in use in the major lead mining districts. In Derbyshire a reckoning was held every six, seven or even thirteen weeks with the 'copers', the equivalent of the tributers. Lead prices were usually more steady than copper prices, but two copers made £60 each in six weeks in 1802, for example. Dead ground miners here were known as 'sinkers' and took work much in the manner of the Cornish tutworkers. In the northern Pennines pay settlements came only six-monthly or even yearly. Young in 1771 thought lead miners in this district averaged around 7s 6d a week, not high by mining standards.[78]

In the great metal manufacturing towns of Birmingham and Sheffield artisan wages were generally high, although because of the variety of specialisms among them, the range was considerable. Young in 1791 gave the range as being from 10-25s in Birmingham, but thought the higher end predominated to make the city's wages the 'highest in Europe'. Twenty years previously he had given the range as from 7s to £3 but

had confessed that this was based on 'slight intelligence'.[79] The height
of the wages earned by Sheffield's cutlery workers astonished him.
Grinders could earn from 18-20s a week in compensation, Young felt,
for the risk of being maimed or killed by flying stone fragments. Common wages in the trade were from 1s 6d to 2s a day, while the highly
skilled razor-polishers could earn a *daily* wage of 10s 6d, truly as he
remarked 'surprising wages for any manual performance'. A report on
the town in 1792 thought wages so high that the artisans commonly
opted for a three-day week.[80]

The most evident general wage trend of the century was the rapid
rise of wages in the inflationary 1790s, which ended the stability which
characterised most of the century (see Table 2.2). Price inflation was
rapid enough, however, to produce a general fall in real wages.

Table 2.2: London Artisans' Wages (1900 = 100)[81]

	Money Wages	Real Wages
1729	42.7	59.8
1749	44.0	53.9
1769	44.0	53.5
1789	44.0	48.7
1799	51.1	40.9
1809	64.2	36.9
1819	65.1	41.4

Dr George thought the real upward movement began around 1793 and
peaked in 1810/11 with some fall in money wages accompanying the
fall in the cost of living around 1816. Saddlers' wages rose from 14-16s
in 1786 to 25-27s in 1811; compositors from 24s in 1777, through 27s
in 1780 to 36s by 1800.[82] The rise was not confined to London. We
have already seen that it occurred in both coal and metal mining. Dr
Gilboy calculated that Lancashire money wages (1700 = 100) rose from
133 in 1750 through 200 in 1780 to 267 by 1793.[83] In the west of
England cloth manufacture the 10s to £1 rates for weavers presented
by Eden for Wiltshire show a rise over the earlier rates given above
(pp. 63-5).[84]

Other less evident trends have been noticed. Dr Gilboy found that
wages increased somewhat over the first third of the century in London,
and she and others have noticed that by the third quarter northern wages
were beginning to show a more favourable aspect than those in other
provincial regions. The annual (300 day) £15 for 1750 becoming in the
north £22 10s by 1775, while in the west £17 10s became £18 15s. For

London £30 remained constant from 1750 to 1790.[85]

Some historians have poured scorn on the idea of a 'golden age' for the labourer in the eighteenth century, claiming it stems from a sentimental view of pre-industrial society. Dr George has been especially severe, but if the idea of a 'golden age' is applied in a qualified way to specific trades and periods it has some meaning, even if loosely applied it is little more than a romantic illusion. For the serge weavers and combers of Devonshire, the 'golden age' was over by the 1720s, but for other groups the 'golden age' looked back at from the nineteenth century was a *recent* memory of better times when rates were high and as much work was put out as a man wanted to take. For cotton hand-loom weavers it lasted roughly from 1788 to 1803, although it did not reach all branches of the trade. Samuel Bamford was born in 1788 at a time when his father and uncle were prospering: 'for there was then a market for anything which the spindle or hand-loom could make'.[86] Machine-produced yarn gave weavers in both cotton and wool a period of real prosperity at the end of the eighteenth century before factory weaving extinguished their livelihood in the nineteenth. Framework knitters had their periods of depression, as in 1778 when only 7s could be made from a week of 16-hour days from which sum deductions of 2s 6d had to be made, but in the 1780s and perhaps down to 1800 they were much more prosperous. When Arthur Young visited Leicester in 1791 he found trade so brisk that there was a scarcity of hands and a man with a frame could earn 20-30s a week.[87] Other groups like wool-combers, shearmen or calico printers also enjoyed a late-century prosperity before machinery threatened their scarce skills by the beginning of the nineteenth century.[88]

The wage levels discussed in this chapter for the most part are approximations of what could be earned in normal times, but, as we have seen, the times were often out of joint. Even if a customary piece rate remained unchanged for half a century, as Adam Smith pointed out they sometimes did in money terms in many places,[89] the amount of work available fluctuated considerably and with it the level of a man's wages. Trade unions were as often concerned to defend standards as to raise them, and their actions to maintain the institution of apprenticeship were a means to this end by controlling the supply of skilled labour. Workers' combinations in a number of trades had, as we shall see in later chapters, their successes in raising wages from time to time, although rarely by very significant amounts before the 1790s. Overall it is difficult to view the impact of trade unionism on wage levels as *persistently* effective in the eighteenth century, even if it was so more often than has sometimes been supposed. Every trade had its ups and downs be they seasonal and regular, or occasioned by external and irregular occurrences, but for the most part a given level of money earnings was a customary expectation and it was the rising prices of essential foodstuffs which were likely to produce quick resentment and rapid action.

Notes

1. Daniel Defoe, *A Plan of the English Commerce* (1728, reprinted Oxford, 1928), pp. 192-3.
2. A.P. Wadsworth and J. de L. Mann, *The Cotton Trade and Industrial Lancashire* (Manchester, 1931), p. 348.
3. T.S. Ashton, *Economic Fluctuations in England 1700-1800* (Oxford, 1959), *Sherborne Mercury*, 21 October 1740; 28 November 1740.
4. Diary of George Wansey, 5 January 1745/6 in J. de L. Mann (ed.), *Documents Illustrating the Wiltshire Textile Trades in the Eighteenth Century* (Devizes, 1964), doc. no. 176.
5. John Wesley, *Journals* (Everyman edn, four volumes, London, 1906), Vol. III, p. 489, entry 27 October 1772.
6. Ashton, *Economic Fluctuations*, p. 53; E.P. Thompson, *The Making of the English Working Class* (Harmondsworth, 1968 edn), pp. 616-18.
7. Defoe, *Plan of Commerce*, p. 69; Henry Fielding, *Joseph Andrews* (Signet edition, New York, 1961), p. 279; *Sherborne Mercury*, 31 November 1741.
8. *Report from the Committee on the Petitions of the Watchmakers of Coventry*, 1817 (504), VI, Minutes, p. 5.
9. D. Wilson, 'Government Dockyard Workers in Portsmouth 1793-1815', unpublished PhD thesis, University of Warwick, 1975, p. 42; A. Geddes, *Portsmouth during the Great French Wars 1770-1800* (Portsmouth, 1970), p. 18.
10. *The Weavers' Pretences Examined* (1719), reprinted in J. Smith, *Memoirs of Wool* (1747, reprinted Farnborough, 1968), Vol. II, p. 186.
11. Ashton, *Economic Fluctuations*, pp. 4-5; *Minutes of Evidence before the Committee . . . on Laws relating to the Woollen Trade*, P.P. 1802/3 (95), VII, p. 69; R. Campbell, *The London Tradesman* (1757, reprinted Newton Abbot, 1969), p. 219; *Report from the Committee on the Apprentice Laws*, P.P. 1812/3 (243), IV, p. 18; *Sherborne Mercury*, 19 February 1739.
12. Campbell, *London Tradesman*, pp. 103-4.
13. Adam Smith, *The Wealth of Nations* (1776, edited by E. Cannan 1904, paperback edn, London, 1961), Vol. I, pp. 115-16.
14. E. Welbourne, *The Miners' Unions of Northumberland and Durham* (Cambridge, 1923), p. 16.
15. Ashton, *Economic Fluctuations*, p. 5; William Hutton recalled a happy break from his child labour at the Derby silk mill when during a dry summer, 'the water would scarcely turn the wheels', Hutton, *Life of William Hutton F.A.S.S.* (London, 1817 edn), p. 91.
16. *Third Report from the Select Committee on Artisans and Machinery*, P.P. 1824 (51), V, p. 97.
17. E. Grose, *A Classical Dictionary of the Vulgar Tongue* (Text of 1796 edited by E. Partridge, London, 1931), p. 109.
18. F.W. Galton (ed.), *Select Documents Illustrating the History of Trade Unionism. The Tailoring Trade* (London, 1896), p. 15; Campbell, *London*

Tradesman, pp. 192-3; *The Times*, 10 January 1789.

19. Campbell, *London Tradesman*, pp. 103-4.

20. Max Weber, *The Protestant Ethic and the Spirit of Capitalism* (Unwin paperback edition, London, 1965), p. 59.

21. F. Mendels, 'Proto-industrialisation: The First Phase of the Industrialisation Process', *Journal of Economic History*, XXXII (1972), p. 241.

22. H. Medick, 'The Proto-industrial Family Economy: The Structural Function of Household and Family during the Transition from Peasant Society to Industrial Capitalism', *Social History*, 3 (1976), p. 298.

23. William Temple, *The Case as It Now Stands etc.* (1739) reprinted in K. Carpenter (ed.), *Labour Problems before the Industrial Revolution* (New York, 1972), pp. 20, 40.

24. W. Hutton, *A History of Birmingham* (Birmingham, 1781), p. 69.

25. Arthur Young, *A Six Months Tour through the North of England*, 2nd edn (London, 1771), Vol. I, pp. 176-7; Vol. III, p. 193.

26. *Commons Journals*, XLIX, 31 March 1794, p. 395.

27. P. Mathias, 'Leisure and Wages in Theory and Practice' in *The Transformation of England* (London, 1979), p. 149.

28. For a useful discussion of Mercantilist wage theories see R.C. Wiles, 'The Theory of Wages in Later English Mercantilism', *Economic History Review*, 2nd series, XX (1968), pp. 113-26; Diary of George Wansey, 15 July 1760, in Mann (ed.), *Wiltshire Textile Trades*, doc. no. 203; J.G. Rule, 'The Labouring Miner in Cornwall c. 1740-1870: A Study in Social History', unpublished PhD thesis, University of Warwick, 1971, p. 75.

29. Smith, *Wealth of Nations*, Vol. I, p. 87.

30. Mathias, 'Leisure and Wages', p. 161.

31. Samuel Bamford, *Early Days* (1848-9, reprinted London, 1967), pp. 4-5; Young, *Northern Tour*, Vol. I, pp. 176-7.

32. For seventeenth-century England see D.C. Coleman, 'Labour in the English Economy of the Seventeenth Century', *Economic History Review*, 2nd series, VII (1956), pp. 280-95; for Europe see Mendels, 'Proto-industrialisation', pp. 241-61.

33. E.P. Thompson, *The Making of the English Working Class* (London, 1963 edn), p. 357.

34. E.P. Thompson, 'Time, Work-discipline and Industrial Capitalism', *Past & Present*, no. 38 (1967), pp. 49-50.

35. D.A. Reid, 'The Decline of Saint Monday, 1776-1876', *Past & Present*, no. 71 (1976), p. 77; *Third Report from the Select Committee on Artisans and Machinery*, P.P. 1824 (51), V, p. 97.

36. G.I.H. Lloyd, *The Cutlery Trades* (London, 1913), p. 181.

37. Rule, 'Labouring Miner', p. 75; Benjamin Franklin, *Autobiography* (London, 1903 edn), pp. 57-8.

38. N. McKendrick, 'Josiah Wedgwood and Factory Discipline', *Historical Journal*, IV (1961), p. 46.

39. Rule, 'Labouring Miner', p. 73.

40. Welbourne, *Miners' Unions*, p. 16.

41. Francis Place, *Autobiography* (edited by M. Thale, Cambridge, 1972), p. 123 (footnote); Smith, *Wealth of Nations*, Vol. I, p. 92.

42. 7 George I c. 13 (1721).

43. Galton, *Tailoring Trade*, p. 52.

44. Campbell, *London Tradesman*, Table of Trades, pp. 331-40.

45. Galton, *Tailoring Trade*, p. 60 (8 George III c. 17).

46. *Third Report from SC on Artisans and Machinery*, P.P. 1824, V, pp. 96-7.

47. Geddes, *Portsmouth*, p. 18; D.C. Coleman, *The British Paper Industry*

1495-1860: A Study in Industrial Growth (Oxford, 1958), p. 278; *Commons Journals*, LI, 21 April 1796, p. 595.

48. *Report from Committee on Apprentice Laws*, P.P. 1812/13, IV, pp. 54, 57; W.G. Hoskins, *Industry, Trade and People in Exeter 1688-1800*, 2nd edn (Exeter, 1968), p. 53.

49. Young, *Northern Tour*, Vol. II, pp. 189, 261-2; A. Raistrick and B. Jennings, *A History of Lead Mining in the Pennines* (London, 1965), p. 286; T.S. Ashton and J. Sykes, *The Coal Industry of the Eighteenth Century*, revised edn (Manchester, 1964), p. 131; Welbourne, *Miners' Unions*, p. 15.

50. Rule, 'Labouring Miner', p. 81; W. Pryce, *Mineralogia Cornubiensis* (Oxford, 1778), p. 173.

51. Rule, 'Labouring Miner', pp. 86-7.

52. *Minutes of Evidence before the Committee . . . on the Woollen Trade*, P.P. 1802/3, VII, pp. 87, 379-80.

53. *Commons Journals*, XXVII, 24 February 1757, p. 731; XXXVI, 25 February 1778, p. 740.

54. *Report from the Committee on the Petitions of Several Cotton Manufacturers and Journeymen*, P.P. 1808 (177), II, pp. 5, 12.

55. *Minutes of Committee . . . on the Woollen Trade*, P.P. 1802/3, VII, p. 115.

56. See the evidence before the *Committee on the Petitions of Several Cotton Manufacturers and Journeymen*, P.P. 1808, II and also that on the *Silk Ribbon Weavers' Petitions*, P.P. 1818 (134), IX.

57. P. Mantoux, *The Industrial Revolution in the Eighteenth Century*, 2nd edn (London, 1964), p. 413.

58. Place, *Autobiography*, pp. 105-6, 112.

59. *Minutes of Committee . . . on the Woollen Trade*, P.P. 1802/3, VII, p. 35; Geddes, *Portsmouth*, p. 18; M.D. George, *London Life in the Eighteenth Century* (Harmondsworth, 1966 edn), p. 166; Welbourne, *Miners' Unions*, p. 14; *Report from the Committee on the Apprenticeship Laws*, P.P. 1812/13, IV, p. 56; *Exeter Mercury*, 11 May 1764.

60. P. Mathias, 'The Social Structure in the Eighteenth Century: A Calculation by Joseph Massie' in Mathias, *The Transformation of England*, pp. 186-7, Table 9.1.

61. Smith, *Wealth of Nations*, Vol. I, pp. 84, 116.

62. George, *London Life*, pp. 168-9.

63. Ibid., p. 160.

64. Smith, *Wealth of Nations*, Vol. I, pp. 114-16; Galton, *Tailoring Trade*, p. 15; Campbell, *London Tradesman*, p. 193.

65. George, *London Life*, pp. 166-7.

66. Wilson, 'Government Dockyard Workers', p. 239.

67. *Commons Journals*, LI, 21 April 1796, p. 595; Coleman, *Paper Industry*, pp. 297-8.

68. J. de L. Mann, *The Cloth Industry in the West of England from 1640-1880* (Oxford, 1971), p. 104; *Commons Journals*, XXVII, 24 February 1757, p. 731.

69. W.E. Minchinton, 'The Petitions of the Weavers and Clothiers of Gloucestershire in 1756', *Transactions of the Bristol and Gloucestershire Archaeological Society*, Vol. 73 (1954), p. 218.

70. Hoskins, *Exeter*, p. 56; E. Lipson, *The Economic History of England, Volume II*, revised edn (Newton Abbot, 1943), p. 34.

71. Young's figures are taken from the various published tours (see bibliography).

72. Smith, *Wealth of Nations*, Vol. I, p. 112.

73. Ashton & Sykes, *Coal Industry*, pp. 136-8; Welbourne, *Miners' Unions*, p. 14.

74. Rule, 'Labouring Miner', pp. 34-60; C.J. Hunt, *The Lead Miners of the Northern Pennines in the Eighteenth and Nineteenth Centuries* (Manchester, 1970), Chapter 3, 'The bargain system'.

75. Rule, 'Labouring Miner', pp. 92-3.

76. Ibid., pp. 46-7.

77. Ibid., pp. 49-50.

78. Hunt, *Lead Miners of the Northern Pennines*, pp. 62-5; N. Kirkham, *Derbyshire Leadmining* (Truro, 1968), p. 23; Young, *Northern Tour*, Vol. II, p. 189; Wesley, *Journals*, Vol. II, p. 68, 29 July 1748.

79. Young, *Tours in England and Wales selected from the Annals of Agriculture* (London, 1932), pp. 257-8; *Northern Tour*, Vol. III, p. 279.

80. Young, *Northern Tour*, Vol. I, p. 123; A. Aspinall, *The Early English Trade Unions* (London, 1949), doc. 6, p. 4.

81. R.S. Tucker, 'Real Wages of Artisans in London, 1729-1935' (1936), reprinted in A.J. Taylor (ed.), *The Standard of Living in Britain in the Industrial Revolution* (London, 1975), pp. 27-9.

82. George, *London Life*, pp. 166-7.

83. E.W. Gilboy, 'The Cost of Living and Real Wages in Eighteenth-Century England' (1936) reprinted in Taylor (ed.), *Standard of Living*, p. 13.

84. F.M. Eden, *The State of the Poor* (London, 1797), Vol. II, p. 643; Vol. III, pp. 781, 800, 797.

85. E.W. Gilboy, *Wages in Eighteenth-Century England* (Cambridge, Mass., 1934), pp. 220-1, 224.

86. M.D. George, *England in Transition* (Harmondsworth, 1953 edn), p. 136; J.G. Rule, introduction to J.L. and Barbara Hammond, *The Skilled Labourer* (London, 1979 edn), pp. xiii-xiv; Bamford, *Early Days*, p. 4.

87. Young, *Tours in England and Wales*, p. 328.

88. For woolcombers and shearmen see Hammond & Hammond, *Skilled Labourer*, Chapters 6 and 11; for calico printers see *Facts and Observations to prove the Impolicy and Dangerous Tendency of the Bill . . . for limiting the number of Apprentices, and other restrictions in the Calico Printing Business. Together with a Concise History of the Combination of the Journeymen* (Manchester, 1807), reprinted in K. Carpenter (ed.), *Trade Unions under the Combination Acts 1799-1823* (New York, 1972).

89. Smith, *Wealth of Nations*, Vol. I, p. 83.

3 WORK AND HEALTH

Although manufactures deserved in many respects the 'high encomiums' bestowed upon them, declared a pamphleteer in 1782, many of them waged a 'secret successful war' bringing 'infirmity, sickness and death' to those they employed:

> Scarcely are we fed, lodged, clothed, warmed, without sending multitudes to their grave. The collier, the clothier, the painter, the gilder, the miner, the makers of glass, the workers in iron, tin, lead, copper, while they minister to our necessities, or please our tastes and fancies, are impairing their health and shortening their days.

Manufactures, he concluded, equalled war in exhibiting a mournful scene of the blind and lame and of enfeebled, decrepit, asthmatic, consumptive wretches 'crawling half alive upon the surface of the earth'.[1] A connection between occupation and health had been observed in the ancient world. Xenophon attributed to Socrates the opinion that the mechanical arts were rightly stigmatised with dishonour: 'For these arts damage the bodies of those who work at them' and through physical degeneration they led to the 'deterioration of the soul'. Lack of leisure left workers culturally deprived and it was evident that they could not be regarded as proper citizens.[2] The modern history of occupational medicine however begins with the publication in 1700 of *De Morbis Artificum Diatriba* by the Italian physician Bernard Ramazzini. This pioneering treatise was widely known in England in a translation by the surgeon Robert James. Ramazzini extended the areas of diagnostic concern laid down by Hippocrates:

> When you come to a patient's house you should ask him what sort of pains he has, what caused them, how many days he has been ill, whether the bowels are working, and what sort of food he eats. So says Hippocrates . . . I may venture to add one more question: what occupation does he follow? . . . This should be particularly kept in mind when the patient to be treated belongs to the common people.[3]

The connection between work and health was sufficiently taken for granted by 1776 for Adam Smith to write simply of 'the peculiar infirmity of the trade' and assume that every class of worker was subject to some special form of affliction.[4] The growth and spread of manufacturing and especially of the factory system produced by the early-nineteenth century widespread accusations of the destruction of health by industry — a destruction which seemed only too evident from the much publicised conditions in which child labourers toiled in the textile mills. Already by 1805, Charles Hall had produced a powerful attack on the emerging industrial society. He declared the manufacturing towns of Europe to be peopled by 'rickety, squalid, dwarfed, distorted objects'; a vivid testimony to the devastation made by manufacturing industry on the human species. There were trades, he contended, which were so destructive of health that 'the workmen's lives are measured with great exactness'.[5]

Hall was a doctor, but his book was a polemic rather than a medical tract. There are, however, sufficient sources on which to base an examination of occupational health in the eighteenth century. There are a few direct medical writings and there are also guides to the various trades intended to inform parents in a matter of fact way of the risks of apprenticing their offspring to them.[6] Some of the authors of descriptions of regions or industries were coincidentally medical men, as was William Pryce who wrote in 1778 a classic work on Cornish mining. Newspapers reported the more dramatic instances of death or maiming from accidents at work. Parish registers can suggest links between occupation and mortality. Employers and employees sometimes raised issues of health in the pamphlet wars which accompanied industrial disputes. Towards the end of the century parliamentary investigations add importantly to the store of information. Language itself affords important clues. The dust-induced lung disease silicosis has been known as: grinders' asthma, grinders' consumption, grinders' rot, grit consumption, masons' disease, miners' asthma, miners' phthisis, potters' rot, rock tuberculosis, stone hewers' phthisis and stone workers' lung. Occupational bursitis in various forms has been known as: bricklayers' or miners' elbow, weavers' bottom, housemaids' knee (sometimes nuns' bursitis), hod carriers' shoulder and tailors' ankle. The paranoia which was one of several symptoms of mercury poisoning explained the madness of the hatter.[7]

The results of investigations carried out after the eighteenth century provide valuable retrospective evidence if used with special care. They afford the advantage of more systematic presentation and a superior basis of medical knowledge, but it must be firmly established that working or environmental conditions as well as the materials in use in an occupation had not changed in any health-affecting way in the intervening period. One such investigation, that of Charles Turner-Thackrah in 1831, is indispensable.[8] Sir John Simon regarded him as the man who made the effects of employment on health 'common knowledge'. A Leeds physician, he concentrated on that district investigating in a systematic way with a team of pupils, talking both to employers and to 'the more intelligent workmen' and using what statistical data he could obtain. He came to the conclusion that workmen were less thought of than machinery which was frequently examined to 'entertain its capabilities' while the workman was scarcely ever so considered.[9]

In our examination we will use this retrospective evidence. Indeed we must for part of our argument will be that although there was an awareness of the link, it was an *accepting* one. And the fact that the health of workers was not a matter of serious *concern* explains a lack of documentation for something which was seen but not noticed. The labouring poor you had always with you, but not, in many occupations, for very long.

An investigation of occupational health needs to be controlled by the realisation that the poor health of manufacturing workers could have been produced or intensified by factors other than their employment; such as insanitary and unhealthy living conditions, poor or inadequate diet, or excessive drinking. Willan in his investigation of the health of London artisans placed emphasis on the miserable accommodation of the poor in their ill-ventilated, over-crowded dwellings. He wrote of garrets reached through passages and stairways filled with bad air and 'putrid excremental effluvia'. Where work was carried on in the living area, the rooms were not only clogged with furniture but also with the 'utensils of trade' and an 'accumulation of heterogeneous, fermenting filth'.[10] Even if the main cause of affliction was the occupation, its effects need not have been anything like as serious if they had not been worsened by other factors. Young workers might suffer deformities from an activity which would not have unduly affected the body of a mature adult. The health of an adult might suffer from the extra period of exposure to slow-acting effects resulting from having begun the occupation as a child labourer. If a job killed in twenty years, then those who were exposed to its effects from the age of ten died younger than those who commenced it as adults. Much attention was given to the effects of sedentary occupations. Rightly so, but if a trade such as tailoring had been followed for an eight- rather than a 14-hour-day; if good food could have been afforded from its wages, and if time had been available for relaxation and exercise, then the journeymen tailors of London would not perhaps have been the 'wretched emblems of death and hunger' described in 1728.[11] The link between long working hours and the intensification of the 'peculiar infirmity of the trade' was noted by Adam Smith who thought it was the man who worked 'so moderately as to be able to work constantly' who kept his health the longest. Turner-Thackrah was convinced that a shortening of the hours of work was the most urgently needed reform: 'Most operatives in this country prematurely sink from labour if they be not destroyed by acute disease. "Worn-out" is as often applied to a workman as a coach-horse.' Long hours were often the direct result of low piece rates, hence excessive application and insufficient or deficient diet tended to go together. This was strikingly true of female trades like dressmaking where a vicious circle of low wages – long hours – exaggerated infirmity (eye strain) – decreased ability to earn at the better paid work because of the infirmity led to still lower wages, still longer hours and eventual destitution. The pattern was familiar enough too in many male trades. A London carpenter on piece rates, according to Adam Smith, was so apt to overwork himself that he did not last in his 'utmost vigour' more than eight years. A remarkably early realisation of the connection came from the Sheffield scissor-smiths who in 1680 voluntarily adopted three annual holidays of a week each in order to check the physical disablement and bad workmanship which resulted from excessive labour.[12]

Turner-Thackrah was pessimistic enough to associate both low and high wages with adverse health effects. The former led to undernourishment while the latter led to the deleterious effects of drunkenness and improvidence:

> The grand bane of civilised life is intemperance. Greater in towns than in the country, it dreadfully aggravates the evils of our employments; and it produces evils of its own, ten fold more urgent, more rapid and more deadly.[13]

Often habits of drinking at work meant that large amounts of alcohol were taken during working hours as well as in off-work periods. Turner-Thackrah instanced, among others, the printers and shoemakers as work-time drinkers. Eighteenth-century writers had long made similar claims. Few saw as Adam Smith did, that bouts of heavy drinking were very often directly related to excessive and insupportably heavy labour:

> Excessive application during four days of the week is frequently the

real cause of the idleness of the other three, so much and so loudly complained of. Great labour, either of mind or body continued for several days together, is in most men naturally followed by a great desire for relaxation, which if not restrained by force or by some strong necessity is almost irresistible.[14]

Smith's call of nature was perceived by William Hutton to lie behind the working pattern of many of Birmingham's artisans. It was a pattern characterised by laborious employment and irregular conduct. Time was divided between hard working and hard drinking. Men at forty had frequently the appearance of sixty and ended at fifty a life which the 'hand of prudence' would have directed to eighty. The appearance of ill health of the west-country weaver in the early-eighteenth century was attributed by William Temple to 'excesses, sottishness and debauchery', while a physician at the end of the century thought the extent of pulmonary diseases among the working population was a reflection of lives spent in 'labour and drunkenness'. Alcohol is accepted by modern authorities as intensifying some occupationally produced conditions.[15]

Such intensifying conditions must be kept in mind when considering the relationship of health to occupation. The Cornish mine-surgeon, Pryce, was careful to distinguish between diseases which affected only the men who worked underground, and those which also afflicted women and children in the district. A serious attempt to measure the connection between cotton-mill employment and the incidence of pulmonary consumption in 1842 failed to establish a link which medical knowledge can show retrospectively to have existed. Its author failed to emphasise that so prevalent was consumption and so varied and widespread were the conditions which lowered resistance to it, that as Robert Southey remarked factory children would certainly in many cases die of consumption, as would many others for it was the 'disease of the English'. Only modern refined statistical techniques could hope to succeed in isolating occupational factors when pre-disposing conditions were varied and widespread.[16]

Charles Hall divided the occupational causes of ill health into three main categories: those sedentary occupations which denied proper exercise; those entailing forced, strained and unnatural postures of the body and those carried on in 'bad atmospheres' arising from filth, the use of chemical substances, excessive heat or damp, or oxygen-deficient air. Contemporaries may have written of 'miasmata' or 'noxious effluvia', but they did in many instances perceive the harmful nature of many substances used in manufactures.[17] Hall's classification can be usefully extended and modified to produce a classification into these broad categories: (1) ill health resulting from the harmful effects of materials e.g. metal poisoning; (2) resulting from the working environment e.g. from poor ventilation, dust-laden air, dampness or heat; (3) physical deterioration from harmful postures, cramped conditions, the over-strain of particular muscles or organs, or from the lack of an essential amount of exercise to compensate for prolonged sedentary work and (4) direct risk to life or limb from accident such as was common in the mining or building trades.

Contemporaries were too prone to offer 'noxious' gases or poisonous inhalations as the direct cause of ill health. In mining the concentration on supposed poisonous gases emanating from the metals themselves hid for centuries the fact that dust was the real destroyer of miners' lungs. Nevertheless they were often on the right track. Ramazzini described the effects of lead poisoning on pottery workers who used lead in glazing with some accuracy: 'First their hands become palsied, then they become paralytic, spenetic, lethargic, cachectic and toothless, so that one rarely sees a potter whose face is not cadaverous and the colour of lead.'[18] These symptoms were evident to Josiah Wedgwood in his rationalisation of the Staffordshire pottery manufacture, and they were still regarded as normal in less well-regulated factories than Wedgwood's *Eturia* by Turner-Thackrah in 1831. Not surprisingly lead poisoning was also recognised among plumbers and among house painters who according to one authority in 1747 had their nerves and lungs much affected by the lead in paint, and who were still in 1831 regarded as 'unhealthy in appearance' and as not generally attaining full age. Workers in the Whitechapel lead works rapidly became paralytic and seldom lived more than a dozen years in the business. Glaziers were also affected, while Ramazzini thought gilders so affected that when they did not die young they prayed for death.[19]

Lead was not the only substance whose harmful effects were recognised. Mercury was used in the manufacture of felt hats and produced the proverbial symptoms of the 'mad hatter': the palsy known as 'hatters' shakes' and the disturbing mental symptoms of depression, mania, loss of memory and paranoia.[20] The arsenic fumes from copper refining had dreadful effects on employees at Hayle in Cornwall where one visitor in 1794 claimed they became emaciated in a matter of weeks and died within a few years. Fumes at the bottom of large brewing vats could cause the death of men employed to clean them, and chemicals used in textile drying had adverse effects on the health of calico printers. Soot produced the well-known sweeps' cancer.[21]

Many other examples could be produced from less commonly pursued trades, but the effects of harmful working environments were more widespread and affected larger numbers of workers. Miners were commonly described as bearing evident indications of the effects of their employment. Celia Fiennes found the lead miners of Derbyshire in 1695 'pale and yellow' while the one met by Defoe was 'lean as a skeleton', 'pale as a dead corpse' and looking like 'an inhabitant of the dark regions below'.[22] The working conditions of the coalminers of Shropshire were vividly described in 1772:

> The murderers' cell is a palace in comparison with the black spot to which they repair; the vagrants' posture in the stocks is preferable to that in which they labour.
>
> Form if you can an idea of the misery of men kneeling, stooping or lying on one side, to toil all day in a confined place where a child could hardly stand . . . In these low and dreary vaults, all the elements seem combined against them. Destructive damp and clouds of noxious dust infect the air they breathe. Sometimes water incessantly distils on their naked bodies; or bursting on them in streams, drowns them, and deluges their work.[23]

William Pryce as a surgeon employed by the mines, was well aware of the effects of working in bad air on the Cornish miners, especially those who worked in the deeper, worse ventilated levels. He knew several men and boys who perished after a few months of such conditions, while those who lingered on were 'generally grieved with nauseas and reachings to vomit, oppression upon the breast, lassitude and torpor of the limbs, till at last the whole habit becomes tabid and they die hectick or consumptive'.[24] If the effects of dust on miners' lungs was for a long time missed because of the concern with the 'effluvia' of metals, the iron-filing laden air of the cutler's workplace was sooner recognised as responsible for the terrible toll of lung disease. Turner-Thackrah found grinders in particular to be 'almost all unhealthy' and remarkably short-lived, while a treatise on London diseases (1800) noted the effects of dust on the lungs of a variety of workers from coal-heavers through masons, bricklayers, chimney sweeps to bakers and hairdressers.[25]

Even a 'good' trade like confectionery or baking involved labour over charcoal fires in excessive temperatures. Woolcombers worked over charcoal stoves as well and were forced by their fumes to keep windows open even in cold weather. Such conditions persisted in this trade until the mid-nineteenth century when its practitioners were described as 'pale and cadaverous, few reaching fifty years of age'.[26] Forge workers were especially vulnerable to great heat, smoke, sulphurous fumes and noise:

> Stop to consider the sons of Vulcan confined to these forges and furnaces. Is their lot much preferable? A sultry air, the clouds of smoke and dust are the elements in which they labour. The confused scene of water falling, steam hissing, fire engines working, wheels turning, files creaking, hammers beating, ore bursting and bellows roaring, form a dismal concert that strikes the ears, while a continual eruption of flames, ascending from the mouth of their artificial volcanoes dazzles their eyes with a horrible glare . . . See them cast; you would think them in a bath and not a furnace; they bedew the burning sand with their streaming sweat, nor are their garments dried up by the fiery fires they attend or the fiery streams they manage.[27]

The lower levels of mines were often as excessive in heat as they were deficient in pure air. Frequently they were also wet, and miners suffered accordingly from extremes of heat and cold. Preparatory washing stages in the production of ores, cloth and leather, involved workers, often women and children, in working for prolonged periods in cold water, and rheumatic problems were frequently associated with such activities. Outside workers in the building trades needed hardy constitutions to stand up to extremes of weather in an age when they were neither as well-fed or as well-clothed as present day workers in the industry. Some tasks were so exhausting as to be destructive to health from sheer intensity of effort. Severity of labour must have worn down many a common labourer or porter. Pryce has left a vivid description of a method used to drain mines in Cornwall with a rag and chain pump. Such a pump of four inch diameter required five or six fresh men every six hours to draw a depth of 20 feet. The pump consisted of a metal chain with leather-stiffened knobs of cloth placed nine inches apart, turned by a three foot wheel through a wooden pipe of three to five inch bore, the knobs bringing up a stream of water. The men worked naked to the waist in turning the wheel and 'suffer much in their health and strength from the violence of the labour, which is so great that I have been witness to the loss of many lives by it'.[28]

Cramped working positions in low-ceilinged levels meant miners often laboured in stooping or even lying positions, but they were not alone in suffering from the physical strain of imposed working postures. Occupational cramps sometimes known as 'craft palsies' were conditions whereby symptoms were aggravated by the necessity of performing a customary act involving a repeated muscular action in a particular position. The necessary co-ordination of movement breaks down and spasm, tremor, pain, weakness and loss of control occur in the muscles concerned. Work becomes less careful and the finer kinds soon pass beyond the capabilities of the sufferer. Writers' cramp is a well-known form, but cotton-twisters, shoemakers, nailmakers, saddlers, sawyers and tailors were common victims.[29] These cramps, like eyestrain, limited efficiency and denied to the sufferers the opportunity of working on the better paid tasks, thus reducing their earning power as their time in the trade lengthened. Tailors suffered such deterioration in their eyesight that the best paid work was said to have been beyond most of them by the time they reached 40 after long years of winter working by dim candle-light. Watchmakers, too, fairly soon lost the acuteness of sight necessary for making the best wages by the time they reached early middle age, and many were forced to leave the profession altogether at an even earlier age.[30]

Standing often involved leaning or stooping postures which had adverse effects. Weavers complained both of this and of pressure on the chest when operating looms. Some even returned to the old loom where the shuttle had to be returned by hand because they complained the flying-shuttle loom needed too much strength. But for a man in reasonable physical condition the new looms may have been beneficial for Turner-Thackrah thought that weaving with them was an occupation in which more old men were to be found than most.[31] A part of the Black Country was locally known as 'Humpshire' because of the humped shoulders and twisted walk of the constantly bending lock makers.[32]

The sedentary trades presented their special problems, especially the widespread ones of tailoring and shoemaking. Plenty of people in the present-day pursue sedentary occupations without undue strain on their health, but they are not only better fed and likely to have sounder constitutions having grown up in healthy environments with well established patterns of infant care, but working only five eight-hour days have time and opportunity for relaxation and recreation. Their health problems begin when they over-indulge in the food and under-indulge in the recreation. It was the long hours of sedentary work which were primarily responsible for the unenviable reputation for ill health of the journeymen tailors and shoemakers of the eighteenth and early-nineteenth century. This reputation went at least as far back as Ramazzini:

It is a laughable sight to see those guilds of cobblers and tailors in their own special feast days when they march in procession two by two through the city or escort to the tomb some member of their guild who has died; yes it makes one laugh to see that troop of stooping, round-shouldered, limping men swaying from side to side; they look as though they had all been carefully selected for an exhibition of these infirmities.[33]

Campbell thought the cross-legged sitting posture of tailors, with the constant bending of the body made them more liable to consumption and coughs than most workers: 'You rarely see a tailor live to a great age'. The journeymen tailors of London reinforced the point themselves during their campaign for higher wages in 1752, complaining of the strains of sitting for so many hours bent double on the shop board with their legs under them.[34] Campbell makes no mention of similar problems for shoemakers, but both Ramazzini and Turner-Thackrah do. The latter thought that sitting with the legs crossed was a peculiar posture which made tailors a little more liable to ill effects than shoemakers. The crossed legs and bowed spine impeded respiration, circulation and digestion and led not to acute diseases, but to frequent stomach disorders and eventual pulmonary consumption: 'We see no plump and rosy tailors; none of fine form and strong muscle'. He gave a description of a representative young tailor:

He is 19 years of age, wretchedly meagre and sallow. He came from the country six years ago blooming and healthy. But since this period he has lived in Leeds, been confined to his baneful position from morning to night in a small low room, in which thirteen other tailors are at work. He cannot take more exercise than about half-a-mile's walk a day, except on Sundays. This case presents nothing rare. It is adduced as a fair specimen of the lamentable state of a great number of artisans.[35]

Shoemakers were a close second. Their digestion and circulation were so impaired that: 'the contenance would mark a shoemaker almost as well as a tailor'.[36] Campbell did not in 1747 single out watchmakers as being subject to any peculiar infirmity, but their own witnesses in 1817 complained that there were many boys who had entered the trade with robust constitutions, but who had rapidly become sickly and emaciated.[37]

Ruptures caused by the strain of lifting heavy loads were common among labouring people. Apprentices complained of being 'bursten',

and the existence of several charitable foundations for the support of
the ruptured poor is indicative of the familiarity of the problem: the
National Truss Society was formed in 1786; the Rupture Society ten
years later and the City Truss Society in 1807.[38]

Risk to life or limb was present in many occupations, but in several
was especially high, and in none were there so many possible sources of
danger as in mining. In addition to the risks inherent in any job which
involved manual labour with heavy and sharp tools in confined places,
there was the risk of explosion from gas or gunpowder and of crushing
from falling rock or cave-ins. Pryce was well aware of the demands of
his position as mine surgeon:

> In the course of a year it is 300 to 1 that trepan or crooked knife
> will be wanted very often . . . besides the ordinary accidents of burns,
> wounds, contusions, luxations or simple and compounded fractures,
> where the knife is spared; and the blasting one or both eyes, and the
> lost fingers of the left hand by gunpowder.[39]

So common was the maiming or killing of Cornish miners that a mine
steward whose letterbooks survive and which are full of solicitations
for the relief of injured miners or the families of dead ones, advised his
employer that it would save trouble if he were allowed to dispense such
sums as he thought fit up to £14 a year and charge it annually.[40] Gunpowder had been introduced into the Cornish mines in the seventeenth
century, as it had been into the lead mines of Derbyshire where the
dangers attending its use had been remarked on by Celia Fiennes in
1695. When it was introduced into the coal mines around 1719 it added
a new risk of explosion to that already existent in the presence of 'fire-
damp' (marsh gas). Defoe recorded a Durham pit explosion around
1700 in which 60 miners were killed. Such colliery disasters were far
from uncommon throughout the eighteenth century.[41] Accidents in
general were so frequent that with no inquests being required before
1814 most of them probably went unrecorded. Explosions were so
frequent in the Northern coalfield that the *Newcastle Journal* was re-
quested not to report them.[42] 'Fire-damp' ignited by a pitman's candle
was dramatic and sudden in its impact:

> Some of the unhappy men have time to prostrate themselves; the
> fiery scourge grazes their backs; the ground shields their breasts,
> they escape. See them wound up out of the blazing dungeon . . . A
> pestiferous steam and suffocating smoke pursue them. Half-dead

themselves they hold their dead or dying companions.[43]

The toll from less spectacular accidents such as falling from ropes while being lowered or being injured by falling rock, was large and is unknowable. The abounding reports in local newspapers can hardly amount to more than the tip of a very large iceberg.[44]

Even today the risk to workers in the metal working trades and in outside construction work is high despite the wearing of protective clothing and more aware and cautious attitudes. There is little point in running through the long catalogue of incidents from eighteenth-century newspapers. However the dangers to Sheffield knife grinders were especially commented on and will serve as a non-mining example. The grindstones they used turned with such speed that they sometimes flew into pieces and the slivers of stone maimed or even killed the men working at them.[45]

That industry extracted such a toll from its workers was hardly unknown in the eighteenth century, but to what extent was it seen as a social and human problem needing attention? Most, but not all, health risks were regarded as inevitable by employers and by employees alike. Indeed carelessness by the latter was often a contributing factor. William Jenkin thought many lives were lost in the Cornish mines through casual attitudes towards gunpowder because 'men in the habit of so working, seem to lose in a great measure a sense of their danger' and failed to take proper care.[46] Colliers contributed to rock falls by 'robbing the pillars' left to support the gallery roofs, or through careless propping.[47] Josiah Wedgwood was aware that bad hygiene habits contributed to the doleful effects of lead poisoning in the potteries, and typically provided remedial regulations. The dipping rooms were to be cleaned with a mop, not with a dry brush. A pail of water, soap and towel with a brush for the nails was to be provided near at hand. No one was to eat in the dipping room and the men and boys employed there were to wear overalls at all times.[48]

Wedgwood was, however, not even typical of pottery manufacturers let alone factory masters in general. Towards the end of the century there were some improvements (more than one of which was resisted or disregarded by the employees). Several improvements were noted in Sheffield. The use of power in iron forgery had sufficiently abridged the intensity of the labour to produce the remark in 1797 that the district no longer 'abounded in cripples and weak, deformed people' as it once had done. Young described the fixing of an iron guard over the grindstone wheels to deflect flying stone slivers, while Turner-Thackrah reported that the use of magnetic mouth pieces to help prevent iron filings from entering the lungs had been introduced 'many years ago'. They must have been to some effect but Young still thought the dangers to grinders from flying stone sufficient to justify very high wages, while Turner-Thackrah still found the filers to be 'almost all unhealthy men and remarkably short-lived'. The dry-stone fork grinders died in their thirties while the wet-stone knife grinders lasted into their forties.[49]

Attempts in the mines to deal both with bad air (choke damp) and with explosive gases (fire-damp) were made throughout the century. There was widespread use of the primitive method of exploding fire-damp by lowering lighted candles, but so long as naked flames had to be taken underground the risk remained a serious one. Even the invention of the Davy lamp in 1815 was not an unmixed blessing for by encouraging the working of deeper more gas-prone levels, it increased the risk of working in bad air even if it substantially lessened the chance of explosion.[50] Ventilation methods improved but only slowly through the century. John Wesley noted the use at Whitehaven in 1759 of a trap door method of making the air circulate, the doors being operated by child 'trappers'. This method spread to the north-east in the 1760s. The sinking of separate ventilating shafts was frequently considered too expensive, but in more profitable mines air pipe ventilation was developed. There is a description of a Whitehaven colliery in 1751 which describes the burning-off of foul air by enclosing a shaft and inserting four inch pipes. The air drawn up through these pipes was directed through a two inch funnel at the surface and ignited to burn in a controlled flame. The directing of a stream of water to carry an air current was well-known in the Cornish mines by the time of Pryce.[51]

It is, however, difficult to accept that conditions in the mines in general improved over the century. In some respects they may have. Cornish miners opening up some old parts of a mine in 1819 were surprised at how narrow and ill-ventilated the old levels were and at how cramped the tinners who worked them must have been.[52] However, the trend in metal and coalmining was towards the deeper and larger workings that the development of pumping technology made possible. This meant increased work at higher temperatures and in worse air offsetting to an extent the improvements in ventilation. In coalmining the introduction of pillar working increased casualties from roof falls.[53] Explosions were perhaps less frequent, but with the increase in scale of operations they were more expensive in terms of human life.

Mining was one of the few trades where there was some compulsory provision for medical care. The practice of paying for a mine surgeon by compulsory deduction from the miners' wages had already existed in Cornwall for more than sixty years by the time Pryce wrote in 1778. Perhaps he can hardly have been expected to have thought himself over-paid but he does record the difficulties of attracting the best doctors into such employment. He was himself the driving force behind the establishment of a miners' hospital, his experience having convinced him that injured miners had poor prospects of recovery if returned to their 'huts' or 'hovels'.[54] Self-help played its part among the artisans, for many friendly and benefit societies not only supported widows and the sick, but also paid for medical attendance. The Saint Helena Society formed in 1793 by London shipwrights provided a surgeon for its sick as well as offering £20 death benefit. It had, however, the inherent weakness of such clubs. Those who formed it grew old, sick and died together, causing the fund to collapse.[55]

Instances of concern and attempts at prevention do not substantially alter an impression of widespread acceptance on the part of masters and men alike of the health and life-destroying conditions of many employ-ments. The one may have been complacent and the other fatalistic, but both could take it for granted that to be short-lived and unhealthy was the normal lot of many workers. The attitude of Socrates was not dead in eighteenth-century middle- and upper-class Englishmen. Acceptance was hardly a matter of choice for the labouring poor. Sir George Barker, a physician who took a special interest in the lead-caused ailments of plumbers, glaziers and painters, thought they could be restored to health if they pursued their employment with greater caution, but that to have remained free from the disease they would have had to quit their em-ployment.[56] Such was not often a possibility. For the most part need not only kept men to trades whose effects they were well aware of, but forced them to bring their children up to those very same employments.

The present-day notion of high wage compensation for dangerous and unpleasant labour was largely non-existent, although Adam Smith offered it as an explanation of wage differentials, using the miner as an example: 'A journeyman blacksmith, though an artificer seldom earns so much in twelve hours as a collier who is only a labourer, does in eight. His work is not quite so dirty, is less dangerous, and is carried on in daylight, and above ground.'[57] The shorter day of the miner was true enough, but higher remuneration probably owed less to the dangers of the occupation than to the problems of labour supply in the remote rural mining districts. The shorter day may have had its origins in a

recognition of the limited number of hours a man could stand underground, but by the mid-eighteenth century it was more of a customary
expectation, than one requiring rational justification.[58]

In general the less healthy trades were among the least well paid.
Since there was little choice about either entering or leaving them, there
was no relevance in thinking of compensating for their conditions.
Workers did sometimes include harmful effects in the catalogue of
'oppressions' they presented when in dispute with their employers, but
they gave them no special place in their lists of grievances, nor sought
specific redress or remedy for them. The Portsmouth shipwrights on
strike in 1775 against the introduction of a piecework scheme designed
to increase their efficiency complained that it would 'occasion pro-
gressive suicide in our bodies'. But their real objections were deeper
seated and more entrenched in their customary work practices.[59] The
London tailors were more specific and gave a more central place to an
argument about health in their disputes in the first half of the century.
Resisting the masters' imposition of a 15-hour day, they linked their
hours of work directly to the deterioration of their eyesight which
made them 'incapable to get their bread after forty years of age'. They
were seeking only a reduction of an hour and the main prop of their
argument was not health deterioration but the custom of 14 hours in
most other trades. In 1752 in seeking a living wage they wove into their
argument a clear statement of the way in which ill health limited their
earning power:

> Their health and sight are soon impaired; insomuch that many in the
> prime of their years are become despised by their masters, by reason
> their sight is decayed, and they cannot see to work so well as others
> . . . and in order to get bread for themselves and their families, the
> poor miserable wretches are obliged to work for masters at an under-
> price.[60]

They were however seeking to explain why they needed higher wages to
subsist, not developing a notion of high wage compensation for the ill-
health effects of their employment. When the weavers of the south-west
drew attention to the miseries of their lives in 1739, the employers
turned the health argument back on them. William Temple argued that
weaving did not make for ill health, rather it offered employment to
the already poor in health:

> The weavers in general are the most feeble, weak and impotent of all

the manufacturers. A male child perhaps is found on a dunghill, bursed up by the parish, through negligence and want of proper care is weak and sickly, and at the age of 8 or 10 years is put an apprentice to a weaver: a parent has a child infirm, deform'd sickly, weak and distorted; he considers his constitution, and how easy the employment of a weaver is, and puts him an apprentice to that trade in which he knows his child can aquire a comfortable subsistence, without the requisites in other occupations of a healthy body and a strong constitution. The father is sensible in this craft his son is not exposed to hard labour, to the inclemencies of the weather, to travel from place to place for employment. He knows if his child is dull, sagacity is not required; if weak, strength is not demanded; if sickly, hardships are not incident; if slow and inactive, agility is not necessary.[61]

The same argument was put in the master clothiers' petition of 1756. The persons employed in weaving were not chosen for strength or robustness. The work was neither laborious nor toilsome. The weak, lame, old, decrepit, puny, women and children were all capable of weaving, as were such whose condition and ability were not equal to other employments. Was it therefore 'just or reasonable' that the labour of such people should be put on a footing with men of stronger and more robust constitutions or more useful abilities? The argument falsely implies that choice of trade existed for the healthy.[62]

Some trades, the worst and the lowest of all, could only be filled by the truly desperate and needy, or by the 'unfree' parish apprentices. For the labourers in lead works or the chimney boys, the meanness of their occupation confirmed the lowness of their being. Their crippled bodies marked and dehumanised them. The shortness of their miserable existence was a blessing. Amid such attitudes there was no place for any notion of compensation.

Technological improvements even when they abridged labour were not always unmixed blessings. The effect of the Davy lamp was, as we have seen, to allow the working of deeper levels. The spring-shuttle reduced the bending needed on the traditional loom, but most agreed that it took more strength to operate. The factory system is beyond the scope of this book, but it should not be forgotten that the numbers engaged in handloom weaving multiplied as the consequence of the emergence of the spinning mills. Machine-produced yarn multiplied their number before machine weaving extinguished them. The overstocking of the trade pushed rates lower and lower as competition with factory weaving intensified. In order to make subsistence wages increasing hours had to be put in at the loom, and the toiling handloom weaver became enmeshed in that pattern of excessive labour inducing ill health regarded by Turner-Thackrah as so destructive of the well-being of the artisan.[63]

It might be argued that the discussion of ill health presented in this chapter is itself so dismal as to suggest that the factory has been held over-responsible for bringing ill health to working people. The cottage of the domestic manufacturer may often have been as unhealthy a place as the factory. It was ill-ventilated, damp and cold. The very fact that work was carried on in the home could in itself add noxious smells and fumes which would have been absent from the pure residence. Nevertheless the cottage was in the country allowing access to pure air and space. The possibility of occasional farming employment and the lack of stress in domestic production rhythms all gave opportunity of renewing the vigour that hard labour sapped.[64]

The debate over the factory belongs to the early-nineteenth century. That debate centres on the health of women and children for they were the labour force of the early mills. Child labour was already widespread in eighteenth-century manufacturing and the vivid illustrations in the Blue Books of the 1840s showing children on all-fours drawing trucks through the narrow levels of the coal pits, could as well have come from the 1770s in Shropshire where a contemporary described children who 'with their hands and feet on the black, dusty ground and a chain about their body, creep and drag along like four footed beasts, heavy loads of the dirty mineral, through ways almost impassable to the curious observer'.[65]

However hard children worked in the manufacturing cottage, and however young they started, the truth about the factory is that it separated child labour from the family economy, systematised it and placed it in a more intolerable environment. Corporal discipline, long hours and the dangers from unfenced machinery mangling over-tired young limbs make it special pleading which denies the substantial difference in form and pace which differentiates child labour in the factory from that in the home. The recognition that it was widespread in eighteenth-century manufacturing and that the lot of these children was not always a happy one, does not permit us to regard the exploitation of child labour by the early factory masters as little more than the continuation of well-established practice. Well before the end of the eighteenth century, observers who, like the Manchester doctor Thomas Percival in 1774, lived close to the early mills reacted against their associated conditions:

It is a common but injurious custom in manufacturing counties to confine children, before they have reached a sufficient degree of strength to sedentary employments in places where they breathe putrid air and are debarred from the free use of their limbs. The effect of this confinement is either to cut them off early in life, or to render their constitutions sickly and feeble.[66]

Ten years later a highly critical report on conditions in the Manchester mills was produced. They were built to contain as many employees in a given space as possible and ceilings were accordingly low to get in more storeys. Floors were crowded with machines. Much oil was used and with the cotton dust in the air adhering to the friction-heated oil a strong and disagreeable smell was always present. At night the situation was worsened by the lack of ventilation and the heat and smoke of great numbers of candles.[67] Aiken, the author of a famous description of the Manchester area in 1797 was also a doctor. He wrote of the poor law apprentice children brought in batches from the workhouses to the mills. They were usually too long confined to work often for the whole night in the 'injurious' air of the mills. Temperature changes from extreme heat to cold predisposed them to sickness and disability and epidemics were general.[68] The evidence produced in the several reports on factory conditions from 1816 through to the well-known Blue Books of the 1840s have been variously assessed, accepted or dismissed, but what little evidence there is on the factory system during its eighteenth-century beginnings seems strongly to suggest a deleterious effect on the health of its mostly young employees.

Sir John Simon, an important figure in the history of public health, thought that general *concern* with as opposed to awareness of the health problems associated with work only came about as a result of Turner-Thackrah's great book in 1831. This made such problems not only a matter of 'common knowledge' but also one of state responsibility since industrial conditions which brought 'painful disease and premature disablement or death' were often of 'an evidently removable kind'.[69] Much publicised parliamentary investigations paved the way for the ameliorative acts of the 1840s on child labour in the factories and mines, but adult male workers were for longer considered no concern of the law. Outside the larger establishments workers in small workshops and outworkers in many trades revealed themselves in the pages of Mayhew and Booth to be labouring in conditions not very different from those of their eighteenth-century counterparts until they too received their share of parliamentary attention around the turn of the nineteenth century.

Even today as I drafted this chapter a single issue of a newspaper revealed both the side-stepping by the powerful asbestos interest of the
issues raised by the revelations of the death-dealing dust of their production processes and the last-ditch resistance by the nationalised coal
industry to the payment of compensation to some breath-gasping
victims of pneumoconiosis.

Notes

1. *Gentleman's Magazine*, LII (1782), p. 526.
2. D. Hunter, *Health in Industry* (Harmondsworth, 1959), pp. 24-5.
3. Bernard Ramazzini, *De Morbis Artificum* (Translation of 1713 edition by
W. Cave Wright, Chicago, 1940), p. 3. The work was first translated into English
anonymously in 1705, but became widely known in an enlarged edition by Robert
James in 1746. This was the edition known to Adam Smith.
4. Adam Smith, *The Wealth of Nations* (1776, edited by E. Cannan 1904,
paperback edn, London, 1961), Vol. I, p. 91.
5. Charles Hall, *The Effects of Civilization on the People in European States*
(1805, rep. New York, 1965), p. 21.
6. For example, R. Campbell, *The London Tradesman* (1747, reprinted
Newton Abbot, 1969).
7. Hunter, *Health in Industry*, pp. 177-8, 246.
8. Charles Turner-Thackrah, *The Effects of the principal Arts Trades and
Professions and of civic states and habits of living on Health and Longevity with
a particular reference to the Trades and Manufactures of Leeds etc.* (London,
1831).
9. Ibid., pp. 5, 121.
10. Robert Willan, *Reports on the Diseases in London* (London, 1801), pp.
133-6.
11. F.W. Galton, *Select Documents Illustrating the History of Trade Unionism:
The Tailoring Trade* (London, 1896), p. 14 (footnote).
12. Smith, *Wealth of Nations*, Vol. I, p. 92; Turner-Thackrah, *Effects*, pp. 118-
19, G.I.H. Lloyd, *The Cutlery Trades* (London, 1913), p. 111.
13. Turner-Thackrah, *Effects*, pp. 111, 114.
14. Smith, *Wealth of Nations*, Vol. I, p. 92.
15. W. Hutton, *A History of Birmingham* (Birmingham, 1781), p. 10; William
Temple, *The Case as It Now Stands etc.* (1739), p. 24. Reprinted in K. Carpenter
(ed.), *Labour Problems before the Industrial Revolution* (New York, 1972);
M. Dorothy George, *London Life in the Eighteenth Century* (Harmondsworth,
1966 edn), p. 205; Hunter, *Health in Industry*, p. 123.
16. D. Noble, 'On the Influence of the Factory System in the Development of
Pulmonary Consumption', *Journal of the Statistical Society of London*, Vol. V
(1832), pp. 274-80; quoted in M. Thomis, *The Town Labourer and the Industrial
Revolution* (London, 1974), p. 112.
17. Hall, *Effects of Civilization*, pp. 19-20.
18. Ramazzini, *De Morbis Artificum*, p. 53.
19. Turner-Thackrah, *Effects*, pp. 58, 55; Campbell, *London Tradesman*,
pp. 103-4, 107; Turner-Thackrah, *Effects*, p. 56; Ramazzini, *De Morbis Artificum*,
p. 33.
20. Hunter, *Health in Industry*, pp. 123-5.

21. W.G. Maton, *Observations on the Western Counties of England* (Salisbury, 1794-6), p. 261; *Exeter Mercury*, 6 January 1764; *Minutes of Evidence taken before the Committee on the Petition of the Journeymen Calico Printers*, P.P. 1804 reprinted as P.P. 1807 (129), II, pp. 6-7.

22. Celia Fiennes, *Journeys 1695* (edited by C. Morris, London, 1949), pp. 102-3; Daniel Defoe, *A Tour through the Whole Island of Great Britain* (1724, Everyman edition, London, 1962), Vol. II, p. 164.

23. John Fletcher quoted in L. Moffit, *England on the Eve of the Industrial Revolution* (1923, reprinted London, 1963), pp. 256-7.

24. W. Pryce, *Mineralogia Cornubiensis* (Oxford, 1778), p. 198.

25. Turner-Thackrah, *Effects*, p. 52; George, *London Life*, p. 204.

26. H. Heaton, *The Yorkshire Woollen and Worsted Industries* (1920, reprinted Oxford, 1965), pp. 334-5.

27. John Fletcher quoted in Moffit, *England on the Eve of the Industrial Revolution*, p. 258.

28. Pryce, *Mineralogia Cornubiensis*, pp. 150-1.

29. Hunter, *Health in Industry*, p. 230.

30. Galton, *Tailoring Trade*, pp. 15, 38; *Report of Committee on the Petitions of the Watchmakers of Coventry*, P.P. 1817 (504), VI, pp. 73-4; Turner-Thackrah, *Effects*, p. 25.

31. *Report from the Committee on the Woollen Manufacturers' Petition*, P.P. 1802/3 (71), V, p. 495; *Report from the Committee on the Silk Ribbon Weavers' Petitions*, P.P. 1818 (134), IX, p. 7; Turner-Thackrah, *Effects*, pp. 20-1.

32. G. Hogg, *Safe Bind, Safe Find* (London, 1961), p. 66.

33. Ramazzini, *De Morbis Artificum*, p. 283.

34. Campbell, *London Tradesman*, pp. 192-3; Galton, *Tailoring Trade*, pp. 52-3.

35. Turner-Thackrah, *Effects*, pp. 15-16.

36. Ibid., p. 22.

37. *Report on the Watchmakers of Coventry*, P.P. 1817, IX, pp. 73-4.

38. George, *London Life*, p. 203.

39. Pryce, *Mineralogia Cornubiensis*, p. 176.

40. Letter books of William Jenkin, Mss. County Museum, Truro, Jenkin to A.M. Hunt, 17 January 1800.

41. Fiennes, *Journeys*, pp. 102-3; T.S. Ashton and J. Sykes, *The Coal Industry of the Eighteenth Century*, revised edn (Manchester, 1964), p. 15; Defoe, *Tour*, Vol. II, p. 249.

42. Ashton & Sykes, *Coal Industry*, p. 43.

43. John Fletcher quoted in Moffit, *England on the Eve of the Industrial Revolution*, p. 257.

44. Ashton & Sykes, *Coal Industry*, p. 57.

45. Arthur Young, *A Six Months Tour through the North of England* (London, 1771), Vol. I, pp. 123-4.

46. Jenkin Mss. Jenkin to A.M. Hunt, 27 February 1801.

47. N. McKendrick, 'Josiah Wedgwood and Factory Discipline', *Historical Journal*, IV (1961), pp. 30-5.

48. Ashton & Sykes, *Coal Industry*, p. 17.

49. George, *London Life*, p. 203; Turner-Thackrah, *Effects*, pp. 50-2; Young, *Northern Tour*, Vol. I, pp. 123-4.

50. R. Pococke, *Travels through England* (1751, edited by J.J. Cartwright, London, 1888), Vol. I, p. 206; Ashton & Sykes, *Coal Industry*, pp. 52-3.

51. Ashton & Sykes, *Coal Industry*, pp. 43, 46, 49; Pococke, *Travels*, Vol. I, p. 16; Pryce, *Mineralogia Cornubiensis*, p. 201.

52. J.G. Rule, 'The Labouring Miner in Cornwall c. 1740-1870: A Study in

Social History', unpublished PhD thesis, University of Warwick, 1971, p. 22.

53. Ashton & Sykes, *Coal Industry*, p. 162.

54. Pryce, *Mineralogia Cornubiensis*, pp. 176-7.

55. *Report from the Select Committee on the Combination Laws*, P.P. 1825 (417, 437), IV, p. 300.

56. George, *London Life*, p. 369, footnote no. 142.

57. Smith, *Wealth of Nations*, Vol. I, p. 112.

58. Rule, 'Labouring Miner', p. 81.

59. A. Geddes, *Portsmouth during the Great French Wars 1770-1800* (Portsmouth, 1970), p. 19.

60. Galton, *Tailoring Trade*, pp. 13, 52-3.

61. Temple, *The Case as It Now Stands*, pp. 12-13.

62. W.E. Minchinton, 'The Petitions of the Weavers and Clothiers of Gloucestershire in 1756', *Transactions of the Bristol & Gloucestershire Archaeological Society*, vol. 73 (1954), p. 222.

63. Turner-Thackrah, *Effects*, p. 119.

64. Heaton, *Woollen and Worsted Industries*, pp. 349-50.

65. From an account quoted in Moffit, *England on the Eve of the Industrial Revolution*, pp. 256-7.

66. Ibid., p. 259.

67. W. Bowden, *Industrial Society in England towards the End of the Eighteenth Century* (1925, reprinted London, 1965), pp. 267-8.

68. J. Aikin, *A Description of the Country from Thirty to Forty Miles round Manchester* (1795, reprinted New York, 1968), pp. 219-20.

69. Hunter, *Health in Industry*, p. 46.

4 APPRENTICESHIP

When in 1814 Parliament repealed part of an act which had been on the statute book for 250 years it threatened an institution which, according to one of the repeal's opposers, had existed 'from time, to the contrary whereof the memory of man runneth not'.[1] That institution was apprenticeship and the threat came from the repeal of the clauses governing it in the famous act of 1563, the Statute of Artificers and Apprentices — the act of 5 Elizabeth as it had become generally known. The relevant clause was:

· It shall not be lawful to any person, other than such as now do lawfully exercise any art, mistery, or manual occupation, to exercise any craft now used within the realm of England or Wales, except he shall have been brought up therein seven years at the least as apprentice.

The act intended the extension to urban England at large of what had been for several centuries a guild practice in the City of London and other corporate towns.[2] The purposes of the framers of the act have never been clear even to specialist historians of the period,[3] but throughout the eighteenth century it remained the main statutory prop of those seeking to preserve the principle of apprenticeship and the main, if all too often ineffective, inhibition on those seeking to destroy or evade it.

Many historians have commented on the significance of the repeal of 1814. Paul Mantoux saw the outcome as marking the triumph in Great Britain of *laissez faire*, while to the Webbs the House of Commons was sweeping away 'practically the last remnant of that legislative protection of the Standard of Life which survived from the Middle Ages'.[4] It was perhaps not as clear-cut as that, but it did represent a definite step in the triumph of *laissez-faire* capitalism in Britain. With the repeal of the apprenticeship clauses of 5 Elizabeth the last major legislative limitation on the labour market had been removed, and the need of capitalist employers for a mobile labour force whose supply and price would be determined by the 'natural' laws of a free labour market was recognised in law as it had long been allowed in practice. The struggle which preceded the repeal and which occupied the several years leading up to 1814 was between organised skilled labour seeking to have re-asserted the sleeping protective functions of the state, and the manufacturing employers resisting any attempt at the reimposition of disregarded restrictions on freedom of economic action. This freedom they had sought and largely achieved well before Adam Smith's *Wealth of Nations* gave economic self-interest a justifying ideology and a new intellectual rigour in 1776. Retrospectively the historian finds it difficult to see the outcome of the struggle as other than inevitable. So completely had the ideas of Dr Smith come to dominate the thinking on social and economic matters of the large majority of Members of Parliament, that to preach the removal of economic restrictions was by 1814 to preach to the converted. To this end the careful findings and uncertainties of Parliament's own committees were ignored.[5] When the clockmakers petitioned Lord Liverpool in 1813 to try and win his support against the Bill, they well knew whose authority would be used to underpin the employers' case:

> we apprehend that even if the enlightened mind of your Lordship should disdain to be bound by the cobweb theories of Dr Adam Smith and other modern specialists on political economy (the temerity of which experience and observation cannot but proclaim), yet that your Lordship might not immediately be able to induce other persons to partake your liberation.[6]

Although the details of the passing of the repeal bill and of the well-organised campaign of the skilled workers on a national basis against it have been described by historians, it has tended to be seen from the retrospective nineteenth-century standpoint rather than from the context of the place of apprenticeship in the labour experience of the eighteenth century.[7]

Whatever the intentions of Elizabethan legislators, there is no doubt that 5 Elizabeth was for two centuries an important symbol to the skilled workers of the better days of Good Queen Bess when a paternalist government had protected their interests against the encroachments of capitalism. Memory or myth, the idea of a concerned government functioned as an important reference point. An Essex woolcombers' verse of the late-seventeenth century put it very clearly:

> From such as would our rights invade,
> Or would intrude into our trade,
> Or break the law Queen Betty made
> Libera nos Domine

Nearly a century later an *Ode to the Memory of Queen Elizabeth* was composed after the London saddlers had been in dispute with their employers:

> Her memory still is dear to journeymen,
> For sheltered by her laws, now they resist
> Infringements, which would else persist:
> Tyrannic masters, innovating fools
> Are check'd, and bounded by her glorious rules.
> Of workmen's rights, she's still a guarantee.
> And rights of artisans, to fence and guard,
> While we, poor helpless wretches, oft must go,
> And range this liberal nation to and fro.[8]

Clearly we are dealing not just with a sustaining memory or myth, but with an essential supportive notion of legitimacy. *Laws* passed in the Queen's reign which protected the artisan were still the law of the land. Labour did not suffer because they did not exist but because they were hardly enforced.

Apprenticeship was much older than the Act of 5 Elizabeth, but that act intended to extend more generally an institution whose essential features, long incorporated into the by-laws of guilds and chartered companies were:

(1) The binding by indenture and the due recording of the articles of agreement therein.

(2) A minimum term of seven years to be served before a trade could be independently exercised.

(3) The binding to be a personal linking of the apprentice to a specific master, and to involve a close supervisory control over private life as well as over training. In fact a *'loco parentis'* relationship was implied including the right to inflict corporal punishment.

(4) The normal age of binding was to be the early teens.

(5) The completion of an apprenticeship would confer an exclusive right to exercise that trade.

(6) No remuneration other than support was required.

Formal binding involved some bother and some expense. In many trades the notion of a 'legal' workman extended to those who had worked seven years in a trade whether or not they had been formally indentured and case law had come to recognise this by the eighteenth century. In

particular where sons were brought up in the trade by their fathers, or
nephews by their uncles there was rarely in the common trades any
formal indenturing. The experience of John Phillips, a Somersetshire
weaver who began to learn the trade about 1770, was probably common
enough:

> I was brought up under my father when about 11 years of age; then
> I had an Uncle, my father's brother, who took me out of charity
> [on his father's death]. No my father was a poor Shearman, and he
> was not able to put me out properly Apprentice, and my uncle took
> me to teach me the trade. My uncle bought a stamp to put me out
> apprentice, he went the cost of the stamp, my father was to pay the
> expenses, but through poverty he did not do it; I was carried to a
> gentleman of our town, Sexton of the Parish, but it was never paid
> for, and I was not apprenticed; I served seven years with my uncle.[9]

In a large rural trade like weaving it was expected that a father would
bring up his sons to his trade. It was a matter of necessity as much as
choice: 'because they cannot put them out to any other trade, or they
would not teach them to weave'. If this was true of the common trades,
especially in rural districts, at the other end of the trade structure were
some groups of skilled men who kept the supply of labour under control by allowing fathers the right to bring up only their first son to the
trade.[10]

Where a formal indenture existed freedom from a bad master, or
from an unsatisfactory apprentice, could only be achieved through the
courts, generally Quarter Sessions, or in the case of the incorporated
London trades through the court of the company. For example the
Manchester magistrates discharged an apprentice from a fustian cutter
in 1789 on the grounds that the apprentice had been worked too hard
at unreasonable hours and subjected to unmerciful beating. Release
could also be obtained for seemingly less oppressive reasons as one
west-country broadweaver remarked, 'A difference in opinion arose,
and I went to a Magistrate and he released me'. A petition for release
from a master printer complains:

> Having suffered many hardships during my Apprenticeship, such
> as my father dying when I had served but two years and left me
> friendless, in so much that I had no one to find me in cloaths but
> my Master, which he refused in consequence of which I had not
> any to appear decent in, and for the last three years of my time was

actually obliged to remain at home for want of them. For trifling faults . . . I have been frequently knocked down, knelt on and beat in a most unmerciful manner.

He continued to complain of long hours, sometimes from 6 am to midnight without any gratuity as reward. To such lads as this the advice to printers' apprentices offered in 1705 must have seemed somewhat hollow: 'I'd reckon my Master and Mistress as another Father and Mother . . . There's no way but this to make the chains of a seven years bondage sit easily without galling'.[11]

By insisting on a seven-year period of service from about the age of 14 it was perhaps the intention of 5 Elizabeth to protect the quality and reputation of English manufactures by ensuring that only the properly trained produced them. Adam Smith was clearly of the opinion that there was hardly a trade that could not be learned in less time. Even the skilled trades like watchmaking could be picked up in a matter of weeks, and as for the common trades, they could be picked up in a few days. Long apprenticeships were no guarantee of good workmanship, indeed they did not form young persons to habits of industry, but rather to idleness.[12]

Many would have agreed with Smith, although perhaps not with his extreme suggestions as to the amount of training needed. It should be borne in mind, however, that young people often assisted their fathers for many years before they became apprenticed in their teens. As a clothier from the West Country admitted:

You do not speak of an instance of a savage from the woods, or a porter taken out of the London streets, but you speak of persons who know something of the trade; he knows the nature of yarn, he puts his hand to one thing and another, and there is hardly a boy who does not put his hand to every part that he can; I have not the least doubt that a boy so circumstanced at the age of sixteen would learn his business perfectly well in about a Twelvemonth.[13]

Those who viewed apprenticeship as more than a simply economic relationship stressed its importance as an agency of social control. The young person learned his trade under the guiding principles of a sound moral supervision within a good Christian family. This aspect was presumed self-evident. The apprentice went to live in his master's house and it is all too easy to absorb a cosy picture of these 'extra sons and daughters'.[14] In the words of a contemporary: 'youth should be under a particular moral restraint during the most dangerous period of their lives, rather than left at large . . . who then shall have nerve enough to say that by one act of legislative licence they will set afloat the great body of the passions of the most helpless part of society; that part from which, poverty and the want of education, is the most subject to error, the most liable to temptation, and the least capable of resisting it'.[15] It was not just customary expectation. This aspect was given full acknowledgement in the usual form of indenture:

> he shall not commit fornication, nor contract matrimony . . . he shall not play at cards, dice, tables, or any other unlawful games, . . . without license of his said masters he shall neither buy nor sell; he shall not haunt taverns nor playhouses, nor absent himself from his said masters service, day or night unlawfully; but in all things as a faithful apprentice he shall behave himself towards his masters.[16]

However, important reservations have to be made before this aspect of apprenticeship can be evaluated. Those who favoured the institution sometimes stressed the authority of the master as being especially beneficial in that it was likely to be more strict than that of a parent. But many young men were bound to fathers or close relatives with or without formal indenturing. Equally important the 'perfect model' of the institution was in many trades seriously impaired by the growth of 'outdoor' apprenticeship, so much so that the traditional living-in form of the institution had to be specified as 'indoor' apprenticeship. One form of outdoor apprenticeship simply implied that the lad received instruction in the home or shop of the master while continuing to be boarded at home by his family. In such cases an allowance was sometimes made by the master towards his upkeep, commonly £5 p.a. at the end of the eighteenth century.[17] This hardly threatened the traditional conception of the relationship but the growth of another form of outdoor apprenticeship clearly did. This was the taking on by masters of large numbers of young lads in the form of apprentices and lodging them out. Such lads were in fact a way of obtaining cheap labour for they would be used to perform tasks for which journeymen would have been paid much higher rates. Naturally the fully trained craftsmen bitterly resented this method of obtaining cheap labour. In the trades where it was widely used e.g. the calico-printing trades in the north, the London printing trades, and the silk-weaving and watchmaking trades in Coventry, the evidence that it brought about considerable unemployment of the skilled workers is strong. The 1790s seem to have been the period in which this use of apprenticeship was most evident.[18]

The obvious hostility of the legal workmen clearly colours their accounts of the iniquities of the outdoor system, but there can be no doubt that they were right in seeing it as bearing no relationship to the traditional conception of apprenticeship. A printers' circular of 1806 suggested that the Society for the Suppression of Vice would be better employed combating outdoor apprenticeship where the lads 'finding no check' were 'hurried into every vice' and ended their lives on the gallows, than in 'hunting lollypop sellers on Sunday mornings'. The bookbinders were sure that this 'novel practice' had 'nothing of the manner of an apprentice in it'. It might as well have been said 'after the manner of a journeyman'. The youths were found in neither food nor lodgings, but were converted into a kind of indentured journeyman: 'every idea of apprenticeship is violated'. It had in London diffused vice and dissipation to a 'lamentable extent' and offered 'numerous victims' to the violated laws of the country. As far as the calico-printing trade in Lancashire was concerned a parliamentary enquiry found that the practice 'altogether extinguished' both 'the duty which ought to attach to an apprentice' and the 'right which ought to belong to a journeyman'. Four years after the repeal of the apprenticeship clauses of 5 Elizabeth, the Coventry watchmakers were deploring the fact that now there were none other than outdoor apprentices:

> they are left to their own conduct to obtain their living at large, without protection, without domestic discipline, without moral or religious instruction or example; so diametrically opposite and re-pugnant to the ancient custom and law of apprenticeship.

They recalled the old times when a master took no more than two apprentices at a time into his own dwelling where he supported and maintained them and acted towards them 'in all respects as of his own family' and taught them properly the whole art of their trade.[19]

Of course this is a romanticised view of the traditional institution. We do not expect the nuclear, let alone an extended family to be in-variably a circle of love and affection with necessary gentle chastise-ment from time to time hurting the master more than the apprentice. Even a casual examination of the columns of newspapers would reveal instances of violence and maltreatment of apprentices. The apprentice was all too often in a vulnerable position if indentured to a brutal master. Corporal punishment was allowed within reason, and if it is remembered that most apprentices were not boys but young men well before their period of indentured service ended, then bitter resentment, hostility and running away and even retaliatory action were hardly surprising responses.[20] Naturally the most extreme atrocities were the ones which made the news, but they still serve to emphasise that the placing of a young person in a household could expose them to savage, even pathologically brutal treatment. The extent of sexual exploitation, particularly of females apprenticed as house-servants can hardly be guessed at. The parish apprentices, those apprenticed by the guardians of the poor, were especially vulnerable. They were usually younger children rather than adolescents. They had no parents in a position to look after their interests, and they were often resented in that they were forced by the poor-law authorities on reluctant members of the rate-paying community. Because of the incentive to remove them from the support of the poor rate as quickly and as cheaply as possible they were often bound to the most unpleasant, health- or even life-destroying employments. Two forms of such employment have been widely discussed: the dispatching of large numbers of children to form the labour force of the cotton mills of the early industrial revolution and the cruel use of undersized boys to climb and sweep chimneys. In both cases child labour was being placed in conditions to which few parents would have willingly consigned their children. The literature both contemporary and modern on these cases is extensive, but a comment on the chimneyboys in 1747 makes the essential point clearly enough:

> The proper business of this black fraternity is expressed by their name, and may be seen in their face; it is true they all take apprentices, and the younger they are the better fit to climb up the chimneys; but I would not recommend my friend to breed his son to this trade, 'tho I know some masters who live comfortably. I think this branch is chiefly occupied by unhappy Parish children, and may for ought I know, be the greatest nursery for Tyburn of any trade in England.[21]

In such trades beatings were commonplace to keep a child attentive to unpleasant and painful tasks.

Theory and expectation do not always correspond to practice and reality. Many masters so long as they were getting their due work from an apprentice were hardly over-concerned to attempt the wearisome and all too often impossible role of disciplining the adolescent. An historian has recently suggested that living-in notwithstanding, the London apprentices of the seventeenth century as a group displayed many of the characteristics which have been ascribed to twentieth-century youth.

They thought of themselves as a separate order or sub-culture, which like the larger culture of which it was a part, was somewhat hierarchical with the gentleman apprentice to a merchant being poles apart from the pauper apprentice to a shoemaker. Nevertheless all shared in the experience of apprenticeship and of adolescence. They had been taken from their families at a crucial stage in their development and put into other families of which they were a part, yet always apart. Their shared experiences bound them into a sub-culture with a 'fraternal affection' not unlike class solidarity or youth solidarity.[22] Certainly Francis Place's description of apprentice life in eighteenth-century London shows that far from being models of good conduct apprentices represented the wild, excessive behaviour frequently associated with youth. The 'industry' of taverns, theatres, gaming houses, pleasure gardens and brothels depended upon their custom. Drinking, hooliganism and consorting with prostitutes were common, and turning to crime was not infrequent. Place himself was an indoor apprentice, but his master cared little what he did once his required quantity of work had been executed. Samuel Drew apprenticed to a shoemaker in Cornwall learned the trade of smuggling in his spare time. Professor Rudé used the fact of a completed apprenticeship to establish the 'respectability' of Gordon rioters, but Dr Linebaugh had shown that the test works in the same proportion for criminals hanged at Tyburn.[23]

When an apprentice lived in his master's household he had to live not only with him, but also with his wife. Many an apprentice found it easier to get on with the former than with the latter. A life could be made miserable by a scolding mistress, or by one whose parsimonious housekeeping provided inadequate and poor meals. William Hutton suffered much in this respect, and the woman was his aunt.[24] In his specially written guide for parents seeking to apprentice their offspring, Robert Campbell warned:

> Such a woman, who has got the better of her husband, in the management of her domestic concerns, must of course rule his apprentice; the youth must be Madam's slave, must fetch and carry, and do all the drudgery of her house, without regard to his business, in which he is never employed but when she has nothing for him to do in the kitchen. This is not learning a trade, but acting the drudge; yet it is the fate of those whose masters are under petticoat government: And such masters, Parents ought to guard against in the choice of a Master for their children.[25]

Some of the extreme cases of violence and maltreatment of apprentices involved members of the family as well as masters.[26] The recollections of an apprentice to a shoemaker in Cornwall of harsh treatment and of being forced to undertake menial tasks about the house were about the mistress rather than the master. It was hardly surprising that he learned his trade badly, for not only was he at the beck and call of the wife, but his master kept a smallholding and the lad was employed for half of his time on that.[27]

One area where apprenticeship did bring a restraint regarded as useful for society, was that it prevented marriage until the indentured period was over. The decline of formal apprenticeship was blamed in the Sheffield cutlery districts for the increasing number of improvident marriages among the young cutlers. In the age of Malthus such arguments had special force.[28]

Because no normal remuneration was involved, apprenticeship provided a cheap form of labour for the master once the early stages of learning the trade were over and the lad was capable of productive work. Francis Place's labour during his apprenticeship was the main support of the family of the drunken leather-breeches maker to whom he was apprenticed. The master paid him 6s a week, less than half the wages fixed by Parliament for journeymen tailors in London. The arrangement between William Hutton and his uncle, a framework knitter, was customary in that trade. The lad received only 'overwork', that is he had to earn 5s 10d for his employer and could keep any earnings over that. Hutton soon discovered that apprentices were more often than not 'under the mark', but he just about managed to keep himself in clothes.[29] In law the earnings of an apprentice belonged to the master and anything paid to the lad was a private matter. A famous case of 1747 involved an apprentice shipwright who left before his time was up and joined a privateer. The ship took such a valuable prize that the apprentice's share was £1,200. The master claimed it. The great lawyer Lord Hardwicke gave verdict that the master was entitled to all that an apprentice earned, even if it was at a different business as a runaway. In the event an out-of-court settlement left the master with £450.[30]

The survival of many small masters depended upon the availability of apprentices as a form of cheap labour. To understand this we must remember the two meanings of 'master' in the eighteenth-century industrial context. In a large number of trades, as we have seen, the independent master craftsman owning his own tools, purchasing, working up and selling his own materials was already long dead. The 'putting-out system' had reduced the master craftsman in a wide range of trades to a labour-selling outworker. In such circumstances the term 'master' meant simply a representative type of industrial worker who had 'mastered' a trade. There were others who although independent worked in poor trades and relied upon the assistance of apprentices as much as did the outworkers. If apprentices brought premiums with them, then so much the better, but in many cases the poorer artisans were glad to get the necessary assistant labour of an available lad. William Hutton cursed his father for binding him to 'the starving business' of stocking weaver, and his uncle who needed two lads at a time was prepared to go to some lengths if he heard of a possible recruit. On one occasion he went ten miles to secure an apprentice, and on another 19 miles to 'employ all the arts of solicitation' on the parents of another lad.[31] When Francis Place rejected his father's intention that he become a lawyer, having no taste for further education, his father, a publican, walked into the tap-room and offered to bind him to anyone present in need of an apprentice. The offer was taken up by a leather-breeches maker, a trade which fashion changes were already forcing into decay. The man came from that marginal area where poor tradesmen shaded into the under-world. His eldest daughter was a prostitute; his youngest was visited by gentlemen, while the middle daughter was kept by a sea captain but traded on her own account during his times at sea. His eldest son worked at the father's trade, but only as a cover for pick-pocketing activities, at which art he was esteemed one of the best in London. His younger son had been a thief but had escaped conviction by enlisting as a soldier, while his wife was a drunk.[32]

The underlying problem in the lower trades was that the compulsion to obtain cheap supplementary labour through apprenticeship exposed them to the danger of overstocking with hands, so that when the indentured period was up there was little prospect of the new journeyman obtaining properly remunerated employment. This was said in 1719 to have been responsible for the rioting among the Spitalfields silk-weavers who were concentrating their resentment on the competition of imported calicoes:

> The grand cause of the weavers wanting work, is the covetousness of both masters and journeymen in taking so many 'prentices for the sake of the money they have with them; not considering whether they should have employment for them.[33]

The argument was contradicted, but only the point about premiums: 'where there is one that has money with an apprentice, there are fifty that have none at all', but there was no denial that too many were being taken.[34] In framework knitting overstocking was very evident. The poor stockinger was caught in a vicious circle. He needed supplementary labour and unless he had family members of a suitable age to assist, being unable to make enough to pay journeymen's wages, he had to rely on apprentices. In other trades the temptation to maximise output when prices were good and work plentiful led to taking on too many apprentices for the good of the trade when less brisk times returned. The smallware weavers of Manchester complained in 1756 that some of their number so determined to 'make hay while the sun shin'd' had taken on each as many as six apprentices: 'And by this means they began to multiply so fast as to be one in the Gate of another'.[35] At the end of the century and into the early-nineteenth, the larger employers in several trades were to make increasing use of so-called apprentices to work at lower rates in doing journeymen's work. In the framework knitting districts such actions brought about the Luddite disturbances, but earlier in the century it was not *directly* the hosiers who were over-stocking the trade, but the poor stockingers with rented frames under the unavoidable necessity of finding cheap supplementary labour.[36]

Adam Smith's view that apprenticeship offended against the 'most sacred and inviolable' property which every man had in his own labour to exercise in whatever manner he thought fit without injury to his neighbour, was in direct contradiction to the view of the skilled workers. They saw completion of apprenticeship as conferring a very special property right:

> That the apprenticed artisans have collectively and individually, an unquestionable right to expect the most extended protection from the Legislature, in the quiet and exclusive use and enjoyment of their several and respective arts and trades, which the law has already conferred upon them as a property, as much as it has secured the property of the stockholder in the public funds; and it is clearly un-just to take away the whole of the ancient established property and rights of any one class of the community unless at the same time, the rights and property of the whole commonwealth should be dis-solved, and parcelled out for the public good.[37]

In the better trades a substantial premium added an element of 'pur-chase' to this property right. The London compositors, threatened by the growth of outdoor apprenticeship, expressed their alarm at the threat of being deprived of: 'the just and honourable means of subsistence' which had been obtained by 'the care and purchase of their parents and friends, and by a legal servitude of seven years'.[38] Even in trades where formal binding had become rare indeed, the same sense of exclusive right persisted among those who had worked their seven years. Ten years after the repeal of the clauses of 5 Elizabeth and from the severely depressed cotton weavers (whose trade had in fact not been covered by the statute) came this reiteration of the craftsman's position:

> The weaver's qualifications may be considered as his property and support. It is as real property to him as buildings and land are to others. Like them his qualification cost time, application and money. There is no point of view (except visible and tangible) wherein they differ.[39]

Against the arguments from economic utility of the employers and those from Common Law of the lawyers, the artisans were putting the statute law and the customary right from time immemorial of the skilled man to the exclusive exercise of his trade.

These were the main features of apprenticeship in the eighteenth century, but how extensive was it as an institution in manufacturing by that time? 5 Elizabeth would seem to have established it as the law of the land. In fact the statute had never been popular with the lawyers and in a series of case law decisions its use had become progressively restricted. The lawyers felt it inhibited the right to exercise a trade which they held to be a basic common law freedom. The great authority of Blackstone was firmly behind the view that although it may have been statute law, it was nevertheless bad law:

> At common law every man might use what trade he pleased but this restrains that liberty to such as have served apprenticeships . . . the resolutions of the courts have in general rather confined than extended the restriction.[40]

Less eminent but much more widely influential was Richard Burn, the author of *The Justice of the Peace*, the century's most widely used legal handbook:

> Indiscriminately to arraign the wisdom of our ancestors in requiring a long apprenticeship in all trades, might justly be deemed rash and presumptuous. It does not, however, follow that regulations adopted in the infancy of trade and commerce, or even in their progress to a

comparative state of perfection, however just and proper they might be when established, are never to be altered in conformity to existing circumstances. Granting . . . that the statutes respecting apprenticeship were in every respect consonant to the dictates of wisdom when originally enacted, yet undoubtedly an alteration in the circumstances relative to trade and commerce, may require, at present some material alterations to be made in them.[41]

The most significant of the changes in interpretation were the acceptance of a period of seven years as equivalent to a formal apprenticeship, and the very important limitation that the act could not be held to extend to trades which were not in existence at the time of the passing of the statute. This latter interpretation destroyed any concept of the universality of the institution. Many of the industries of the eighteenth century were exempt from its restrictions on these grounds. Not only was the great prime mover of the Industrial Revolution, the cotton manufacture, exempt, but so too were many of the trades of such important centres of manufacturing as Birmingham and Wolverhampton. The act was sometimes held, although with less certainty, to extend only to corporate and market towns, and a feature of the period intervening between its enactment and the eighteenth century had been the spread of rural industry. On one ground or another there was, then, often at least a debatable case as to whether the restrictions of 5 Elizabeth were applicable. This does not mean that apprenticeship was unknown in such trades; for the most part it was not, but it was regulated by by-laws or customs of the trade or by the strength of trade unions to enforce it.

Even in trades clearly covered by the act, it had in many cases fallen into decline. Sir Francis Eden doubted whether it was any more stringently enforced in the old chartered towns than it was at Birmingham or Manchester:

> I am persuaded that a shoemaker, who had not served an apprenticeship, might exercise his industry at Bristol or Liverpool with as little hazard of being molested by the corporation of either place as of being disturbed by the borough-reve of Manchester or the head-constable at Birmingham.[42]

In Exeter, however, the serge weavers seem to have effectively controlled entry to their craft for most of the eighteenth century, and at Leicester there were fairly regular proceedings against 'interlopers' in the first half of the century, notably initiated by woolcombers. In Bristol the last case of this kind was brought in 1748 and in Liverpool in 1765.[43]

In the woollen manufacture conditions varied. In the West Riding prosecutions had virtually ceased and formal apprenticeship hardly existed by the end of the century. Professor Heaton has pointed out, however, that if we think in terms of regulation by custom rather than by law and of an 'informal' rather than an indentured relationship, then apprenticeship in this broader sense was 'woven into the fabric of the domestic industry' and was 'part and parcel of the economic structure'. Nonetheless the full letter of the law had clearly lapsed with a general absence of prosecutions after 1750 even in branches where up to that date they had not been uncommon. By the time of the revival of the weavers' agitation on the apprenticeship issue in 1806 the prosecution of the non-apprenticed had become a 'thing unknown'. In their struggle against machinery and the factory the weavers and shearmen were seeking the 're-invigoration of an Act which most of them had transgressed'. Professor Heaton's suggestion of 'transgression' is misleading, for case law had clearly established the equivalence of seven years' working to a fully indentured apprenticeship.[44]

In the west of England although apprenticeship was far from non-existent, only parish lads were usually formally indentured after the middle years of the century. The author of the *Essay on Riots* of 1739 remarked that nobody could think weaving a difficult craft who knew 'how many people practise it who never served a regular apprenticeship to it'. Among the shearmen apprenticeship was more general. Among weavers, as in Yorkshire, seven years' service although without formal indentures was the usual case, and formed the basis for the revival of interest in 5 Elizabeth by their organisations at the end of the century.[45]

London is more difficult to assess. Dorothy George was of the view that, although breaking down in its more rigid interpretation, apprenticeship remained throughout the century the usual path by which youths entered craft trades. In some areas the ranks were only being held with difficulty against illegal workers, and in others it was the organised strength of trade unions backed by the threat of strike action which held the line. The Carpenters' Company seems to have given up the struggle by the 1730s, and even in the seventeenth century had relied less upon 5 Elizabeth than upon its own by-laws. An enquiry in 1813 showed that for some years previously only when the government was itself the employer had the act been enforced with any rigidity: 'In all HM's dockyards, they will not employ any smith without he has his indentures to show, and that he has served a regular apprenticeship for seven years'. Even when the Navy Office had advertised for shipwrights to break a strike at Portsmouth in 1775 it had insisted that would-be takers produced their indentures.[46]

An historian who has made a special study of the act in its first century of operation commented on the striking lack of prosecutions for the illegal employment of journeymen who had not been apprenticed. The act was more commonly used by independent qualified tradesmen against unqualified rivals.[47] It would certainly be possible to compile a list of hundreds of prosecutions of illegal journeymen over England as a whole for the eighteenth century, but that would be an average of only a few a year. If enforcement of 5 Elizabeth was commonplace the total ought rather to be in thousands. This is not to deny any substantial importance to the act. The threat of prosecution may have in many instances been effective without the fact. Employers do not seem to have acted with complete indifference when they heard that journeymen were thinking and planning to bring prosecutions, or organising petitions to Parliament for better enforcement. Even if the higher courts were unsympathetic, the number of prosecutions and indictments implies that at least the statute had to be reckoned with as an 'uncertain but harassing weapon'.[48] Further, the act gave an important sustaining sense of legitimacy to the direct actions of legal workers against illegal workers or those who employed them. Although direct action could also be used in trades not covered by the act, the lack of a basis of statutory legitimacy was an inhibiting one.

The use of the threat of proceedings is well illustrated by an advertisement in an Essex newspaper in 1785 inserted by shoemakers which after specific mention of 5 Elizabeth continued:

> whereas many persons do follow the said trade who have not served a legal apprenticeship, nor wrought at the same seven years . . . and others have taken apprentices for a less term than seven years, or have had more than three at one time without employing the proportionate number of journeymen required by law, to the impoverishment of the craft, and by which means many hundreds of workmen, who have served a legal apprenticeship to the business, are destitute of employment to the great distress of themselves and their families.

The notice continued to advertise the intention of the shoemakers to form a society to prevent such abuses, 'through the example of our brothers in London, Chelmsford, and many other towns in England' and called upon 'every man that hath a right to work at the trade to stand forth and assist in such a lawful undertaking'.[49]

Just after the famous Spitalfields Act of 1773 had regulated the trade of their London fellows, the silk weavers of Manchester published their intent to prosecute all those who exercised the trade in their town without having either served a formal apprenticeship or followed the occupation for seven years 'unmolested'. They insisted that such men were working 'contrary to many statutes in that case made and provided' and instanced 5 Elizabeth as well as Weavers' Acts of 1555. Their real intent was clear: it was 'rather to deter from offending than punish offenders'. The London society of masons published their intention to enforce apprenticeships in 1777 as far afield as the Manchester newspapers.[50] When William Lovett who had served his time as a ropemaker was offered employment as a carpenter, his would-be employer was intimidated into discharging him by the threat of proceedings from the journeymen, even though by this time the relevant clause had been repealed for six years![51]

The threat of legal action was probably less effective than that of industrial action, although the two were often part of the same campaign. Eighteenth-century trade unionism will be discussed in the following chapters, but it is important to note the association of early unionism with attempts to restrict entry to skilled trades. It has been suggested that English trade unionism originates in the failure of authority to enforce the apprenticeship clauses of 5 Elizabeth.[52] The by-laws of eighteenth-century unions which survive show a determination to regulate the number of apprentices in the trades, and to resist the influx of the unapprenticed. In some cases 5 Elizabeth was the sole basis of this restriction, in other cases e.g. the hatters and the silk weavers, special clauses from subsequent legislation specific to the trade gave extra emphasis to legitimacy. Direct action could range in form from well-organised attempts to enforce a 'closed shop' backed by strike action, through the smashing of machinery, materials or premises of employers using illegal workmen, to hostile mob action against offending individuals, sometimes employers and sometimes workmen. When the London hatters learned in 1742 that a man named Cripps was working at the trade without having served an apprenticeship (in fact he had served one at Oxford) they surrounded the public house in which he was drinking, dragged him out and rode him on a rail through Southwark. He was beaten and subsequently died.[53] The hatters had the number of apprentices regulated by an act of James I which survived until 1777 limiting the numbers allowed to an employer in proportion to his journeymen. It is perhaps a measure of the popular image of 'Good Queen Bess' that one of their leaders incorrectly described it as an act of her reign. They had a highly effective union organisation which enforced closed-shop conditions on the London trade by its ability to call widely supported strikes if illegal men were taken on. In fact so strong was their organisation that despite the modification of the special statutory restrictions in 1777 and the repeal of 5 Elizabeth in 1814 a disgruntled employer could still complain in 1824 when asked if he could have more than two apprentices: 'According to the laws of the land I could, according to the regulations of the trade I could not'.[54]

The weavers of Banbury were equally well-organised. They had 'laws of their own' and when one of their society transgressed them by taking an apprentice too many, they assembled in a large body and demanded that the master straightaway dismiss him. When this was not complied with the whole body struck work. The shipwrights in the royal dockyards had their way of dealing with any unapprenticed men. They were 'horsed', that is put astride a piece of timber, rushed on the shoulders of the men through the gates and dumped to the accompaniment of three cheers. The London coopers kept control of the number of apprentices by refusing to work with 'illegal' men, but they were especially favoured by the brisk competition for their services between the navy victualling yards and the private employers. In the cloth trade, unlike the weavers, the shearmen were few in numbers and well enough organised to preserve the institution of apprenticeship. From time to time they took direct action to protect it, as in 1738 at Warminster when they threatened to demolish the houses of two of their number who were teaching boys unapprenticed.[55]

The cotton-check weavers of Manchester were employed in a trade which had grown up since the reign of Elizabeth and as such were not regarded as covered by its restrictions. By the 1750s they had strongly organised trade societies and were seeking to resist what they regarded as 'illegal' entrants into their trade. The problem was acute, for many who normally undertook agricultural employment in the summer were taking loom work at under-cutting prices in the winter. After a period of riotous skirmishing with their employers, they sought in 1759 the advice of Thomas Perceval, a sympathetic local gentleman, as to whether their occupation was covered by the clauses of 5 Elizabeth. He gave his opinion that it was not. Whereupon the weavers decided to petition Parliament to have their trade brought under that act. Before that petition was presented several of their number were brought before the assize on charges of illegal conspiracy. The summing-up of the judge is significant. If, he argued, apprenticeship were to be enforced, 'that liberty of setting-up trades, the foundation of the present flourishing condition of Manchester would be destroyed'. He was not content to confine his remarks to the local case in question, but went on to suggest that the apprenticeship clauses of 5 Elizabeth should be in general repealed:

> In the infancy of trade, the Acts of Queen Elizabeth might be well calculated for the public weal; but now, when it is grown to that perfection we see it, it might perhaps be of utility to have those laws repealed as tending to cramp and tye down that knowledge it was at first necessary to obtain by rule.[56]

We have already remarked on the dislike of lawyers for the statute which they saw as restraining common law rights, this judgement with its emphasis on the desirability of unrestrained freedom of trade for industrial and commercial expansion serves to link the legal with the commercial antagonism towards compulsory apprenticeship. Lipson has shown that the need of capitalism to draw freely upon an unlimited supply of labour had even by the early decades of the eighteenth century influenced the legislature towards an unfavourable attitude towards apprenticeship. Examples from the late-seventeenth century, however, still show that Parliament and the courts had not altogether changed its stance. The west of England clothiers were refused a repeal of the apprenticeship clauses in 1693, for example, and an Essex court hearing complaints of fullers and tuckers found them 'much wronged' by intruders into the trade, and noting that the regulations in the by-laws of their own 'ancient book of record' were not entirely in agreement with the penal laws of the realm, advised them on its revision.[57] What was in process was a piecemeal attack on the old restraints. While it is true that Parliament and the courts would from time to time show that threads of the old paternalist tradition were still grasped, the trend was unmistakable. Examples from the 1750s show how far the attack had proceeded by the mid-century. A parliamentary committee reporting in 1751 strongly recommended the repeal of many laws relating to trade and manufacturing: 'particularly such as require the serving an apprenticeship for seven years'. They remarked on the scarcity of prosecutions as evidence of irrelevance.[58] Two years later another parliamentary inquiry declared the by-laws of the London Framework Knitters Company, which it had with vigorous journeyman participation been struggling for half a century to enforce over recalcitrant employers in the East Midlands, to be 'injurious and vexatious to the manufacturers'.[59] The famous judgement in the check-weavers case of 1759 already noted, reflected the comprehensive ruling of Lord Mansfield in the case of Raynard v. Chase of 1756, when he roundly declared the apprenticeship clauses of 5 Elizabeth to be in restraint of natural rights, of the general rights conferred by the common law of the kingdom, and of the interests of trade. The 'liberal interpretation' of the judges had, he remarked, already confined penalty and prohibition to cases 'precisely within the express letter'.[60]

The famous Spitalfields Act of 1773 which lasted until 1823 was clearly an exception to the trend in that it not only enforced apprenticeship but regulated the number of entrants. It was an exception which gave false hope to artisans in other trades and districts that they too might be the recipients of regulatory statutes, but it was an exception none the less. In 1777 the employers in the dyeing trades were specifically exempted from the restrictions of 5 Elizabeth, and in the same year the hatters lost their special act regulating apprenticeship.[61]

These views on the need for unrestrained freedom in the employment of labour were clearly and purposively articulated as a reflection of existing practice well before Adam Smith gave them in 1776 their purest ideological and intellectual expression. Smith strongly opposed apprenticeship because it restrained competition in some trades to a smaller number than might otherwise have been disposed to enter into them, because it impeded the free movement of labour from one trade to another and because it lead to workers' combinations 'reducing the whole manufacture into a sort of slavery to themselves' and raising the price of their labour 'much above what is due to the nature of their work'.[62] This last remark is the key to the understanding of the nature and reason for the struggle between workers' and employers' organisations which preceded the repeal of 1814.

If the act was so little used and its effectiveness so limited by successive legal rulings, why did it re-emerge as a major issue in the early years of the nineteenth century? The short answer is because these years saw a determined attempt by workers' organisations to revive, and even to extend the restrictions of 5 Elizabeth. In fact the employers were faced with the barking of a dog they had thought deeply asleep. They had in response to organise themselves to prevent it developing a bite.[63] Although the struggle was to reach its most developed form in London, the apprenticeship issue had also risen again independently in the provinces. Around the turn of the century workers in the west of England woollen industry thrust the issue to the fore. Two innovations were threatening their well-being. The shearmen were being displaced by the introduction of shearing machines, and after an initial period of machine-breaking they settled to fight the issue by insisting on an observance of legal apprenticeship to prevent the machines being worked by cheap labour. The weavers were threatened by the determination of some clothiers to erect weaving-shops where the work would be under their supervision instead of being done in the weavers' own homes. The weavers saw the enforcement of apprenticeship legislation as the most effective way of ensuring that a cheap-labour factory industry did not displace them. A lawyer, Jessop, was employed and notices of intention to prosecute were served on 'illegal' weavers. Their petitions to Parliament for better enforcement of 5 Elizabeth were countered by a well-organised campaign by the clothiers for the repeal of that statute in so far as it applied to the woollen trades, as well as other inhibiting statutes.[64] An exhaustive parliamentary enquiry was undertaken, and although the repeal bill was initially stopped in the Lords in 1803, the victory went firmly to the employers for the regulations in question were suspended year by year until they were finally repealed in 1809, five years before the repeal of apprentice clauses of 5 Elizabeth was made general.[65]

By the beginning of the nineteenth century the calico printers of the Manchester area had been suffering severe unemployment as a result of their employers taking on large numbers of outdoor apprentices as cheap labour. The trade was too new to be covered by 5 Elizabeth and the men were organising a petition to Parliament for statutory regulation of apprentices in the trade. The trade had originally been based in London and had taken to the north a strong tradition of unionism as a result of the removal of a firm to Manchester, along with its skilled workers in 1783. Once there the London experience was used to good effect in resisting the introduction of machinery by widely-supported strikes in 1785 and 1786. A union fund was built up for the support of strike action against employers who employed illegal men, known as 'knobsticks' to work the new machinery. However, success in resistance was only temporary, for the employers broke the men by the widespread use of so-called outdoor apprentices. It was for this reason that the journeymen were seeking a parliamentary regulation of apprenticeship. A parliamentary committee was appointed to investigate. It found the allegations of the men to be true beyond doubt of a trade where one master had been employing apprentices and journeymen at a ratio of 55 : 2. Unemployment and distress were rife, and the committee wished it were otherwise. They roundly condemned the way in which the masters were conducting the trade. They thought it best that the 'general custom' of two apprentices to a master should be re-established 'through an understanding between the masters and the journeymen'. However they declared themselves unfriendly to legal restrictions on manufacturing and commerce, despite the evils they admitted to have discovered. No regulating act was in the event forthcoming.[66]

A third major provincial context for struggle over apprenticeship was the outbreak of machine-breaking in the framework knitting areas of the East Midlands — known as the Luddite disturbances. This misused word is popularly applied to persons who resist machinery because they misguidedly conceive that its use would affect their interests by making their skills redundant. In fact dislike of machinery as such was not an issue in the East Midlands in 1811-12. What was at issue was the use of unskilled labour to manufacture inferior products. It was after attempts to get a parliamentary regulation of the trade had failed that the machines, only of those employers who had used untrained labour ('colts') to produce cheap products ('cut-ups') were smashed. The outbreaks of 1811-12 were not new in the trade. As early as 1710 when the trade had been still London-based, the frames of masters who breached company regulations on the use of apprentices had been destroyed, and machines had also been broken during the campaign of 1778-9 to get a parliamentary regulation of apprenticeship.[67]

These three examples are all examined more fully elsewhere in the book. They serve here to show that in the provinces the apprenticeship agitation of the early-nineteenth century was closely connected with resisting the introduction of machinery or with innovatory practices connected with the use of existing machinery. The old paternalism was being sought as a refuge from *fresh* attacks by *laissez-faire* capitalism. It was however, in London that the main organised attempts of working men to obtain a strengthening of apprenticeship regulations centred. An important background factor is the passing of the general Combination Laws in 1799 and 1800. These famous enactments by forbidding trade unionism for straightforward wage demands, made a *legal* issue such as the enforcement of 5 Elizabeth especially valuable. To organise journeymen for the purpose of petitioning Parliament, or for the purpose of funding prosecutions under the law could not be regarded as illegal, even if attempts directly to sanction employers on the issue were.[68] London journeymen employed the services of a lawyer named Chippendale, to inaugurate from 1809 a series of prosecutions under the act. There is no direct evidence as to who was actually employing him, but the 19 cases which he brought over three years covered some 13 trades, so that some general representative body of tradesmen was clearly behind

the campaign. The ineffectiveness of the act was shown up by the results
of the prosecutions. Twelve of the 19 prosecuted were acquitted and
costs were high and could not be recovered. A journeymen's association
proposing to bring an action against employers employing illegal men
had to be prepared to pay its own costs and risk those of its opponents
in pursuit of a penalty which could not exceed £12.[69]

This experience led in the summer of 1812 to the formation of a
united association of the London journeymen calling themselves the
'mechanics of the metropolis' with the purpose of campaigning nationally for the restatement and extension of the apprenticeship clauses of
5 Elizabeth:

> to devise such measures as may secure the regular bred artisans in
> future the exclusive enjoyment of the trade he has been brought up
> to ... which we consider is our exclusive privilege of following, in
> so much as it is purchased by large premiums, and other incidental
> expenses, incurred by our friends, and seven years servitude on our
> part.[70]

A letter from employers sent to the Home Secretary speaks of a convention of two delegates from each trade meeting regularly in London,
under the name of the Artisans General Committee or the United Artisans' Committee. In the provincial towns delegates and subscriptions
were to be sent to London. Little is known about the campaign outside
London. At Bristol advertisements were placed informing the journeymen of the campaign, and presumably the same happened elsewhere.
The agitation undoubtedly centred on London, but had nevertheless a
considerable claim to be a national movement. In addition to 62 London
trades, contributions came in from over 70 places in the country, and
a national petition carried 32,735 signatures half of which came from
outside the capital.[71]

The true nature of the struggle soon became open. The employers
described 5 Elizabeth as a 'constant and prosperous rallying point to
further the measures of the journeymen against their employers'. The
opportunity was, they claimed, being taken to build up a united front
of the City's tradesmen, 'an irresistable phalanx ... greatly superior
to the united energies of the masters'.[72] This was the issue picked out
by the employers themselves in an 'official' pamphlet presenting their
case. The pamphlet makes one or two somewhat dubious historical
references, for example that the Statute of Artificers had 'originated
under the feudal government and tyranny of the ancient Barons', but

was at pains to emphasise the central issue:

> The mischief . . . strikes at the root of all our prosperity. It is that
> which arises from the pretensions it countenances, and the colour
> it gives to the combination of workmen for the raising of wages,
> and the prevention of improvement. Under the influence of the pre-
> tended privileges given by this act, many masters are not permitted
> to hire their own workmen. No, the 'Shop committee' must be
> applied to. They must be assured that all is right − that every work-
> man has, as they pretend, been 'legally apprenticed, that is in fact,
> that he belongs to 'the Club'. For they make a distinction if he
> leagues with them. They choose too what articles shall be made, and
> impose large fines on whoever disobeys *their* laws. They fine men
> also that work for masters who conduct their business in a manner
> not approved by them. Aye, and they compell payment too, by out-
> lawry and proscription.[73]

The fear is echoed elsewhere. The master fellmongers of London thought
that 'if the men were compelled to be bound for seven years, and those
who have been so bound were to combine together, that let their demand be ever so exhorbitant we must comply with that demand'.[74] The
master printers had expressed the opinion in 1805 that 5 Elizabeth was
an 'enabling statute', which empowered the workmen to enter into
combinations against their masters, and dictate their own terms.[75] Ten
years after the repeal, Alexander Galloway, by then a successful en-
gineering employer, who had been one of the leaders of the employers'
campaign, looked back with satisfaction:

> previous to the Act for the repeal of 5th Elizabeth . . . combinations
> were much more frequent than they are now, and while that law was
> in existence, every trade was subject to its most mischievous pro-
> visions; but after its repeal, when a man was allowed to work at any
> employment whether he had served one, two, or three years or not
> at all, that broke the neck of all combinations, because then the ex-
> cluding party were so overwhelmed by new men that we could do
> without them.[76]

The importance of the 'closed shop' for effective trade unionism was
clearly perceived by both sides. Despite the thousands of signatures on
the petitions which came pouring in, the outcome of the struggle, which
has been fully told elsewhere, has an air of inevitability. Parliament

received the petitions and appointed a committee to report. It would not perhaps have even gone this far, had not some members voted for the committee on the grounds that once attention was focused on the act, its apprenticeship clauses would be exposed for speedy repeal. In this they were right. No bill for strengthening and extending the clauses was ever submitted, instead a repeal bill introduced by Mr Seargeant Onslow passed through its parliamentary course without serious opposition.[77] The support of one or two Members of Parliament, and the thousands of artisans' signatures from all over the kingdom were as nothing in the scales against a few pages of Adam Smith and the growing fear that, despite the Combination Acts, organised working men represented a growing and serious threat. The place of trade unionism in the eighteenth century, its aims, methods, and its concerns, which were not only those of maintaining apprenticeship, are the subject of the following chapter. Those trades with long traditions of organisation were presumably able to resist dilution, if technological advance did not make their exclusive skills redundant.[78] In other trades the outcome of the repeal in removing the last vestige of legal protection against the employment of cheap labour confirmed the disastrous trends for the artisan against which the re-assertion of his powers had been sought. After considering the complaints of the silk weavers of Coventry in 1818, by which time so much use of cheap labour by employers had been made that the skilled journeymen could hardly find half-time work, a parliamentary committee was forced to remark that 'whilst the statute of 5th of Elizabeth was in force . . . the distressing circumstances now complained of, never occurred'.[79]

Notes

1. *Speech of Randle Jackson Esq. presented to . . . Committee . . . on . . . Woollen Manufacture . . . on behalf of the cloth workers and Shearmen of . . . Yorkshire, Lancashire, Wiltshire, Somersetshire and Gloucester* (1806), reprinted in K. Carpenter (ed.), *The Spread of Machinery* (New York, 1972), p. 62.

2. For the text of the Statute, 5 Elizabeth, c.4, see: A.E. Bland, P.A. Brown and R.H. Tawney (eds.), *English Economic History. Select Documents* (London, 1914), pp. 325-33.

3. For recent discussions of the Tudor context of the statute see: B.A. Holderness, *Pre-industrial England. Economy and Society from 1500 to 1750* (London, 1976), p. 106 and D.C. Coleman, *The Economy of England 1450-1750* (Oxford, 1977), p. 180.

4. P. Mantoux, *The Industrial Revolution in the Eighteenth Century*, 2nd edn (London, 1964), p. 393; S. and B. Webb, *The History of Trade Unionism* (London, 1911 edn), p. 55.

5. For the discomfort and hedge-sitting of a committee faced with an obvious abuse of the apprenticeship system but unable to bring itself to the point of urging regulation, see the *Report on Calico Printers' Petition, Commons Journals*, LXI, 17 July 1806, reprinted in Bland, Brown & Tawney, *Select Documents*, pp. 574-6.

6. S.S. Atkins and W.H. Overall, *Some Account of the Worshipful Company of Clockmakers of the City of London* (London, 1881), p. 281.

7. See for example: I. Prothero, *Artisans and Politics in Early Nineteenth-century London. John Gast and His Times* (Folkestone, 1979), Chapter 3, 'The Apprenticeship Campaign'.

8. Quoted in E.P. Thompson, 'English Trade Unionism and other Labour Movements before 1790', *Bulletin of the Society for the Study of Labour History*, no. 17 (1968), p. 23.

9. *Minutes of Evidence before the Committee on . . . Laws relating to the Woollen Trade*, P.P. 1802/3 (95), VII, p. 61.

10. For example the woolcombers in their regulations of 1812 (reprinted in A. Aspinall (ed.), *The Early English Trade Unions* (London, 1949), p. 128).

11. *The Times*, 22 January 1789; *Minutes of Committee on Woollen Trade*, P.P. 1802/3, p. 8; J. Child, *Industrial Relations in the British Printing Industry – The Quest for Security* (London, 1967), p. 41.

12. Adam Smith, *The Wealth of Nations* (1776, edited by E. Cannan 1904, paperback edition, London, 1961), Vol. I, pp. 136-8.

13. *Minutes of Committee on Woollen Trade*, P.P. 1802/3, p. 251.

14. The phrase is used by Peter Laslett, *The World We Have Lost*, 2nd edn (London, 1971), p. 3.

15. *Speech of Randle Jackson*, p. 61.

16. *Report on the Petitions of the Watchmakers of Coventry*, P.P. 1817 (504), VI, p. 79. Indenture of William Mayo to Samuel Smith and John Wontner, watchmakers, Coventry, 1800.

17. A.K. Hamilton Jenkin (ed.), *News from Cornwall* (London, 1951), p. 25.

18. For the calico printers see *Report on the Calico Printers' Petition* in Bland, Brown & Tawney, *Select Documents*, pp. 574-6; for the London printers see E. Howe (ed.), *The London Compositor: Documents Relating to Wages, Working Conditions and Customs of the London Printing Trade 1785-1900* (London, 1947), Chapter 4, 'The Apprenticeship Question 1568-1818'; for the Coventry ribbon weavers see *Report from the Committee on the Silk Ribbon Weavers' Petitions*, P.P. 1818 (134), IX, p. 5.

19. Howe, *London Compositor*, doc. XXIX, p. 119; Child, *Printing Industry*, p. 65; *Report of the Committee on the Petition of the Journeymen Calico Printers*, P.P. 1800, reprinted 1807 (129), II, p. 4; *Report from the Select Committee on the Laws relating to Watchmakers*, P.P. 1818 (135), IX, p. 5.

20. Among celebrated runaways was William Hutton who ran away at the age of eighteen after his pride had been hurt by a thrashing from his uncle to whom he had been apprenticed: *Life of William Hutton F.A.S.S.*, 2nd edn (London, 1817), pp. 102-6.

21. For an account of the development and forms of pauper apprenticeship see: Jocelyn O. Dunlop, *English Apprenticeship and Child Labour – A History* (London, 1912), Chapter XVI. The comment on the chimney boys is from R. Campbell, *The London Tradesman* (1747, reprinted Newton Abbot, 1969), p. 328. It is not suggested that most or even very many masters and mistresses were deliberately sadistic, however the frequency of *reported* cases emphasises the vulnerable position of the apprenticed pauper child. In a period of ten months the *Exeter Mercury* reported the case of a man and wife and his son and his wife indicted on suspicion of murdering a girl apprentice by 'beating and barbarously using her' (9 March 1764); the sentencing of a man for castrating two eight-year-

old apprentices (23 March 1764) and the ill-treatment of a thirteen-year-old girl parish apprentice by her master and mistress who branded her on her bare buttocks with a hot iron, chained her for six hours to an apple tree, and then beat her before making her work (4 January 1765).

22. S.R. Smith, 'The London Apprentices as Seventeenth-century Adolescents', *Past & Present*, no. 61 (1973), pp. 149, 157, 160-1.

23. Francis Place, *Autobiography* (edited by M. Thale, Cambridge, 1972), p. 73; J.H. Drew, *Samuel Drew, M.A. – The Self-taught Cornishman* (1861), p. 33; P. Linebaugh in *Bulletin of the Society for the Study of Labour History*, no. 25 (1972), p. 14.

24. Hutton, *Life*, p. 95.

25. Campbell, *London Tradesman*, p. 23.

26. See note 21 above.

27. Drew, *Self-taught Cornishman*, pp. 26-7, 36.

28. D. Hey, *The Rural Metalworkers of the Sheffield Region* (Leicester, 1972), p. 58.

29. Place, *Autobiography*, p. 74; Hutton, *Life*, p. 95.

30. J.R. Burn, *Justice of the Peace*, 13th edn (London, 1776), Vol. I, pp. 75-6.

31. Hutton, *Life*, pp. 99, 120.

32. Place, *Autobiography*, pp. 71-2.

33. *The Weavers' Pretences Examined* (1719), reprinted in J. Smith, *Memoirs of Wool* (1747, reprinted Farnborough 1968), Vol. II, p. 186.

34. *The Just Complaints of the Poor Weavers Truly Represented* (1719), reprinted in Smith, *Memoirs of Wool*, Vol. II, p. 197.

35. A.P. Wadsworth and J. de L. Mann, *The Cotton Trade and Industrial Lancashire 1600-1780* (Manchester, 1931), p. 348.

36. William Felkin, *History of the Machine-wrought Hosiery and Lace Manufactures* (1867, reprinted Newton Abbot, 1967), pp. 115-16, 227.

37. *Report from the Committee on the Petitions of the Watchmakers of Coventry*, P.P. 1817 (504), VI, p. 47.

38. Howe, *London Compositor*, doc. XXIX, p. 129.

39. J.L. and Barbara Hammond, *The Town Labourer* (edited by J. Lovell, London, 1978), p. 205.

40. *Considerations upon a Bill now before Parliament, for repealing (in substance) the whole Code of Laws respecting the Woollen Manufacture of Great Britain and dissolving the Ancient System of Apprenticeship* (1803), pp. 51-2. Reprinted in K. Carpenter (ed.), *The Spread of Machinery* (New York, 1972).

41. Burn, *Justice of the Peace*, quoted in J. Anstie, *Observations on the importance and necessity of introducing improved machinery into the woollen manufactory etc.* (1803), pp. 82-3. Reprinted in Carpenter, *Spread of Machinery*.

42. Quoted in Arnold Toynbee, *Lectures on the Industrial Revolution of the Eighteenth Century in England* (London, 1908 edn), pp. 52-3.

43. For Exeter see Joyce Youings, *Tuckers' Hall Exeter: The History of a Provincial City Company through Five Centuries* (Exeter, 1968), p. 120 and W.G. Hoskins, *Industry, Trade and People in Exeter 1688-1800*, 2nd edn (Exeter, 1968), p. 50. For Leicester see G.A. Chinnery (ed.), *Records of the Borough of Leicester. Vol. III* (Leicester, 1974), pp. 31, 36, 47-9, 52-3, 61, 90, 95-6. For Liverpool and Bristol see Wadsworth & Mann, *Cotton Trade*, p. 352.

44. H. Heaton, *The Yorkshire Woollen and Worsted Industries* (Oxford, 1920), pp. 308-11.

45. *Essay on Riots* (1739) reprinted in Smith, *Memoirs of Wool*, Vol. II, pp. 302-3; *Committee on Laws relating to Woollen Trade*, P.P. 1802/3, VII, pp. 57, 141, 250, 263; *Report from Select Committee on Woollen Clothiers' Petition*, P.P. 1802/3 (30), V, pp. 4-6.

46. M.D. George, *London Life in the Eighteenth Century* (Harmondsworth, 1966 edn), p. 268; B.W.E. Alford and T.C. Barker, *A History of the Carpenters' Company* (London, 1968), pp. 137-8; *Report from the Committee on the Apprenticeship Laws*, P.P. 1812/13 (243), IV, pp. 13-14, 18; A. Geddes, *Portsmouth during the Great French Wars 1770-1800* (Portsmouth, 1970), p. 19.

47. M.G. Davies, *The Enforcement of English Apprenticeship 1563-1642. A Study in Applied Mercantilism* (Cambridge, Mass., 1956), p. 263.

48. Wadsworth & Mann, *Cotton Trade*, p. 252.

49. A.F.J. Brown (ed.), *English History from Essex Sources 1750-1900* (Chelmsford, 1952), p. 206.

50. Wadsworth & Mann, *Cotton Trade*, pp. 370-1, footnote to p. 383.

51. W. Lovett, *My Life and Struggles etc.* (1876, reprinted London, 1967), pp. 16-17.

52. Webb & Webb, *Trade Unionism*, footnote to p. 40.

53. *Sherborne Mercury*, 18 October 1742.

54. *Second Report from the Select Committee on Artisans and Machinery*, P.P. 1824 (51), V, pp. 87, 99.

55. Aspinall, *Early Trade Unions*, doc. 22, p. 19; D.A. Baugh, *British Naval Administration in the Age of Walpole* (Princeton, 1965), p. 317; *Report of Committee on the Apprenticeship Laws*, P.P. 1812/13, IV, pp. 30-1; Diary of George Wansey of Warminster, 5 December 1738, reprinted in J. de L. Mann (ed.), *Documents Illustrating the Wiltshire Textile Trades in the Eighteenth Century* (Devizes, 1964), p. 32.

56. See Perceval's own account, *A letter to a friend: occasioned by the late disputes betwixt the check-makers of Manchester, and their weavers etc.* (Halifax, 1758), reprinted in K. Carpenter, *Labour Disputes in the Early Days of the Industrial Revolution* (New York, 1972) and the accounts in Wadsworth & Mann, *Cotton Trade*, pp. 361-9, and in H.A. Turner, *Trade Union Growth, Structure and Policy. A Comparative Study of the Cotton Unions* (London, 1962), pp. 59-60; E.P. Thompson, *The Making of the English Working Class* (Harmondsworth, 1968 edn), pp. 303-4.

57. E. Lipson, *The Economic History of England Vol. III. The Age of Mercantilism* (London, 1943 edn), p. 291; J. de L. Mann, *The Cloth Industry in the West of England from 1640-1880* (Oxford, 1971), p. 105; Brown, *English History from Essex Sources*, p. 4.

58. Committee on the Laws relating to Trade and Manufactures, *Commons Journals*, XXVI, 21 June 1753, p. 292.

59. Webb & Webb, *Trade Unionism*, p. 45.

60. I. Burr. 3, pp. 156-68, Raynard v. Chase, 12 November 1756.

61. *Commons Journals*, XXXVI, 18 February 1777, p. 194; 17 Geo. III c. 55.

62. Smith, *Wealth of Nations*, Vol. I, pp. 140-1.

63. The most comprehensive account of the struggle and the employers' reaction is T.K. Derry, 'The Repeal of the Apprenticeship Clauses of the Statute of Apprentices', *Economic History Review*, III (1931/2), pp. 67-87.

64. A convenient summary of the struggles in the West Country is provided by K.G. Ponting, *The Woollen Industry of South-west England* (Bath, 1971), Chapters 9-14.

65. W.E. Minchinton, 'The Beginnings of Trade Unionism in the Gloucestershire Woollen Industry', *Transactions of Bristol and Gloucestershire Archaeological Society*, vol. 70 (1951), pp. 129-31.

66. The main source for the calico printers is the pamphlet, *Facts and Observations to prove the Impolicy and Dangerous Tendency of the Bill . . . for limiting the number of Apprentices, and other Restrictions in the Calico Printing Business. Together with a Concise History of the Combination of the Journeymen*

(Manchester, 1807), reprinted in K. Carpenter (ed.), *Trade Unions under the Combination Acts 1799-1823* (New York, 1972). For subsequent developments see *Report of Committee on the Petition of the Journeymen Calico Printers*, P.P. 1800, reprinted 1807 (129), II, p. 107.

67. For early machine-breaking see Felkin, *History*, pp. 227-8. For summaries of the major debates on Luddism see J.G. Rule, introduction to J.L. and Barbara Hammond, *The Skilled Labourer* (London, 1979), pp. xx-xxvii and J. Dinwiddy, 'Luddism and Politics in the Northern Counties', *Social History*, vol. 4, no. 1 (1979), pp. 33-63.

68. See the view of the Home Office on the prosecution of a combination of Lancashire Weavers in Aspinall, *Early Trade Unions*, doc. 28, p. 26.

69. For Chippendale's activities see Derry, 'Repeal of the Apprenticeship Clauses', pp. 71-2 and Prothero, *Artisans and Politics*, p. 51. Some of the cases reported are: 3 Camp. 119, 1326, 5 December 1811; 3 Keble 398, 24 May 1809; 5 Esp. 110, 24 February 1811; 2 Camp. 293, 1160, 4 December 1809 and 3 Camp. 13, 5 June 1811.

70. Derry, 'Repeal of the Apprenticeship Clauses', p. 73.

71. Aspinall, *Early Trade Unions*, doc. 145, p. 163; Prothero, *Artisans and Politics*, p. 52.

72. Aspinall, *Early Trade Unions*, doc. 145, p. 163.

73. *The Origin, Object and Operation of the Apprentice Laws; with their application to Times Past, Present and to come. Addressed to the Committee of General Purposes of the City of London. By the Committee of Manufacturers of London and its Vicinity* (1814), p. 237. The pamphlet is reprinted in *The Pamphleteer* III (London, 1814), pp. 217-42.

74. *Report from Committee on the Apprenticeship Laws*, P.P. 1812/13, IV, p. 55.

75. Child, *Printing Trade*, p. 66.

76. *First Report of the Select Committee on Artisans and Machinery*, P.P. 1824 (51), V, p. 27.

77. Derry, 'Repeal of the Apprenticeship Clauses', argues that it was not as clear-cut as has been supposed but puts forward no very telling argument against regarding the repeal as an important step in the establishment of the *laissez-faire* orthodoxy.

78. Thompson, *Making of the English Working Class*, p. 284; W.H. Chaloner, *The Skilled Artisans during the Industrial Revolution 1750-1850* (Historical Association Aids for Teachers, no. 15, 1969), p. 8.

79. *Committee on the Silk Ribbon Weavers' Petitions*, P.P. 1818, IX, p. 2.

5 EXPLOITATION AND EMBEZZLEMENT

'The cause of the poor', complained a clothier in 1739 'is popular with those who don't really know them'. They would have changed this opinion if they had but known of the 'insolence, idleness, debauchery, frauds and dishonesty' of the manufacturing population as well as did the employers.[1] The factory system was not a prerequisite for conflict between capital and labour, but the forms of conflict appropriate to the pre-factory context and the nature of the grievances articulated were not in all cases the same under domestic and putting-out systems of manufacture as they were to become in the nineteenth-century factory economy.

Certainly there were confrontations over wages and hours and the strike was the usual form that they took, but there were other important areas of conflict. Employers complained repeatedly of the 'dishonesty' of their work people, both by fraud and by embezzlement, and of bad workmanship and idleness as often as they complained of 'riotous and un-lawful combinations' to increase or defend wages. The workers counter-complained of 'oppressions' in the form of late, or even non-payment of wages; of being forced to take payment in the form of truck or kind; of 'stoppages' (fines) for supposed bad work being used to clip wages; of effectively cutting wages by increasing the size of the piece or the number of items required for the 'customary' price; of deducting excessive rents for equipment or premises and of supplying over-priced materials as well as of forming combinations for the direct purpose of lowering wages. The author of an essay on the west-country weavers' riots of 1739 urged that a commission be set up to investigate:

(1) If any combinations have been entered into to lower the price of weaving, spinning etc. and by whom.
(2) If any masters have forced the poor manufacturers to take truck, and at what price.
(3) If any masters have obliged their work people to buy bread etc. at any particular shops, and how they have been served.
(4) If some particular manufacturers do not give extravagant rents for their tenements, etc. and if they are not under compulsion in that article.[2]

Wage demands from combinations of workmen are discussed in later chapters. Here we are concerned to examine the context of the recriminations and counter-recriminations of masters and men which fall within the general areas of oppression, dishonesty, exploitation, embezzlement etc. Examples will be used from a wide variety of industries, but three for which especially good documentation survives will be examined in greater detail. They are the woollen and worsted manufacture, the royal dockyards and Cornish tin and copper mining.

Employers' accusations of embezzlement of materials by their employees need to be considered in three contexts: the area of perquisites (wages supplemented by kind); the characteristic form of circulating property which was the basis of the putting-out system and the long delays between work completion and pay which characterised many industries.

In 1762 the house of a labourer earning nine shillings a week from the gunpowder mill on Hounslow Heath was searched. In it were found more than £100 in cash, almost a cartload of matches, a large number of deal boards, a great quantity of candles, 70 bottles of lamp oil, two bushels of new nails and 103 bags of saltpetre. Such booty pointed to systematic embezzlement over a long period, but the newspaper account accepts that some of it was legitimate since workers at powder mills had 'liberty at their leisure' to split deal and dip it into the brimstone prepared for the making of the gunpowder, thus supplementing their wages from the sale of matches.[3] The idea of an exclusively money wage was not an established but a developing one in eighteenth-century manufacturing. Dr Linebaugh in a brilliant study of the relationship of crime to the development of English capitalism in the eighteenth century, has suggested that much 'criminal' activity occurs in the transformation of the wage from a form in which monetary payment constituted a part (although a substantial one) of the wage, to one based exclusively on a money payment:

Bugging to the hatter, cabbage to the tailor, blue-pigeon flying to plumbers and glaziers, chippings to shipwrights, sweepings to porters, red sailyard docking to navy yard workers, fints and thrums to weavers, vails to servants, privileges to west country clothiers, bontages to Scottish agricultural workers, scrappings and naxers to coopers, wastages to framework knitters, in all these the eighteenth-century labourer appropriated a part of his product or a part of the materials of his labour.[4]

Such perquisites could be either directly disposed of, or worked up into articles to be sold. Dictionaries of the 'vulgar tongue' abound with colloquialisms for perquisites appropriated by workers, some of which, like 'cabbage', remain in use today to describe the pieces of cloth appropriated by tailors in cutting out cloth already bespoken to customers. The origin is probably late-seventeenth century and a modern dictionary quotes: 'Your tailor cabbages whole yards of cloth' from 1712 as an example of an early use.[5] Campbell writing in 1747 took it for granted that cabbage was part of the remuneration of the cutting-out tailor. It was not of course available to the poorer class who simply sewed what others cut out.[6] 'Shreds' judged of little use rapidly pass the label of perquisite to pieces of usable size.

The use of specific colloquialisms for such practices instead of general slang terms such as 'pinching' or 'nicking' suggests a different view of legitimacy. In fact not all such activities involved simply taking materials. 'Bugging' in the hat making trade was the 'exchange of some of the dearer materials of which a hat is made for others of less value'.[7] This substitution was claimed by a witness in 1777 to make the master hatters 'great and daily sufferers by the journeymen'.[8] Similar practices existed in the shoemaking trade where masters complained that their journeymen defrauded them by buying cheap leather from the curriers and substituting it for better quality leather put out to them by the masters. They then converted the quality leather to their own use.[9]

Perquisites which were of little value to the employers were not contested. The sawdust perquisite of the sawyer seems to have lasted unchallenged into the nineteenth century,[10] but in many trades there was direct confrontation over the issue. In Essex there was a bitter and long-lasting dispute in 1757/8 over weavers' 'thrums'. Thrums were the weft ends left on the loom after the finished cloth had been removed. Legally they belonged to the clothier who had put out the yarn, but they had long been regarded by the weavers as a customary perquisite. Trouble began in the winter of 1757 when Colchester clothiers indicated their intention of prosecuting weavers who did not return thrums, and in fact a man and a woman were publicly whipped for retaining them. Braintree and Bocking clothiers followed suit, but after initially demanding the return of thrums outright, they modified their demand by offering 3d a thrum compensation. This modification implies some recognition of thrums being part of the 'customary' wage whatever the legal ownership. The weavers did not regard the sum as suffcient compensation and responded with a 14-week strike. In the course of the dispute the Braintree weavers inserted a notice in the *Ipswich Journal*:

> They made a demand of our waste, without offering any allowance
> for the same; (and by degrees did we tamely submit, we should be
> brought under a yoke, which would have some affinity to that of the
> Egyptian Bondage). Though we would not presume to deny, but that
> afterwards through the negociation of the Right Hon. Robert Nugent
> Esq. they offered us 3d per bay in lieu thereof. The waste is a small
> perquisite that hath been granted us for several hundred years past,
> which we are able to prove by our ancient Books of Record, which
> have been no less than 14 or 15 times ratified and confirmed at the
> General Quarter Sessions.[11]

The sense of legitimate right here goes far beyond the simple assertion
of a customary practice, and is strengthened by the involvement of the
local Member of Parliament and by the confidence that it has been ratified by the justices. More than 500 weavers struck insisting that they
would conduct themselves in a 'regular' and 'decent' manner without
causing any disturbance. They acted only in defiance of their masters
to 'support our ancient custom'. The weavers held out from 6 November
1757 to the February of the following year before going back on the
masters' terms of 3d a piece compensation.[12]

Thrums were an expected perquisite in the south-west too. A
Gloucestershire clothier stated in 1802 that although they belonged
without doubt to the employers, they did not insist on having them
returned and they were commonly kept by the weavers.[13] The fact that
the Essex weavers gave in, and the whipping of two of their number at
Colchester suggests that in one important area of a major manufacture
the employers had succeeded in placing a non-monetary form of the
wage within the criminal sanction. Henceforth the weaver in Essex who
retained thrums was committing a criminal act, but a long time would
elapse before he would be seen by his fellows as in breach of any moral
sanction.

In some coalmining districts a coal allowance was an important source
of fuel to the colliers. Dr Hay has described how Midlands coalowners,
especially instancing the Earl of Uxbridge in Staffordshire, attempted in
the mid-eighteenth century to end this perquisite. He maintained that
the miners did not content themselves with taking customary small
amounts sufficient for their own fuel needs, but removed larger amounts
to sell at a profit. It was estimated that in a three-week period before
Christmas 1750, colliers sold £3 worth of undeclared coals each. In
Staffordshire perhaps from one-third to one-half of colliers' expected
wages were made up of perquisites in the form of an allowance of two

draughts of coal a week of around 5s in value. The Earl preferred to
see it as theft cutting into profits, and in 1757 ordered that no burning
coals were to be allowed to the miners, or to retired miners, wives or
widows. In practice it was not easy to end an ingrained expectation and
one Midlands owner who followed the Earl's example heard from his
agent in 1805, that although the men had been prohibited from carrying away 'what they call fire coal', they expected the clerk to pay them
3d a day in lieu.[14]

No perquisites attracted more attention than those claimed by the
shipwrights of the royal dockyards. Here the government was directly
involved as employer, and it was the public purse which bore the cost.
The most aggravating from the Admiralty's point of view was that of
'chips'. In origin these were the waste scraps of wood conceded to the
men as firewood. Already by the mid-seventeenth century chips had
developed into a valuable, and indeed essential, part of the shipwright's
remuneration. From the point of view of the government the practice
amounted to an amazingly costly loss of timber. In 1634 a boat full of
wooden tree-nails loaded by a shipwright was seized at Deptford. 'If',
wrote a worried official, 'every carpenter can claim such nails, the
King's purse will deeply waste for it'. The seized load contained 3,500
one foot tree-nails made while they were out of work by a man and his
master out of chips collected over a previous period of six years' working in the royal yards. They were open about the fact that they had
converted their accumulated chips into saleable tree-nails instead of
burning them as firewood as most of their neighbours did, and they
maintained it was 'lawful' for them to have done so. The receiver of the
nails was to have been a government-employed shipwright who ran a
small private yard on the side.[15] By this time chips had become a deeply
established customary expectation. Workmen were described as removing them three times a day from the yards, and even to be building huts
from some waste timber in order to store the rest. An attempt in 1650
to settle the issue by a wage increase of 1-3d a day was ineffective —
clearly indicating the value of the perquisite to the men. In 1662 an
order restricting the carrying out of chips to once a week was resisted
by the men who claimed that they could not subsist without their perquisite, and around 1677 the Admiralty gave up the struggle for the
time being.[16]

Attempts to restrict the practice were resumed in the eighteenth
century. In 1753 a rule was introduced that no more could be removed
from the yard than could be carried untied under one arm. Such con-
trived limitations indicate the realisation of the futility of attempts at

prohibition. And in fact the restriction was not regarded. Men were still said to be not only 'manufacturing' chips by cutting up large pieces of timber, but what was more, doing it in their work time.[17] No more successful was the attempt at rigid definition in 1741 which decreed the only 'lawful' chips to be those made with axes or adzes and not sawn-ends or slabs or old wood of any kind. Had this been observed then chips would have been in effect confined to their original firewood purpose.[18] Complaints of the enormous waste of navy timber through the practice were still being emphatically made in 1792. Then each workman was said to carry home daily sizeable amounts of timber deliberately cut off, and to be finishing their proper work an hour early to do the cutting, commonly into useful-size pieces which could be sold for one shilling each.[19] The practice of taking chips died out in the nineteenth century. It was at long last replaced by an allowance in 1805, and even this was discontinued in 1830.[20]

Timber chips were not the only materials lost from the yards. Ropes and cordage were an obvious target for larceny, and at Deptford sail-makers made breeches out of the canvas.[21] The Thames yards were not alone in suffering. At Plymouth a night-guard was posted in 1764, and the first three men it took were all artificers employed at the yard, while the apprehending of several yard employees at Portsmouth in 1773 was expected to lead to further discoveries of 'this iniquitous practice, which has been carried on for some years past'.[22] The use of the broad-arrow and the running of coloured threads through ropes was introduced as early as 1661 and were aimed not only at preventing the depradations of artificers, but also the illegal disposal of naval stores by higher placed officials. Shifts which involved working after dark were discouraged because of the 'roguery and villainry they commit when it is beginning to grow dark'. In 1764 the ineffective nightwatchmen were replaced by marine guards and in 1770 by a regular dockyard police.[23]

Pilfering and the taking of chips must be viewed in the context of two aspects of naval administration. First, corruption was rife right through the hierarchy of the yards. As a leading authority has written: 'There was no branch of the Navy or victualling departments, and no class of officer, civil or executive, free of similar fraudulent practices'. This aspect has been much discussed in the standard authorities already cited. More important in the context of explaining the determination of the shipwrights to hold on to their perquisite was the second aspect: long arrears of pay. Delayed wage payment was normal in the yards from the seventeenth century when chip taking became established. Under the Commonwealth artificers were fortunate if their wages were only a year behind, while a Chatham petition of 1667 when a year's wages were due complained of the workmen 'starving' and having become so inured to stealing that no half-cut work could be left in the open even overnight. The Chatham commissioners in 1693 reported the men's situation to be 'truly deplorable' and wondered how they survived.[24] Any improvements in the eighteenth century were marginal. Wages were fifteen months behind in 1762 and the men were having to discount pay-tickets at 7½ per cent to local moneylenders, the 'selling' of future wages having long been a necessary practice. When pay notes did eventually arrive the clerks were not above charging fees to process them with any rapidity.[25] The fact that six months' wages due at the end of 1766 were paid by the end of the following March was seen by one Devon newspaper as evidence of the 'honour and humanity' of the naval administration.[26] In such circumstances the clinging of the yard workers to perquisites which could be reasonably quickly converted into cash, rather than agreeing to money commutation is understandable.

The putting-out system which was based on unsupervised home labour on materials belonging to a capitalist entrepreneur, was the mode of production most clearly associated with the embezzlement of materials by workmen. This special 'invasion of property' came to be increasingly seriously regarded as the form of organising production on the basis of circulating raw materials came to dominate important industries. Out-working shoemakers were said to have 'constant opportunities' for defrauding their masters because they 'seldom work in their master's shop'. Clock and watchmakers also worked at home and distressed their employers by pawning valuable materials.[27] Almost all the putting-out trades suffered. Sheffield nail makers frequently embezzled iron wire, and greater strictness in bringing them to court was urged in 1747. In the metal-working trades of the Black Country, iron, lead and brass were easily disposed of among the thousands of small forges which characterised the district.[28]

In the textile trades part of the yarn given out to spinners could be stolen and the loss hidden by 'false reeling'. At the next stage in the chain of production more could be taken by the weaver or knitter, who could attempt to disguise his action by weaving more loosely. Stockingers could easily purloin enough yarn to make up an extra pair of hose for sale on the side.[29] The records of the London sessions indicate a high level of embezzlement of silk by Spitalfields weavers.[30] The specific eighteenth-century statutes which deal with industrial larceny reveal how much the circumstances of the putting-out manufactures were in the minds of the legislators. 9 George I c.27 (1722) deals with journeymen shoemakers exchanging cheap for expensive leathers, or pawning boots and cut leather. 13 George II c.8 (1739) dealt with several putting-out trades including iron working, the issue of wefts, thrums and yarn-ends in the woollen manufacture, reeling short or false yarn, and with similar practices in the leather and skin trades. 22 George II c.27 (1749) put certain practices in the hat manufacture on the same basis as those included in the 1739 law, while 27 George II c.27 (1754) extended similar sanctions to watchmaking. The famous Worsted Acts of 1777 (17 George III c.11 and 17 George III c.56) which set up an inspectorate to work under a prosecuting committee of employers, has been justly viewed by some historians as an outright piece of 'class' legislation. The Hammonds condemned the acts for allowing conviction on the oath of the employer who owned materials in question, and for giving open-ended powers of search and arrest on 'reasonable suspicion' that embezzled yarn was concealed. These aspects made the acts contrary to the accepted principles of English law in that they presumed guilt and not innocence.[31] In fact in this last respect they do not seem to have differed significantly from the other statutes mentioned above, that on the hatters for example made failure to return surplus materials within 21 days an acknowledgement of guilt.

The Yorkshire worsted manufactures who, unlike the small clothiers of the woollen cloth districts of the same county, were putting-out capitalists on a significant scale, petitioned the Commons in 1777 complaining of 'great frauds' by spinners who embezzled and reeled false. Several years before 1777 a subscription fund had been set up to facilitate detection through the employment of inspectors. This had had some effect, but was proving difficult to fund at an adequate level. The masters were now seeking the establishment of a full-time inspectorate financed by a duty drawback on the soap used in the trade. They had been finding that popular resistance was almost certain to be met with if they sought to punish workmen for embezzlement of yarn. An insistent employer might bring upon his head the 'wrath of the labouring classes in his locality, and might suffer severely for his temerity'. The act which was secured allowed only eight rather than 21 days for the return of surplus yarn before guilt was assumed, and Professor Heaton has seen the act as part of a struggle of combined capitalist interest against a 'keen sense of the solidarity of labour'. With the establishment of a seven-man inspectorate, the clothiers intended 'the wicked world' to be 'cleansed and purged'. In fact their efforts were not an unqualified success. The inspectors themselves seemed not always perfectly suited to combat the delinquency of the weaver. By 1779 three of the original seven had had to be discharged and two had resigned. But the major impediment to the employers' campaign was the open reluctance of local magistrates to act in the same spirit. Heaton suggested that the country justices offered 'ignorance, apathy or actual hostility' because they objected 'to being taught their duty by an upstart industrial organisation'. However the evidence which he presents suggests that reluctance or even refusal to act on the part of the local magistracy, came rather from their sympathy with poor weavers and spinners whom they considered the victims of an oppressive act secured by an interest group of capitalist employers. Thus the Recorder of Pontefract in association with other justices complained that the inspectors were being too severe in their prosecution of spinners and asked for greater leniency. Some Lancashire magistrates refused to hear the evidence of an inspector, while the Mayor of Doncaster was such a stubborn opponent of the acts that in 1784 he was threatened by the employers with Kings Bench proceedings for refusing to hear cases brought under it and for allowing women spinners to escape the district before they paid their fines. The justices of Richmond refused to convict under the acts describing them as 'arbitrary and not fit to be put into execution'. The Worsted Committee showed its true colours when in 1791 it went beyond its 'moral' purpose of combating dishonesty by prosecuting Halifax woolcombers for a conspiracy to raise wages, and expressing in the following year its opinion that friendly societies should be discouraged as leading to illegal combinations.[32]

The Worsted Acts applied to Yorkshire and parts of Lancashire. Clothiers in the West Country had long been troubled by similar problems. A Gloucestershire clothier giving evidence in 1774 in support of a campaign for tougher laws instanced the various forms of theft and deception to which he was subject. Pickers embezzled one pound in 20 and disguised the lost weight by throwing the wool on wet stones to impregnate it with water. Scribblers kept back wool and added oil to make up the expected weight. They could take out a pound of Spanish wool worth about 3-4s in this way. Spinners held yarn over a boiling pot impregnating it with the steam — a disguise sufficient to conceal the removal of half-a-pound in every six. Weavers could keep five or six pounds (worth 4-5s) out of every amount put out for weaving at a 60-pound piece a time, a fraud which was difficult to detect as the wool was delivered wet.[33] The clothiers of Minchinhampton were said in 1784 to have become so wary of the local people that they sent their wool further afield to have it spun. A search conducted in Frome in 1786 produced several hundredweight of embezzled wool. Several suspected weavers absconded, but others were taken and the wool publicly burnt. The persons receiving it were not discovered. They may have been outsiders, but it is known that certain weavers at times acted as receivers from other spinners and weavers.[34] In 1802 a magistrate claimed that weavers who worked at home were still being accused of embezzling large amounts of yarn, while another who could recall no very recent case had attended the conviction of eleven persons for receiving from eight weavers in 1801. The Weavers' Association striving to emphasise its 'respectability' as it organised itself for petitioning Parliament on the apprenticeship issue, was reported to be very anxious to stop the practice among its members.[35]

Apprentices who received for the most part little in the way of wages, did not find it difficult to find shopkeepers willing to receive materials purloined from their masters. An Exeter woman was whipped through the streets at the cart's tail in 1765 for 'slocking' (enticing) an apprentice rug-maker to steal. Stockings could be easily disposed of in the hosiery districts while the 'bagmen', a class of manufacturers who put out work in a small way at the lower quality end of the manufacture, were regular buyers of yarn embezzled from the large hosiers.[36] Some receiving networks linked with professional crime. John Carmichael, a sometime London weaver, travelled around Coventry in the 1760s receiving silk from weavers in exchange for hardware which he ostensibly hawked. He passed the silk to a London silk-master through a receiving network which included a burglar and a highwayman.[37] Yorkshire weavers seem to have dealt with as little sense of impropriety with gold coin counterfeiters to whom they sold clippings from any gold pieces they received in wages.[38] Pawnbrokers were regarded as receivers from the tradesman as well as from the street criminal. Watchmakers especially were accused of pawning valuable components. One writer in defence of pawnbrokers in 1744 argued that the mischief would be prevented if employers would only pay their workmen as soon as the work was done, and this was what Campbell had in mind when he opined that the poor could not live without the pawnbroker.[39] Watchmaking employers, however, regarded the 'Pawning Act' (27 George II) as inadequate and were claiming in 1817 that its provisions were easily evaded.[40]

Concern with strict example demanded public punishment. We have already noted the public whipping of Essex weavers for retaining thrums. A woman was publicly whipped through Wakefield in 1764 for false reeling, with the town bailiff bearing the reel before her. The whipping of embezzlers occasioned riots in Manchester in 1750 and in Stockport in

1772. Miners who stole from the mines in Cornwall were publicly whipped at the mine at the beginning and end of their prison sentences.[41]

After embezzlement employers complained most stridently of being
cheated in the measurement of piecework. In the coal mines where
pitmen were paid by the filled 'corve', there were constant allegations
that they falsely filled them. One of the earliest known guides to the
industry, *The Compleat Collier* of 1708, cautions that there should be:

> strict notice taken dayly by the said Bancks-Men, if Honest, of the
> filling of the Corves with Coals, for otherwise both the Hewers, and
> Barrow-Men, will confederate under Ground, and if the Coals be
> Hewed or Wrought pretty Round and Large Coals, they will be some-
> times so Roguish as to set these big Coals so hollow at the Corfe
> bottom, and cover them with some small Coals at the top of the
> Corves, and make it look like a full Corfe.[42]

It was a persistent practice and its prevention was the main purpose of
an act in 1800 designed to prevent 'the great fraud of stacking coal . . .
by which colliers obtain money beyond what they earn'.[43]

In the tin and copper mines of Cornwall there were sophisticated
forms of wage payment designed to insure maximum productivity: the
tutwork and tribute systems. Tutworkers paid by the fathom for sinking
shafts and driving levels were said sometimes to bribe the mine captains
to over-measure their work. Tributers, who were paid according to the
value of the actual ore which they raised, having previously agreed a
rate in the pound which varied according to the expected ore content
of the part of the mine contracted to them, developed a form of fraud
known as 'kitting'. This involved two tributing gangs. One who had
contracted for a high rate because they were working in a 'pitch' of low
potential, and the other at a low rate because they were working where
ore was plentiful and of good quality. If the rates had been, for example,
12s in the £1 and 2s in the £1, then meeting underground, ore raised
from the richer pitch would be passed to the group working at the
higher rate for presentation. The extra sum thus obtained would be
shared between the two groups.[44]

A tributer who had taken a pitch at a high rate, but who discovered
on working it that expectations had been wrong, and in fact plenty of
good ore was present, was assured of high earnings for the period of his
contract. However, he was also aware that at the end of the two-month
or one-month period of his 'bargain' the pitch would only be reset on
less favourable terms, and accordingly it was not uncommon for tributers

in such circumstances to hide ore underground under piles of dead rock, in the hope that by giving a misleading impression of the yield from the pitch, they could gain a second period at the more favourable rate, at the end of which the concealed ore could be presented along with the product of the second period's excavation.[45]

Cheating over the measurement of piecework was very difficult to discover in the extensive underground workings of a mine, but even in a well-regulated factory like Wedgwood's *Eturia* the problem existed:

> We have with great difficulty detected one of our workmen in seducing three different and successive sets of men, and instructing them how to cheat the overlooker, and have a part of their work told twice over. The clerks had suspected him long, but could bring nothing positive against him or the men he had corrupted, 'till the last week, when the latter, being detected impeached their grand instructer, and informed us of two other sets of men who had been educated before them by this arch villain, and followed the same course in a train for five or six years past.[46]

Cheating over time was not often relevant to the conditions of home workers. In the dockyards however, the practice of 'basseying' that is escaping over the wall after first answering the morning call was the most common offence in a list of men punished in the Deptford yard between 1733 and 1737, while next came 'idling in the tap-house'.[47] In the northern coalfields pitmen were also regularly fined for absenteeism and drinking at work.[48]

The accusations of the employers were met by counter-accusations of 'oppressions' by the men. Oppression was the most commonly used word to convey the idea of the exploitation of labour by the masters. A remarkable poem from the end of the seventeenth century, *The Clothiers' Delight*, depicts in scathing verse the methods used by west-country clothiers in amassing fortunes by 'griping and grinding the poor':

> In former ages we us'd to give,
> So that our work-folk like farmers did live;
> But the times are altered, we will make them know
> All we can for to bring them under our bow;
> We will make to work hard for sixpence a day,
> Though a shilling they deserve if they had their just pay.

And first for the Combers, we will bring them down
From eight groats a score unto half a crown.
If at all they murmur, and say 'tis too small,
We bid them choose whether they will work at all:
We'll make them believe that trading is bad:
We care not a pin, though they are ne-er so sad.

We'll make the poor Weavers work at a low rate;
We'll find fault where there's no fault, and so we will bate;
If trading grows dead, we will presently show it;
But if it grows good, they shall never know it;
We'll tell them that cloth beyond sea will not go,
We care not whether we keep clothing or no.

Then next for the Spinner we shall ensue,
We'll make them spin three pound instead of two;
When they bring home their work unto us, they complain,
And say that their wages will not them maintain;
But if that an ounce of weight they do lack,
Then for to bate threepence we will not be slack.

But if it holds weight, then their wages they crave,
We have got no money, and what's that you'd have?
We have bread and bacon and butter that's good,
With oatmeal and salt that is wholesome for food;
We have soap and candles whereby to give light,
That you may work by them so long as you have light.

But if to an alehouse they customers be,
Then presently with the ale wife we agree;
When we come to a reckoning, then we do crave
Twopence on a shilling, and that we will have,
By such cunning ways we our treasure do get,
For it is all fish that doth come to our net.

The poem is fittingly sub-titled: 'Wherein is exprest (sic) the craftiness and subtility (sic) of Many Clothiers in England, by beating down their Workmen's Wages'.[49]

The verses point to several distinct exploitative practices. These include forcing down wages on false premises, making workers accept truck, fining (bating) for producing work wrongly declared underweight and non-payment of due wages. Not all clothiers acted alike of course, but the persistence of complaints and their acceptance as justified from time to time by local persons not connected with the clothing trade, as well as by Parliament, suggests that the methods of exploitation were widespread. A west-country clothier gave a little away by implication when he recorded in his diary a promise if the Lord would allow his business to pick up:

> Now if it please God to do this great thing for me. To deliver me out of my present difficulties, to open for me a free and advantageous vent for my goods, and grant me a good trade according to the desires of my heart; . . . I would be just in my dealings with everybody . . . I would be charitable to the poor, and would be a kind master to all my servants, not be pressing to have my work done at the lowest rates of anybody, but be glad to see the poor live comfortably by my work.[50]

Combinations of employers to reduce wages were regarded by Adam Smith as a normal fact of manufacturing life. The extent to which this is supported from other documentation is discussed fully below. That workers suffered from late or even non-payment of due wages is evident from the number of statutes passed to remedy this grievance. Long waits for pay have already been shown to have been characteristic of the royal dockyards. In some trades they were not so much the result of delay as of a 'long pay' form of settlement. In the lead mines of the north Pennines a system of payment was in use whereby settlement of contracted agreements with the miners took place at six-monthly intervals, a fact noted by John Wesley in one of his journeys.[51] However, where such long pay systems were in use workers were usually paid a subsistence allowance at regular intervals in anticipation of their eventual settlement. A similar practice was employed in the Cornish mines where three- or two-monthly account periods were usual before a regular monthly account became normal in the nineteenth century.[52]

Where piece-rate systems were in use, employers more commonly tried to effect wage cuts by increasing the quantum rather than by directly cutting the rate. This avoided the appearance of changing rates which may have been 'customary' for a generation or more. Gloucestershire weavers complained in 1756 that the clothiers had 'laid the chain four or five yards longer on the barr', and instead of paying 2s a cloth for stopping (repairing flaws) they had first reduced it to 1s and then refused to pay any extra at all, although stopping added a fifth to the time it took to weave a piece of cloth. The clothiers of Essex in 1758 added to both the length and width of the cloth they expected for the usual rate. Wiltshire clothiers in 1801 changed the time on which they based their rate calculations from 23 hours to a piece to 20.[53] Outside of the clothing industry a clear example comes from the Sheffield cutlery trades in 1787 when there was a strike against the master Jonathon Watkinson who insisted on 13 knives to the dozen rate. This insistence produced one of the cutler songwriter Joseph Mather's most bitter efforts:

> That monster oppression behold how he stalks!
> Keeps picking the bones of the poor as he walks.
> There's not a mechanic throughout this whole land
> But what more or less feels the weight of his hand.
> That offspring of tyranny, baseness and pride
> Our rights hath invaded and almost destroyed
> May that man be banished who villainy screens,
> Or sides with big W......n and his thirteens
>
> And may the odd knife his great carcass dissect:
> Lay open his vitals for men to inspect
> A heart full as black as the infernal gulf
> In that, greedy, blood-sucking, bone scraping wolf.[54]

Complaints about payment in kind or in truck were persistent in many trades throughout the century. The weavers of Somerset complained in 1726 of suffering great hardship 'from their masters, by paying their wages in goods, and setting extravagant prices on such goods'. In 1739 it was complained that weavers were being forced to take remnants of cloth as payment, and the practice of paying in commodities 'above the market price' was described in 1693 as a 'great mischief to the country'. Devonshire weavers were 'up in arms' in 1743 'on account of their masters forcing them to take corn, bread, bacon, cheese, butter and other necessaries of life, in truck, as it is called, for their labour'.[55] These examples all come from the west-country clothing areas, but workers there did not uniquely suffer. Around Sheffield the practice was known as the 'stuffing system' and with prices said to be overvalued threefold, there were riots there in 1756 against an attempt to force cutlers to take half their wages in this form.[56] Journeymen watchmakers were forced during the depression of their trade to take payment in cheap watches which they could only sell at a loss, or else to accept bread tickets for inferior bread, or even paid entirely in bread, some of which they had to sell to pay rent and other expenses.[57] West-country clothiers were suspected of obliging their work people to buy over-priced bread at particular shops as well as forcing them to rent cottages from them at excessive rents.[58]

That the paying of truck and related activities was a *general* practice was consistently denied, but that it existed to some degree was recognised even by spokesmen for the employers. Evidence for the widespread nature of this form of payment does not come entirely from the unspecified complaints of protesting workmen. The west of England woollen trade is among the best documented trades of the early-eighteenth century, and the newspapers of that district from time to time pointedly record prosecutions of clothiers for paying in truck.[59] A clothier giving evidence in 1726 from the serge manufacturing area of the far south-west claimed that most clothiers paid in money and that even those who did not would 'willingly be obliged to pay the whole in money'. A pamphleteer writing on behalf of the clothiers in 1739 acknowledged that the practice, 'not only illegal, but scandalous', existed, but was very glad to hear that 'a large body of clothiers are so heartily disposed and engaged to put a stop to truck'. William Temple similarly recognised that 'trucking masters' existed, but argued that the weaver knew before-hand that he would be paid in kind, and that these masters were the ones who generally accepted poor quality work, and he had known weavers leave ready money clothiers to go to trucking ones.[60]

Established 'gentlemen' clothiers were apt to blame newcomers with little capital for sometimes 'paying the poor in truck in lieu of ready money' and using other oppressive methods which 'have given pretence to them to raise tumults and disturb the peace of the country'. Such newcomers were, they argued, the ones guilty of 'distress, injustice and abuse'.[61] However, the proportion of good to bad masters was differently judged by a claimed 'third party' in 1739. He thought it rare indeed to come across a clothier who paid in ready money, unless he at the same time obliged the workmen to lay it out again with himself or friends. The employers offered no answer at all to the suggestion that clothiers who paid in ready money when competing for labour in times of brisk trade, would resort to truck during times when trade was stagnant and workers would have to take work on any terms.[62]

After truck payment the most frequently articulated grievance was that employers used claims of embezzled materials or bad workmanship to 'stop' fines from wages. Even the clothiers' most ardent polemicist, William Temple, admitted to knowing one employer who stopped wages and defrauded his workers 'in the most base and flagrant manner' and who actually became a JP, but thought him a rare exception. The weavers' claim was that *in general* the clothiers 'load them with intolerable weights and starve them by stoppages'. In one town it was claimed that the clothiers had: 'got into a way of making themselves judges in their own cause, by passing the cloths in the market, after which mark of public infamy, the weaver goes off with a deduction of about 8s and can hardly ever get another chain'. Clothiers set too rigorous standards for the closeness of the weave, and then extracted arbitrary penalties from the weavers for failing to satisfy them.[63]

Temple dismissed such claims as generally untrue. If a clothier did deduct on false pretence of bad workmanship, waste or embezzlement of materials, then the weaver had recourse to a magistrate, who, according to Temple, never failed to do the weaver 'more than justice'. Such a course of action was certainly open in theory under 13 George I which empowered magistrates to put it 'out of the power of any clothier to oppress or defraud any manufacturer in any shape whatsoever'. In fact in most cases, he argued, the stoppages were not at all unreasonable: 'if a manufacturer wastes, embezzles, works bad or injures the manufactures committed to his care'. Whatever the law allowed in theoretical redress, the bringing of a clothier to court was hardly likely to be regularly resorted to by common weavers intimidated by the prospect of obtaining little further work from any source if branded trouble-makers; as Temple himself admitted discharge of employees was a much used weapon.[64] Like payment in kind, stoppages were more likely to have been used in times of bad rather than good trade, when workers had little or no choice of employer and a desperate need for work. Certainly in such times independent accusations appeared to add to the evidential weight of workers' own petitions and pamphlets, such as that of the 'Gentleman of Wiltshire'. James Wolfe, sent as a young officer to command the troops sent to restore peace in the troubled clothing districts, and the Secretary of State at the time, the Duke of Newcastle felt there was a real basis for the weavers' complaints.[65] Complaints about stoppages came from other trades and districts. The London hatters complained that masters were in the habit of stopping 'hundreds of pounds' for alleged faults 'when trade has been slack'.[66]

The rejection of badly-filled corves on the grounds of intentional false filling was a running grievance through the century in the northern coalfields. Attempts to get miners to spend time separating coal from stone underground in one coalfield in 1751 led to a strike which was ended when compensation for the time spent was added to wages.

However, the owners insisted on retaining a heavy penalty clause if too much stone were sent up.[67] Abatements for alleged negligent or fraudulent work was a frequent cause of friction in the framework knitting districts too. In disputes over the amount that should be tolerated for waste, the masters were themselves accused of deceit in that they gave out yarn by weight and on weighing it again when it was taken in made too little allowance for normal waste, so that they could allege a misdemeanour and bate accordingly. Some hosiers put-out silk damp so that when goods were later weighed dry they showed a deficiency.[68]

Stoppages in the hosiery manufacture probably cut into wages far less than did a series of fixed and exploitative standard deductions. Loom rent was far from unknown in some areas of the woollen manufacture, but in no other industry did renting become so common and characteristic as it did in framework knitting. Stocking frames were costly, around £50-60, and the practice of renting them out to the knitters developed in the seventeenth century and progressed steadily through the eighteenth so that by 1800 a knitter owning his own frame was rare. Why was this so? When times were slack trade frames could be bought second-hand very cheaply. In fact exploitation centred on the fact that even if a knitter owned his own frame he needed to take in work from the hosiers. Nottingham masters were said not to employ a man unless he rented a frame from them or else to charge a man 'half-rent' for undertaking their work on his own frame. Hosiers took care to keep their rented frames in sufficient work to allow the deduction to be made. William Hutton borrowed £10 from his brother-in-law to buy his first frame in 1746, but it was a bad time for such an investment: 'The stocking-frame being my own, and trade being dead, the hosiers would not employ me. They could scarcely employ their own frames.' At times when the frame-owner could not provide work even for his own frames, knitters taking work from other hosiers were asked for a payment in lieu of rent. As the eighteenth century wore on rents tended to become increasingly oppressive with the growth of middlemen 'putters-out' between the large hosiers and the knitters, for these men drew their income by deducting higher rent from the knitter than they paid to the hosier. There was no logical system of rent related to the value of a frame or to the expected income from working at it. Indeed rents seem to have increased after 1780 when the cost of second-hand frames was low and when earnings were declining. The explanation lies in the fact that the hosier frame-owners enjoyed a certain profit from the rent whether the knitter was in full work or not as the rent was deducted from wages, and it could even be demanded if the unfortunate knitter was without work.[69]

Rent was not the only deduction. If seaming of the stockings was not done at home by a wife, that too was charged to the knitter. For the journeyman knitter there could be deduction for frame standing — the use of a corner of a master-knitter's workplace — and a charge paid to a small master for taking in work as an agent for his journeymen. A list of 1811 gives the range of deductions:

Seaming	1s	1d
Needles		3d
Oil		½d
Candles		3d
Coals		1½d
Frame standing		3d
Expenses taking in work	1s	0d
Frame rent	1s	0d
Deductions	4s	0d from a wage of 13s 3¼d[70]

The London coal-heavers suffered from the control of their labour by 'undertakers', usually publicans who contracted with the collier-vessel masters for the unloading and thereby took total control over who got work. The heavers, apart from having to give a cut of their earnings to the undertaker, were also forced to hire their shovels and other supplies from them at excessive rents. So strong was the hold of the undertakers over the trade that they evaded with ease an act passed to protect the men, and won against the competition of an alternative employment office set up in 1768 by the sympathetic (to the heavers) magistrate Ralph Hodgson.[71] In other trades too essential supplies were monopolised by the employers. Pryce noted that Cornish miners drew their candles from the mines, and although he gives no indication of the level of charges, mine account books from the nineteenth century show that large profits were then taken from supplying the miners with essential supplies.[72]

The London tailors had a different form of grievance. The statutory fixing of their hours of work in 1721 had not divided the day into equal parts. Before the act, master tailors wanting to offer only a half-day's work commonly turned off journeymen in the middle of the day. The statute however made the afternoon session an hour longer than the morning one, and the employers 'took advantage of the poor journeymen' by letting them 'play in the morning' and calling them from their 'houses of call' for the afternoon period. Not only did they then get an extra hour's work for the same pay, but even avoided paying the required 1½d breakfast allowance.[73]

Social historians who take pains to unravel the structures and relationships which provide the context in which such activities as the embezzlement of materials take place are likely to be accused of being 'soft' on the simply criminal, or of ignoring the obvious link between poverty and the temptation to steal. The light-fingered and the desperate account in any age for a large proportion of embezzlement. There is no way of quantifying motivations. All that can be done is to place the increasingly widespread and insistent allegations of employers and their representation in new statutes in the context of an expanding capitalist mode of production: the putting-out system. The accusations and counter-accusations of masters and men are part of the special forms of conflict appropriate to that system.[74]

Notes

1. William Temple, *The Case as It Now Stands etc.* (1739), reprinted in K. Carpenter (ed.), *Labour Problems before the Industrial Revolution* (New York, 1972), p. 5.

2. *An Essay on Riots etc.* (1739), reprinted in J. Smith, *Memoirs of Wool* (1747, reprinted Farnborough 1968), II, p. 302.

3. *Sherborne Mercury and Yeovil Advertiser*, 21 February 1762.

4. P. Linebaugh, summary of paper in *Bulletin of the Society for the Study of Labour History*, no. 25 (1972), p. 13.

5. Entry under 'cabbage' in *The Shorter Oxford English Dictionary*.

6. R. Campbell, *The London Tradesman* (1747, reprinted Newton Abbot 1969), p. 192.

7. Francis Grose, *A Classical Dictionary of the Vulgar Tongue* (text of 1796, edited by E. Partridge, London, 1931), p. 124.

8. *Commons Journal*, XXXVI, 5 February 1777, pp. 118-9.

9. Ibid., XXXIII, 15 March 1737, p. 93.

10. *Fourth Report of Select Committee on Artisans and Machinery*, P.P. 1824 (51), V, p. 240.

11. A.F.J. Brown, *Essex at Work 1700-1815* (Chelmsford, 1969), p. 25 and *English History from Essex Sources 1700-1900* (Chelmsford, 1952), pp. 204-5.

12. Brown, *Essex at Work*, p. 25.

13. *Minutes of Evidence before the Committee on the Laws Relating to the Woollen Trade*, P.P. 1802/3 (95), VII, p. 320.

14. D. Hay, 'Crime, Authority and the Criminal Laws in Staffordshire 1750-1800', unpublished PhD thesis, University of Warwick, 1975, pp. 87, 92-3.

15. *Calendar of State Papers Domestic 1633-34*, cclx.

16. M. Oppenheim, 'The Royal Dockyards' in W. Page (ed.), *Victoria County History of Kent. Vol. 2* (London, 1926), pp. 348, 358.

17. Ibid., pp. 374-7.

18. D.A. Baugh, *British Naval Administration in the Age of Walpole* (Princeton, 1965), p. 321.

19. *Commons Journal*, XLVII, 13 February 1792, p. 229.

20. Oppenheim, 'Royal Dockyards', p. 386.

21. Ibid., p. 368.

22. *Exeter Mercury*, 16 November 1764; *Hampshire Chronicle*, 15 February 1773.

23. Oppenheim, 'Royal Dockyards', pp. 352-3, 377.

24. Ibid., p. 347. The corruption in the yards is fully described by both Oppenheim and Baugh. Late pay references from Oppenheim, pp. 350, 355, 363.

25. Baugh, *Naval Administration*, p. 315; Oppenheim, 'Royal Dockyards', pp. 376, 380.

26. *Exeter Mercury*, 20 March 1767.

27. *Commons Journal*, XXIII, 15 March 1737, p. 93; S.E. Atkins and W.H. Overall, *Some Account of the Worshipful Company of Clockmakers of the City of London* (London, 1881), p. 275; *Report from the Select Committee on the Petitions of the Watchmakers of Coventry*, P.P. 1817 (504), VI, p. 12.

28. David Hey, *The Rural Metalworkers of the Sheffield Region* (Leicester, 1972), p. 48; Hay, 'Crime, Authority and the Criminal Laws', pp. 94-6.

29. G.A. Chinnery (ed.), *Records of the Borough of Leicester Vol. VII* (Leicester, 1974), pp. 136, 143, 149.

30. M. Dorothy George, *London Life in the Eighteenth Century* (Harmondsworth, 1966 edn), p. 185.

31. J.L. and B. Hammond, *The Skilled Labourer* (edited by J.G. Rule, London, 1979), pp. 190-1.

32. *Commons Journal*, XXXVI, 29 January 1777, p. 85, 29 January 1777, p. 113; H. Heaton, *The Yorkshire Woollen and Worsted Industries* (Oxford, 1920), pp. 421-32.

33. *Commons Journal*, XXXIV, 26 January 1774, pp. 451-2.

34. J. de L. Mann, *The Cloth Industry in the West of England from 1640-1880* (Oxford, 1971), p. 114; *Sherbourne Mercury*, 10 and 24 July 1786.

35. *Report from the Committee on the Woollen Clothiers' Petition from Somerset, Wiltshire and Gloucestershire*, P.P. 1802/3 (30), V, pp. 16-17.

36. *Exeter Mercury*, 12 September 1765; E.A. Wells, *The British Hosiery and Knitwear Industry: Its History and Organisation* (1935, reprinted Newton Abbot, 1972), p. 63.

37. Linebaugh in *Bulletin of the Society for the Study of Labour History*, no. 25 (1972), p. 13.

38. J. Styles, '"Our Traitorous Money Makers": The Yorkshire Coiners and the Law, 1760-83' in J. Brewer and J. Styles (eds.), *An Ungovernable People. The English and their Law in the Seventeenth and Eighteenth Centuries* (London, 1980), pp. 172-249.

39. *SC on Watchmakers' Petitions*, P.P. 1817, VI, p. 12; quoted in T.S. Ashton, *An Economic History of England: The Eighteenth Century* (London, 1955), p. 210; Campbell, *London Tradesman*, pp. 296-7.

40. *SC on Watchmakers' Petitions*, P.P. 1817, VI, p. 12.

41. Heaton, *Woollen and Worsted Industries*, p. 419; J.G. Rule, 'The Labouring Miner in Cornwall c. 1740-1870: A Study in Social History', unpublished PhD thesis, University of Warwick, 1971, p. 58 (footnote).

42. J.C., *The Compleat Collier* (1708, reprinted Newcastle 1968), p. 38.

43. E. Welbourne, *The Miners' Unions of Northumberland and Durham* (Cambridge, 1923), p. 21.

44. Rule, 'Labouring Miner', pp. 57-60.

45. *Quarterly Review*, LXXII (1827), p. 86.

46. Ann Finer and G. Savage (eds.), *The Selected Letters of Josiah Wedgwood* (London, 1965), p. 238.

47. Baugh, *Naval Administration*, pp. 312, 314.

48. *A Pitman's Notebook of 1749* (Newcastle, 1970), p. 14.

49. The poem is reprinted in full in P. Mantoux, *The Industrial Revolution in the Eighteenth Century* (revised edn London, 1961), pp. 75-7.

50. Diary of George Wansey of Warminster, 10 September 1741 in J. de L. Mann (ed.), *Documents Illustrating the Wiltshire Textile Trades in the Eighteenth Century* (Devizes, 1964), p. 31.

51. John Wesley, *Journals* (Everyman edn, London, 1906), Vol. II, pp. 69-70, entries 27 July 1748 and 29 July 1748.

52. Rule, 'Labouring Miner', pp. 49-50.

53. W.E. Minchinton, 'The Petitions of the Weavers and Clothiers of Gloucestershire in 1756', *Transactions of the Bristol and Gloucestershire Archaeological Society*, vol. 73 (1954), p. 219; Brown, *English History from Essex Sources*, p. 204; *Minutes of Evidence before the Committee on the Laws Relating to the Woollen Trade*, P.P. 1802/3 (95), VII, p. 212.

54. G.I.H. Lloyd, *The Cutlery Trades* (London, 1913), pp. 241-2.

55. *Commons Journals*, XX, 7 March 1725(6), p. 627; Gentleman of Wiltshire, *The Miseries of the Miserable etc.* (1739), reprinted in Carpenter (ed.), *Labour Problems*, p. 21; quoted in C.R. Dobson, *Masters and Journeymen. A Pre-history of Industrial Relations 1717-1800* (London, 1980), p. 21.

56. Lloyd, *Cutlery Trades*, p. 215.

57. *SC on Watchmakers' Petitions*, P.P. 1817, VI, p. 15; *Report from the Select Committee on the Laws Relating to Watchmakers*, P.P. 1818 (135), IX, p. 4.

58. *Essay on Riots etc.* (1739) reprinted in Smith, *Memoirs of Wool*, Vol. II, p. 302.

59. *Sherborne Mercury*, 12 and 26 May 1783 and 28 March 1785.

60. *Commons Journals*, XX, 31 March 1726, p. 648; *Remarks on the Essay on Riots* (1739) reprinted in Smith, *Memoirs of Wool*, Vol. II, p. 305; Temple, 'The Case as It Now Stands etc.', p. 59.

61. *Sherborne Mercury*, 2 March 1742.

62. Gentleman of Wiltshire, *Miseries of the Miserable*, p. 6.

63. Temple, *The Case as It Now Stands etc.*, p. 5; *The Devil Drove out the Warping-bar* (1727), p. 7. Reprinted in Carpenter, *Labour Problems*; Gentleman of Wiltshire, *Miseries of the Miserable*, pp. 19-20.

64. Temple, *The Case as It Now Stands etc.*, pp. 5-8.

65. See the interesting chapter on the west of England in D.G.D. Issac, 'A Study of Popular Disturbances in Britain, 1714-54', unpublished PhD thesis, University of Edinburgh, 1953.

66. *Commons Journals*, XXXVI, 13 March 1777, p. 289.

67. *A Pitman's Notebook*, pp. 48-51; Welbourne, *Miners' Unions*, p. 21.

68. Wells, *Hosiery and Knitwear Industry*, pp. 69-70.

69. Ibid., pp. 63-7; W. Hutton, *Life*, p. 130.

70. Ibid., p. 68.

71. *The Conduct of Ralph Hodgson etc.* (1768), pp. 3-5, 7. Reprinted in K. Carpenter (ed.), *Labour Disputes in the Early Days of the Industrial Revolution* (New York, 1972).

72. W. Pryce, *Mineralogia Cornubiensis* (Oxford, 1778), p. 180; Rule, 'Labouring Miner', p. 48 (footnote).

73. F.W. Galton, *Select Documents Illustrating the History of Trade Unionism: the Tailoring Trade* (London, 1896), p. 56.

74. Linebaugh has made an interesting comment on this: 'The divergence between the themes of criminality and the labour movement cannot be assisted

by the anachronistic transposition of the nineteenth-century triad, respectable artisan, unskilled labourer, criminal classes to the eighteenth century, when the basis for the perennial struggle between capital and labour was fundamentally different'. (*Bulletin of the Society for the Study of Labour History*, no 25 (1972), p. 15.)

6 TRADE UNIONISM AND INDUSTRIAL DISPUTES: THE NATURE AND EXTENT OF TRADE UNIONISM

Adam Smith regarded the separation of labour and capital as normal, believing that in Europe 20 workmen served a master for every one that was independent: 'the wages of labour are everywhere understood to be what they usually are, when the labourer is one person, and the owner of the stock which employs him another'. A separation in fact and function meant a separation of interest. Smith's view of industrial relations in operation in the eighteenth century, as opposed to his expectation for the ideal *laissez-faire* economy, was a conflict one. The workmen sought to get as high wages as possible, while the employers sought to pay as little as possible: 'The former are disposed to combine in order to raise, the latter in order to lower the wages of labour'. But while accepting that industrial action was a commonplace and expected phenomenon, he had little doubt that the advantage lay with the employers who could in normal conditions affect a compliance with their terms. This advantage stemmed from several causes. The masters being fewer in number could combine more easily and more solidly. The law did not prohibit their combinations while it did that of the workmen. The masters had the resources to hold out much longer than the men in any strike. He recognised that combinations of workmen came about both from attempts to raise the price of labour, not only because of cost of living pressures but sometimes when employers were believed to be making great profits, and from defensive reactions against attempts to lower wages. Whether offensive or defensive, the problem for the workers was that lacking resources they had to bring matters to as speedy a decision as possible and this too often implied 'the loudest clamour, and sometimes the most shocking violence'. Their actions became a matter of public order, and repressive law denied them any advantage from their dispute, which ended only in their sullen return on the masters' terms and the imprisonment of their leaders.[1]

Charles Hall echoed Smith's views in his *Effects of Civilization* in 1805. Workmen constantly endeavoured to raise wages, but 'being unequally matched', for the most part with little success:

It has been taken notice of, that the manufacturers in their disputes with their masters are generally worsted. If they strike their work with this view, as what they have beforehand is generally very little, they cannot hold out long, but are, like a garrison short of provisions, obliged to capitulate on the best terms they can get. We need not observe that this, the only method they have of redressing their grievances is frequently crushed by the military.

Whatever Hall thought of the effectiveness of the strike weapon, he was convinced it should not be taken away by law. To do that was to remove: 'the right and advantage that all other people have in their dealings — of refusing to take what is offered to them'.[2]

The effectiveness of collective action by labour will be assessed in the following chapter. The first concern is to examine the extent and nature of combined labour action in the eighteenth century. That it was widespread and frequent cannot be doubted. An historian has recently listed 383 disputes between 1717 and 1800, of which 230 took place before 1780. There is little meaning in Dr Dobson's averaging his listed disputes in terms of years or regions (he offers three strikes a year as the 'average' for the British Isles). In the first place his list can only be a proportion of an unknown total reported in provincial newspapers or only locally documented, and in the second place even if the total *reported* were recoverable it would still represent only an unknown proportion of the number which actually took place.[3] If we resist the temptation to do anything too 'mathematical' with it, Dr Dobson's data together with that supplied several years ago in a too little-used article by Dr Mary Rhys Baker, is most valuable and confirms overwhelmingly that industrial disputes were known in most parts of the country and in most artisan trades as well as in many smaller and less skilled ones. Of Dobson's sample, 18 took place in Scotland, 32 in Ireland and none at all in Wales. Of the 333 which took place in England, London the great centre of the artisan trades headed the list of recorded disputes 1717 to 1800:

London	120	Midlands	27
South-east	21	East and West	
South	7	Midlands	15
South-west	47	North-west	38
Eastern	24	Northern	34

A breakdown by trade of the 383 British disputes shows the great lead of the woollen workers (combers, weavers and spinners) with 64 incidents. Only the seamen and ships'-carpenters with 37 and the tailors with 22 also exceed 20. Between 10 and 20 brings in the coalminers; shipwrights, ropemakers and sailmakers; keelmen; silk weavers; framework knitters, textile workers other than in wool or silk; shoemakers and the bricklayers, carpenters and other building workers. Between 5 and 10 covers the farmworkers and market gardeners; harvesters, wheelwrights; curriers, hatters; bakers; papermakers; printers and bookbinders; cabinet and chairmakers; bargemen and lightermen; and coalporters and carmen. This still leaves 89 instances to be divided among other trades in which there were less than five instances.[4]

No London trade is as well-documented as the tailors', however. In complaining of a combination in 1721, their employers instanced curriers, smiths and farriers, sailmakers and coachmakers as being among other trades in which 'unlawful combination' existed, and carpenters, bricklayers and joiners as being about to form such combinations.[5] Disputes do not necessarily imply the presence of a permanent or continuous association of workers in a form which resembles a modern trade union. Adam Smith does not seem to have been concerned to distinguish spontaneous or ephemeral combinations, formed to contest specific issues on particular occasions, from disputes which stemmed from an underlying organisational base in existence to defend or advance the interests of its members. The insistence on such a differentiation has come rather from the traditional historians of the labour movement, especially the Webbs. Their insistence on a rigid definition of trade unionism depending upon the existence of a 'continuous association' has, together perhaps with Adam Smith's insistence on the ineffectiveness of collective labour action, restricted and distorted views on eighteenth-century labour combinations.[6] Even if their narrow emphasis on 'continuous' organisation is accepted, then it may be applied to possibly 50 eighteenth-century 'clubs' or societies among wage earners including hatters, woolcombers, tailors, weavers, cabinet-makers, wheelwrights, curriers, blacksmiths, carpenters, bricklayers, masons and calico printers.[7]

The Webbs' definition has been criticised by historians for being historically inapplicable to the actual conditions of eighteenth-century industrial workers. An industrial relations expert, who although not an historian has produced an important study with a major historical perspective of the cotton workers, has remarked that whereas general historians of the labour movement report only sporadic trade unionism among workers in that industry in the eighteenth century i.e. passionate struggle intermittent with abject submission, historians of the district or of the industry tend to write on the assumption of a continuous labour collective presence.[8] Following too closely the line of the Webbs leads to an over-readiness to fasten on to ephemerality as being evident from the surviving documentation of intermittent eruptions. Professor Turner points out that 'continuous association' need not imply permanent organisation. Members of a trade regularly brought together in work-place or community, could acknowledge regular leaders, develop customs of work regulation and systematic trade practices and produce disciplined observance of the latter without necessarily embedding these procedures in any formal record. Such a collective presence could readily submerge but not necessarily disappear in times of trouble. Thus Turner argues that the flickering appearance of early trade unionism among cotton weavers arose not from the absence of any continuing current of collective association but from the 'intermittence of the actual need for collective action'. When that need did arise there is a clear indication from the promptness of organised response that the elements of a continuing association had in the meantime been preserved.[9]

Thus labour historians have missed the point in looking for origins of a formally constituted movement, while industrial historians of the cotton trade have been nearer the truth in noting in the 'persistence of certain reiterated collective pressures', a tendency towards collective action. It is in these rather than in particular institutional forms, Professor Turner argues, that the 'essence of trade unionism consists'. For the rural weavers the habit of association was probably in itself sufficient to produce at need an organisation to handle deputations or strikes, and this habit was reinforced rather than created by continuing and more formal links such as village friendly or burial clubs. The habit of association among handloom weavers could last as long as the class of workmen concerned itself lasted, or until it became too unstable and diluted to preserve it. Unlike modern 'professional' leadership there was no existence independent of the members' activity. It is indeed possible that balloting and the rotation of office may have been intended to prevent the emergence of an élite separate from the rank and file and there is accordingly little relevance in modern notions of official versus unofficial workers' action.[10]

Association developed informally from the weavers' conditions of work and life. The village social meeting, a convivial social forum – the smallware weavers claimed in 1756 to have been long accustomed to meet weekly at a public house to discuss trade matters – developed easily into the friendly society with its 'box' (fund) and found itself exercising union functions. The town weavers in places like Manchester worked in small numbers in workshops. The 'shop' was in itself a natural unit which could through delegation of representatives to a central meeting develop organically into a structured union. The very simplicity of the structure meant that even formal disbanding might be only a temporary interruption, since the essential units survived to make reconstruction a straightforward matter. Professor Turner concludes that so far as the cotton weavers are concerned there is no problem in reconciling persistence with evidence of sporadic incidence, since the true foundation was the durable one of the habit of association between workers of a settled occupational group.[11]

There have been too few studies of other industries which compare in detail and insight with Turner's, but his general line of argument is a convincing one, and might reasonably be expected to have a more general applicability. Edward Thompson has also pointed out that the Webbs' position inhibits a functional perspective on the effectiveness of eighteenth-century forms of collective action, especially in the area of popular disturbance.[12]

The Webbs' insistence on the exclusion of the 'innumerable instances' in which workers formed 'ephemeral combinations against their social superiors',[13] is better replaced with one which, while it accepts that in many important cases industrial action stemmed from the prior existence of unions whose existence continued after the ending of the specific issue, also recognises that both the strike weapon and the industrial disturbance and riot were widespread and expected occurrences in eighteenth-century industry. Perhaps stress should be laid not on 'ephemeral' but on 'innumerable'. It is not useful to think of a polarisation of organised trade union activity at one pole and sporadic 'one-off' actions at the other. Instead there was a spectrum of responses with *recurrent* forms linking the ephemeral with the continuous. By recurrent is understood a situation in which groups of workers although not necessarily keeping an organisation for trade-protecting purposes in permanent being, nevertheless preserved in experience and tradition a sufficient knowledge of possible forms of action. From these they selected and employed the appropriate one when a point of stress arose if defence were in question, or when favourable circumstances occurred if advance were the object. The idea of recurrent behaviour is equally relevant in the food-riot when forms of action could reappear in a strikingly repetitive form after half a generation had lapsed since the previous food-riot in that district. There would seem to be no reason why such should not also be the case with industrial disputes.

Several trades for which good documentation survives can be used to illustrate the growth of trade unionism. The tailors of London, the woollen workers of the south-west, the hatters and the cotton weavers of Lancashire offer the best possibilities. In all of these trades the Webbs' view that: 'whilst industrial oppression belongs to all ages, it is not until the changing conditions of industry had reduced to an infinitesimal chance the journeyman's prospect of becoming himself a master, that we find the passage of ephemeral combinations into permanent trade societies'.[14] Although in some trades a split might develop along a line of cleavage between journeyman and small master on the one side and the large master on the other, as it did in the framework knitting trades.

Their employers complained during a dispute in 1810 that they had had to endure a combination of the journeymen tailors which had subsisted for nearly a century and had become 'ripened by experience'. Over this time it had been able to impose 'arbitrary and oppressive laws' upon the trade.[15] In fact the origins probably went back for more than a century, for around 1700 five clubs of journeymen confederated to form a central union. The union first drew public notice to its existence and activities in the dispute of 1720/1 which led up to the passing of the well-known act prohibiting combinations of journeymen tailors in London and Westminster, and fixing by statute their wages and hours. According to the committee whose examinations were the basis for the act, large numbers of journeymen had 'departed from their services without just cause and have entered into combinations to advance their wages into unreasonable prices and lessen their hours of work'. When trade was brisk they were 'very often' able to insist on 7s or 8s a day, setting a very bad example to other artificers and labourers.[16] They were well-organised around their 'houses of call', the public houses on which their organisation was based and which functioned as 'labour exchanges' from which employers drew their short-term labour needs, and had been able to keep their wages up. The masters' petitioning of the Commons which had resulted in the act of 1721 fixing wages at 2s in the summer and 1s 8d in the winter for a 14-hour day, had stemmed from a combined and determined resistance to the effectiveness of the union: 'For the masters are now subscribing and make purses of money to prosecute the journeymen, as much as the journeymen are to defend themselves'.[17] From the employers' viewpoint a statutory fixing of wages allied to a prohibition of combinations would inhibit wages from moving upwards in brisk periods and seasons, although the act did allow re-adjustment by justices in sessions and was itself revised in 1768 to reduce the hours to 13 and increase the daily rates to 2s 7½d.[18] Adam

Smith had little doubt who were the gainers from statutory settlements: 'whenever the legislature attempts to regulate the differences between masters and their workmen, its counsellors are always the masters'.[19] Despite the act the Tailors' Union persisted and throughout the century descriptions of its procedures and the breaking of the surface from time to time in open confrontation confirm its permanence. Trouble broke out in the winter 1744/5, in 1752, 1764 and 1768. The pattern which brought matters periodically to a head was a natural one. Levels fixed by the act were made unrealistic by rises in the cost of living, as claimed by the journeymen in 1752, when a large part of the masters sympathised and 'for several years past' paid 2s 6d a day all the year round, when the most recent Quarter Sessions fixing had been only 2s in the winter.[20] It is clear that the wealthier employers who had lobbied and secured the parliamentary intervention did not represent the whole body of masters. Smaller men closer to the journeymen were in sympathy with them and many of these were paying in 1745 2s 7½d when the statute wage was 1s 9½d. In brisk trade even the larger employers' avidity for labour led many of them to evade the act which they had solicited. Some large employers moved to Marylebone outside the limits of the act and offered seductive wages to journeymen. In 1760 the daily wage of 5s, far above the official rate, was being described as 'customary', but that can have applied only to the few whose special skills were much sought, for in 1762 a union meeting of 42 society houses set 3s as a 'fair' rate.[21]

The act most probably increased conflict since the existence of a legal maximum, although they disregarded it when it suited them, encouraged employers to take advantage of its existence whenever market conditions worsened. They combined to cut by the differential between what was actually being paid and the legal rate of the time. In this they were attempting cuts which tended to go beyond those likely to be attempted in other trades, intensifying the deep-rooted grievance of the journeymen that they had been especially singled out by law for oppressive treatment: describing themselves in 1745 as 'picked out as the only class of men among His Majesty's subjects on whom such extraordinary and singular hardships are laid'.[22] The very existence of the act was in itself a focal point for organisation to get it removed as in 1768.[23] Sir John Fielding thought the statute so ineffective that by 1756 as many as 40 box clubs had confederated into an impressive organisation with a central delegate conference (the House of Representatives) and an executive committee (the Grand Committee for Management of the Town):

The master taylors ... have repeatedly endeavoured to break and suppress the combinations of their journeymen to raise their wages, and lessen their hours of work, but have ever been defeated, notwithstanding the excellent provision of the ... statute; and this has been in some measure due to the infidelity of the masters themselves to each other; some of whom, taking advantage of the confusion, have collected together with some of the journeymen, whose exhorbitant demands they have complied with, while many other masters have had a total stop put to their business, because they would not be guilty of a breach of so necessary a law.[24]

At the time of the major strike of 1764 the masters were complaining that the union which had existed since 1720 had recently become so strong that not only had it extracted greater wages and shorter hours 'then by law allowed', but had formed itself into a 'kind of republic' holding meetings at 42 different houses of call to appoint delegates to the 'Grand Committee' which made rules and orders 'for the direction of the masters and the whole body of journeymen tailors'. Masters or journeymen who did not comply were sanctioned: the former by being 'blacked'; the latter by fines, and by not being allowed to take any work until the fine had been cleared. In that year a massive petition had succeeded in persuading the Middlesex magistrates in January to raise the daily rate to 2s 6d all year round, instead of a winter drop to 2s, and to take an hour off the winter working day. The journeymen felt strong enough to hold out for the shorter day in the summer as well, and accordingly on a Monday in July they all left work at seven instead of eight o'clock.[25] Greatly fearful of the growing confidence of the union, the employers made a move against the houses of call. Ironically these cells of the union organisation had originated primarily to serve the needs of the employers:

The master taylors, in order to be secure of having a sufficient number of journeymen always ready to answer their occasions, did long ago, amongst themselves, contrive to encourage the journeymen to assemble daily at certain publick houses of call, from whence they could at a minutes warning, be employ'd with any number of journeymen they wanted.[26]

They enjoyed the convenience of taking men they wanted for as short a period as they wanted, perhaps for only two days out of a week, while the men awaiting call were at the expense of meeting the publicans' expectations: 'Custom has established it into a kind of law, that the House of Call gives them credit for victuals and drink, while they are unemployed; this obliges the journeymen on the other hand to spend all the money they earn at this house alone'.[27] The not surprising development of the house of call as a box club centre and base for union activities turned the advantage around. In 1764 the employers tried to boycott the existing houses by setting up others under their own control. By recruiting only from these they would break the combination:

> It will be in vain for the journeymen to stand out any longer against the laws of their country; if they do they will bring poverty and distress upon themselves and families, and perhaps a more severe punishment than they at present apprehend, for the masters are determined to break the combination.[28]

The employers claimed to have brought in more than 1,000 hands from outside London in the course of just six weeks, but it was not enough to break the union and, losing patience, the chairman of the employers' committee entered a house of call and seized and carried off to prison 45 journeymen. He was to learn that the law had its limitations. There was no evidence that the men had been engaged in anything illegal at the time, and not only was their release ordered but the employers were required to compensate them a guinea a man for their overnight stay in prison. Bitter hostility dragged on for several years with conspiracy proceedings against union leaders taking place in 1767.[29] Massive petitioning for repeal of the act in 1768 was unsuccessful, but in 1778 journeymen were still not infrequently taking strike action.[30]

The organisation described by Francis Place in 1824 reflected the experience of more than a century. He described the journeymen as having 'a perfect and perpetual combination':

> Their system is all but a military system. The orders come from their Executive, and are always obeyed. There are upwards of twenty regular or 'Flint' houses of call in London; each house has a delegate, and they elect five other delegates, who are technically called the 'Town'. In many cases the power of the five men is almost unlimited over the trade, and obedience follows as a matter of course. The whole body never in any instance, discuss the propriety of a strike, as that would subject them to prosecution under the Combination

Laws. Unlimited confidence is, therefore, given to the five, and this
it is which constitutes their power.

The men generally did not know who these 'regulators' were. It was
whispered among them that there was to be a strike: 'but they never
discuss the subject; they strike when bid'. The 'Town' fixed the sum
to which the men conformed. Organisation was confined to the 'flints',
the day-rate journeymen who received the same wages. Less skilled
workers, the 'dungs' generally worked by the piece. Masters tried to
bring in more of the latter in times of dispute to break the hold of the
'house'.[31]

The Tailors Acts applied only to London, thus the areas of dispute
specific to the context of the statute did not occur in the provinces.
Provincial tailors were nevertheless organised in many towns. The
Birmingham journeymen undertook a long strike in 1777 when their
employers tried to replace day rates by piecework. Here, too, the house
of call was the focus of the dispute. The employers advertised for new
men to come to the town to be employed without the medium of the
house: 'none will be employed but such as call at the masters' houses,
and are free from all combinations'. The men responded that it was well-
known that the house of call had been an ancient customary institution
both in London and 'in all the other capital towns in this kingdom for
our trade, and that it is more to the master's advantage than a man's'.[32]
Comparatively little is known about organisation in other towns. A
famous conspiracy case in 1721 involved a combination of journeymen
in Cambridge, and a similar case arose from a Liverpool dispute in 1783.
There had been an earlier strike in that city in 1756.[33]

The journeyman hatters had a history of combination at least as long
as that of the tailors.[34] A Commons committee in 1777 heard evidence
on the extent and power of that combination. For several years previously a scarcity of skilled men had presented the opportunity for
repeated demands for advances in wages and shortening of hours. The
journeymen had entered into what they termed a 'congress' which
made by-laws, extracted fines and prevented many masters from taking
apprentices beyond a prescribed limit. At the time of the hearing the
men were all out. The masters had been forced to give into wage demands made following meetings of the congress in 1772 and in 1775.
The congress levied a weekly subscription of 2d. One employer complained that when five of his 50 employees refused to join, his shop was
visited by a large body of journeymen, who told him not to employ the
five, and by threatening to bring out his other workers forced him into

compliance. Later he put some work out to one of the men he had been forced to discharge, but the journeymen returned, demanded he withdrew the work and demanded further a contribution of 3 guineas from him for their loss of time in attending to 'this act of justice'; when he refused all his employees quit.[35]

The events of this year clearly indicate that the influence of the combination reached beyond London. The Manchester employers in February were expressing their determination not to employ any hatter who would not declare his intention not to submit to 'any pretended laws made by a Congress, Committee or any other Combination of piece-makers or journeymen'; be concerned in any strikes or contribute towards the support of those who were on strike. Neither were they to pay any fines to the congress. While the employers' petition was before the Commons, counter-petitions from journeymen were received from: London, Manchester, Newcastle-under-Lyme, Burton-on-Trent, several towns in Leicestershire, Derby, Bristol, Liverpool, Chester and Hexham.[36] The masters secured their objective, which had not been just the statutory prohibition of combinations, but a modification of the special legislation which limited the number of apprentices they were allowed to take. This was in fact the main prop of the journeymen's ability to control the supply of labour into the trade. However the strength of the union was such that the journeymen were able in most times to insure an effective limitation through their own collective refusal to work with those whom they did not regard as 'fair' workmen. To the extent that they were able to reflect this, the employers got less from the act than they had hoped.[37] There were further strikes in Manchester in 1780 and 1783 and a confrontation over apprenticeship in Manchester and Salford in 1785. At Leicester in 1780 four journeymen hatters were prosecuted for having 'lately entered into a contract, covenant, rule or order of an illegal club, society or combination' contrary to statute, and for having demanded a subscription under threat of blacking from another journeyman, 'for the use of an unlawful club'. Dr Dobson has noted disputes involving hatters since 1777 in London in 1786, at Dereham, Swaffham and Manchester in 1791 and in Stockport in 1799.[38]

Union activities continued while the Combination Laws were in force (1799-1824); a witness told a select committee that conflicts in 1802, 1810, 1817 and 1820 had all begun with the men usually over the issue of the employing of 'foul' men, i.e. those who had served their time with masters who had taken more than two apprentices at a time 'contrary to the bye laws of the journeymen'. So jealously did the journeymen guard their rights in London that nine out of ten men were 'fair'.[39]

The Stockport hatters, who numbered several thousand and who had drawn up a very comprehensive and detailed set of regulations in 1808 'to be observed by every member of the Associated Feltmakers of Stockport', stood firm for more than three months against their employers in 1809. Hatters at Atherstone were reported to be holding secret meetings in 1817, and in 1818 those of Newcastle-under-Lyme were meeting to arrange a subscription for the support of their striking colleagues in Manchester. The hatters at Ashton-under-Lyne presented in 1819 'a very aggravated case of combination' having turned-out in large numbers, and journeyman hatters were represented at the delegate meeting from the Manchester trades who met in 1818 to form a 'Union of all the Trades' to be known as the *Philanthropic Society*.[40]

Pride of place for early unionism outside London is usually given to the woollen workers, weavers and combers, of the West Country. Historians have tended to write as if the recorded incidents took place within a homogeneous 'west of England' clothing trade, which was characterised above all by the clear separation of large capitalist employers from the weavers. In fact the fullest evidence of early union organisation comes from the small towns which made up the Devonshire serge manufacture, reaching, just, into Cornwall (Callington) and into Somerset around Taunton, and even to Bristol. Here a product quite distinct from the famous woollen broad cloths of Wiltshire, Gloucestershire and parts of Somerset was manufactured. Serge was predominantly a worsted cloth. In one sense the difference between the two regions was immaterial, for in both the separation of capital from labour was evident. Josiah Tucker most probably had the Gloucestershire region in mind when he wrote: 'As the master is placed so high above the condition of the journeyman, both their conditions approach much nearer to that of a planter and slave in our American colonies than might be expected in such a country as England'. The master was tempted to be proud and over-bearing, to consider his people as the scum of the earth, 'whom he has a right to squeeze whenever he can'. The journeymen were equally tempted 'to get as much wages and to do as little for it as they possibly can' and to look upon their master as their common enemy with whom no faith was to be kept. The motives to industry, frugality and sobriety were all subverted by 'this one consideration, viz. that they shall always be chained to the same oar, and never be but journeymen'.[41]

Such a description would have been equally broadly true of the serge districts further west. But there were some differences which may be significant. In the serge districts the weaver was more likely to have been a town dweller, in Exeter, Tiverton, Taunton, Crediton etc.; while in the area of the woollen-cloth manufacture, 'country weavers' predominated living in the villages surrounding the clothing towns. Hence in the former case the town 'clubs' offered an organisational basis for union activities, as at Tiverton where clubs both of weavers and combers were probably in existence by the very early-eighteenth century.[42] Serge being a part-worsted cloth involved a combing process, unlike the pure woollens of the Wiltshire/Gloucestershire/east Somerset region. Since woolcombers were a very early group to unionise and exceptionally thorough and effective in their organisation, weavers in worsted areas were likely to have become influenced by their example. The specific organisation of the combers will be examined below, but it should be noted that the earliest reports from the south-west clearly refer to combinations of both weavers and combers.

Large numbers of weavers in the towns, notably at Taunton, had formed themselves into clubs by the first decade of the century. Employers began to petition Parliament for action against such organisations of workers. By 1706 the Bristol weavers had effected a 'closed shop', and were demanding that no master-weaver was to take an apprentice without the permission of the 'confederacy'. Any apprentice taken was to be enrolled in their books and no journeyman who could not produce a certificate of membership of the Bristol or some other weavers' confederacy was to be offered employment. At Taunton the weavers' club had 'a common seal, tipstaffs and colours' which they openly displayed, while meeting as often as they chose at their clubhouse, an inn. Four or five persons had been appointed 'supervisors'.[43] These weavers' and combers' organisations were causing much concern. In the course of strikes at Tiverton, Bristol and Taunton weavers were said to have intimidated those who refused to join them and even to have rescued their imprisoned leaders from gaol.[44] The society of woolcombers at Tiverton formed in 1700 as a benefit club and for preserving 'due claims, rights and privileges' had been involved in violent disputes in 1706 and in 1720.[45] In 1717 complaints from Devon claimed that weavers and combers had been confederating into clubs 'for some time past'.[46] Conflict built up over the next few years to reach a peak in 1725, when a petition from Tiverton complained that the weavers and combers having formed 'unlawful assemblies' had taken on themselves 'an arbitrary power to ascertain their wages'. Outrages had been committed not only against masters, but also against fellow workers who refused to join. Intimidation included breaking into houses and spoiling wool and cutting cloth from looms. Petitions making similar allegations were received from Exeter and Bristol. From these petitions and from a parliamentary inquiry held as a result, it can be learned that the Taunton weavers had been attempting to raise their wages for 'some years past', and that those at Exeter, among other places, had set up clubs 'where they make byelaws, to among other things, appoint places of meeting, fix officers, make allowances for travelling workmen, and to ascertain their wages'. Witnesses claimed to have seen mobs headed by a 'captain' threatening at Crediton to murder masters who would not raise wages and displaying a piece of cut-off cloth as a symbol of their feelings, and at Callington a master who refused the increase was 'coolstaffed'.[47]

Not noticing that the Proclamation of 1718 and the Act of 1726 which prohibited combinations among woollen workers, seem to have been primarily in response to the troubles in the serge districts, the editors of a well-known documentary collection which reprints both of them, proceed to draw misleading conclusions. The proclamation instances a particular concern with Taunton and the Devonshire towns and refers to the activities of combers as well as of weavers. Although the act of 1726 made no specific district references it once again refers to the clubs of both weavers *and* combers.[48] Despite the clear references to 'clubs' in both documents, Cole and Filson argue that the combinations were ephemeral ones of 'country weavers' which extending over large areas were 'unlike' the local trade clubs of the artisans in being unable to maintain a continuous existence.[49] However true this may have been of the woollen broad cloth districts, it was evidently not so of the serge area further to the south-west. The evidence of 1717 and of 1725/6 clearly reveals an organisation based on town clubs in such places as Exeter, Tiverton, Crediton, Taunton and Bristol. It would seem that in this area of cloth manufacture workers' organisations may have had as much in common with the trade club-based manifestations of unrest which from time to time appear among woollen workers in towns separated from the main producing centres, such as at Alton (1725), Newbury (1760) and Kendal (1760) as with the widespread actions of the rural weavers of western broad cloth areas.[50]

Professor Hoskins has remarked that after the Act of 1726 prohibited combinations no more was heard of trade unionism in Exeter until the 1780s.[51] If this was true of Exeter it was not so of the serge districts as a whole. In Tiverton the clubs of weavers and combers clearly remained a potent force in the intervening period, while at Bristol agitation was continuous between 1728 and 1733 and disputes have been recorded at

Bradninch in 1743 and Taunton in 1764.[52]

Apart from the weavers and combers, the woolsorters in Exeter belonged to a national organisation by 1785, the Woolstaplers Society, and although only 43 of its total 478 members were in the south-west, the Exeter branch had a printed book of orders including one to 'forsake the service of every master' who took an apprentice contrary to their rules. At Exeter the club met regularly and members subscribed 1d a week to support a travelling fund. The union was unsuccessfully involved in a strike in 1787. By 1784 the fullers and other finishers were also clearly organised when they struck over control of apprenticeship.[53]

If the act of 1726 represents, however imperfectly, a finishing point to the most significant period of labour unrest in the serge districts, it rather serves as a starting point for the form of labour agitation which was to become most characteristic of the other district. It is to this area, particularly to Wiltshire and Gloucestershire that the attention of labour historians is best directed after 1726. The act and a follow-up statute in 1727 while they prohibited combinations aimed at raising wages, also restated the Elizabethan principle of periodic wage adjustment by the justices at Quarter Sessions. The struggle between the weavers and their clothier employers centred thereafter on attempts by the weavers to get legal wage rates drawn up and enforced by the justices. The clothiers to a great extent ignored the regulated rates and formed associations to resist their implementation even though the lists of 1728 were restated in 1729 and 1732. This action produced widespread and serious rioting at the end of the twenties. A weavers' petition stating their grievance had been received by the Privy Council, and there was certainly sympathy for their cause, outside the ranks of the clothiers, both locally and nationally. The pattern of petitioning for the enforcement of the wage fixing legislation, accompanied by widespread and heavy rioting was established.[54] When better trade returned after the end of the 1720s the agitation dropped away, presumably because brisk trade increased the competition for labour and was thereby productive of 'natural' wage increases. With the trade depression of 1755/6 the issue came to the fore again. A prolonged and bitter dispute began when the clothiers refused to pay rates fixed by the justices following weavers' representation. The course of events has been described by several writers. The clothiers' non-compliance led to a petition from the weavers to the House of Commons stating this grievance (and several others as well). Catching their employers by surprise the weavers had actually got a statutory re-statement of wage regulation, but the employers counter-petitioned, arguing that the law was not only a bad one, but in the real world of trade an impossible one with which to comply; which fact they were amply proving by their non-compliance with it. Parliament accepted their case and in 1757 ended the principle of wage regulation in the west of England clothing trades more than 50 years before the relevant clauses of 5 Elizabeth were generally repealed.[55]

During the agitation the weavers' riots continued for six or seven weeks, as they strove to prevent anyone from working at the employers' offered rates. Not surprisingly their 'tumultuous manner' of assembly and their committing great 'outrages' were the elements fully played-up by the clothiers. In fact we know rather little of the precise nature of the weavers' organisations. Clearly the preparation of an articulate and forceful petition and its presentation to Parliament is especially impressive coming from scattered country weavers. Equally so is the careful calculation of piece rates presented to the justices. Organisation was clearly effective but there are no descriptions of clubs with their insignia and by-laws such as came from the south-west serge district. As Professor Minchinton has pointed out sporadic demonstrations do not deny the underlying existence of continuing trade clubs. The fact that activity concentrated on attempts to get the law enforced, perhaps denied any advantage in making such denunciations of 'unlawful' clubs as came from the employers of Devonshire. Hence rhetoric concentrated instead on riot, 'violence' or 'outrage' rather than on exposures of illegal organisations. The importance of weavers' clubs with built-up funds, which would be used to finance disputes is implied in an employer's comment of 1739 that the weavers had by their clubs, 'a stock of several hundred pounds capital', which they could have used to prosecute truck-paying masters.[56]

The proclamation of 1718 had depicted the serge-weavers of Devon and the adjacent parts of Somerset as being formed into 'lawless clubs and societies', which had illegally presumed to use a common seal and act as 'bodies corporate' by making and unlawfully conspiring to execute by-laws and orders on the matter of how many apprentices and journeymen should be kept by a master 'together with the prices of all their manufactures, and the manner and materials of which they should be wrought'. Such comprehensive and confident demands were not the product of crisis-desperation. They were contained within the region's most noted period of prosperity, and were put forward at the seasonal trade peaks, especially in the spring when the demand for goods was at its highest and work was plentiful.[57]

In contrast, the main periods of activity in the other district were associated with trade depressions and were *defensive* in object to preserve standards of living against scarce employment and falling wages: the depression of 1726/7, the disturbance to trade at the onset of war in 1739 and the protracted crisis of 1755/6.[58] The first and last of these were associated with agitation for statutory wage regulation to hold levels. The second, that of 1738/9, was reflected in widespread popular disturbances as the trade crisis brought long-smouldering grievances to a head. These included delayed payment of wages, truck, 'abatements', and employers' combined attempts to force down wages. A feature of the disturbances was fierce action against individual clothiers, the best known being the attack on the premises of Mr Coulthurst at Melksham in November 1738 by a large crowd of weavers and shearmen. His goods were ransacked, his instruments of trade destroyed, house demolished, cloth cut, yarn and wool thrown in the river, mills pulled down and several houses belonging to him treated likewise. The rioters 'lived upon free quarter upon the people of Melksham' and 'extorted money from many' before proceeding to Trowbridge for a further demonstration of strength.[59]

Although there had been several previous instances of machine-breaking, for example the destruction of a gig-mill at Warminster in 1767 by shearmen who claimed that with it one man and a boy could do the work in two hours that usually would occupy 30 men for a day, and similar instances at Shepton Mallet in 1776 and Frome in 1781,[60] the next major period of agitation in the industry was the shearmen's campaign against shearing-frames in the 1790s. A period of frame destruction and the sending of threatening letters to clothiers attempting to introduce the machines was followed by a period, as we have seen, when an attempt to defeat the clothiers' intentions was made through a rigid enforcement of apprenticeship regulations which would have denied the employers the unskilled labour to operate the machines. Attacks on gig-mills, frames, and the cutting of cloth became in the 1790s matters of regular report in the west-country press, reaching a peak in 1798 with acts of destruction or the sending of anonymous letters threatening such action recorded from Trowbridge, Bath, Exeter, Bradford-on-Avon, Chippenham and Melksham.[61]

Among the weavers serious agitation also revived in the trade depression of the 1790s, taking the form of the organised campaign over the apprenticeship issue which reached its culmination in 1803-6. The campaign, aimed at limiting the spread of the factory system by preventing the employment of unskilled labour, clearly revealed the strength of the weavers' clubs in their ability to obtain effective legal advice, organise massively supported petitions to Parliament, bring prosecutions against 'unfair workmen' (over 50 were charged[62]) and support their fellows when counteraction was taken against them.

The involvement of combers in the agitation in the south-west serge district has already been noted. Adam Smith acknowledged the special position of strength occupied by these skilled workers at a strategic point in the worsted manufacture:

> Half-a-dozen wool combers, perhaps are necessary to keep a thousand spinners and weavers at work. By combining not to take apprentices they can not only engross the employment, but reduce the whole manufacture into a sort of slavery to themselves, and raise the price of their labour much above what is due to the nature of their work.[63]

Societies are known to have been in existence in the Essex district by 1688, where their rules were ratified in 1709, and by 1700 in Tiverton where they rioted in 1709 for a cause not known and again in 1720 against the importation of ready-combed Irish wool which ended in a long-remembered 'Battle of Oat Hill' against the magistrates and constables of the town.[64] At Leicester the combers had regulations in 1741 that no master should employ anyone not of their club, and several cases brought before the local sessions indicate their persistent attempts to exclude the non-apprenticed.[65] A much quoted description from Yorkshire of the wool-combers' organisation in 1741 claims that 'for a number of years past' the combers had formed themselves into a sort of corporation, 'though without a charter'. The first concern had been with their sick and unemployed and a regularly meeting 'box' club had developed to maintain funds for this purpose. They had become formidable enough to give 'laws to their masters, as also to themselves'. These 'laws' fixed piece rates, and by threat of strike and intimidation prevented the employment of men not of the club. What especially seemed to pose a threat was that their organisation was rapidly taking on a *national* character: 'They are become one society throughout the kingdom . . . if any of their club is out of work they give them a ticket and money to seek for work at the next town where a box club is'. At that town the unemployed comber was subsisted before passing on to the next town and so on until work was found.[66]

This 'tramping system' was known in many trades and was a key organisational feature of early trade unionism. Dunsford described the system among the Tiverton combers where the presentation of 'blanks' (tickets) by tramping members ensured support 'by every wool-combers' society in league and friendship with it throughout England'. The system described to Parliament in 1794 was one in which in its essential forms had been in existence for perhaps a century. The single men were described as leading 'itinerant lives, travelling the kingdom'. The tramping linked societies in 'all the manufacturing parts of the country', so that their strength was such as to allow them to 'counteract all the interests and pursuits of their employers'.[67]

Weavers had a tramping system by 1741, and on a more local basis and in a more rudimentary form by 1707. The curriers had such a system by 1750 and the hatters by the 1770s. Professor Hobsbawm in the best known study of the subject has indicated that among compositors, paper-makers and calico printers the practice was sufficiently well-established by the end of the century to suggest significantly earlier origins. By the early-nineteenth century 'blanks' existed among shoe-makers and Preston carpenters, while Francis Place reported the system among tailors, hatters, smiths, carpenters, boot and shoemakers, metal workers, bakers, plumbers and painters. The Birmingham carpenters formed a society in 1808 to appoint a house for 'the reception of workmen travelling for the purpose of getting employment, and who are commonly called tramps'. Hobsbawm points out that the level of organisation suggests a system that must have been erected on a 'well-built foundation of custom'. Its importance in the development of trade unionism is evident. It became in many of the older craft trades 'the very backbone of union'.[68] The federation of trade clubs into larger organisations could hardly have happened without it. But its importance was more basic than even this: it was the means by which information about rates, conditions and disputes could be spread, and through which union leaders could move away from local victimisation. Assistance for the funds of brother members in dispute in a particular locality could also be forthcoming, both directly in the form of contributions and indirectly by allowing single men to remove themselves from dependence on the local strike fund by resorting to the tramp.

However, the existence of a tramping system does not in itself confirm that a trade had entered a 'national' phase of existence. The system was rather a link between trade clubs from which considerable mutual benefit was secured, and power of resistance to employers increased. Deliberate attempts at organising national unions came later, even among the combers from whom a congress of delegates met in 1812 from 'several different societies in various parts of the kingdom' in Coventry to draw up regulations for 'The United Societies of Woolcombers'.[69]

In the areas of the woollen and worsted manufacture there is evidence of weavers' combinations in both Essex and East Anglia.[70] It is in the

West Riding of Yorkshire that the lack of separation of the small domestic clothiers from their journeymen has been held to have produced an
industrial context inappropriate to the development of a distinct labour
interest. This was broadly true of the main woollen cloth production,
but there were other branches of the manufacture where capitalist
organisation was dominant even in Yorkshire. This was so in the worsted manufacture around Leeds where there were industrial actions by
weavers in 1770 and 1772 which clearly indicate an underlying organisation. It was also the case in carpet weaving where a wage strike lasted
for several weeks in 1787.[71]

The actions of the shearmen in resisting gig-mills and frames in the
West Country has already been noted, and in the West Riding before
they had to face in desperate manner the threat of machinery, a decade
later than in the west, they were a confident and well-organised body
of skilled men. The Leeds manufacturer Gott, in dispute with them in
1802 over an apprenticeship issue, complained of their power while
gloating over their impending redundancy:

> They are the tyrants of the country; their power and influence has
> grown out of their high wages, which enable them to make deposits
> that puts them beyond all fear of inconvenience from misconduct.
> They are however, an order of men not necessary to the manufacturer
> and if the merchants had firmness to do without them their conse-
> quence would be lost, their banks would waste, their combinations
> would fall to the ground, and we should hear no more of meetings
> of any sort or description.[72]

The final struggle of the shearmen, or 'croppers' as they were more
often known in the West Riding, against the shearing frames lies beyond
the chronological limits of this study. As the Yorkshire phase of the
Luddite disturbances of the Regency period it has been much written
about, with very considerable controversy, elsewhere.[73]

Workers' combinations in Lancashire began a little later than in the
woollen and worsted districts, but became well-established by mid-
century. The first union which can be properly dated was that of the
Manchester smallware weavers whose first articles were drawn up in
1747. Within ten years there were similar societies among the check-
weavers and among silk weavers with the object of limiting apprenticeship and of instituting a 'blank', membership card system. The structure
of the smallware weaving trade was town based and characterised by a
clear division between the small master weavers known as 'undertakers'

and their journeymen on the one hand and the large master manufacturers who put-out the work on the other. Organisation based on town
clubs was a natural development.[74] The check-weavers were the rural
workers of the cotton trade and were scattered over the country parishes.
Organising them presented different problems. The necessary devolu-
tion to cope with wide dispersal of workers was provided by having a
central 'box' in Manchester, and local boxes in the parishes. Each local
box club had its own president, clerk and steward elected for three
months only, to prevent the emergence of an elite group. These met
monthly to communicate with and inform the society of anything
necessary to be done, 'regulated or redressed'. A quarterly general
meeting was held in Manchester attended by the local officers. The
rules of the Manchester 'box' applied to all the others, and there were
kept all the membership 'blanks' which were delivered out as required.
Local officials received allowances for lost time in attending meetings
or when on 'trade business'. The society had begun early in 1758 and
was open to all in the weaving trade on January 16 of that year, but
after that membership was to be restricted to those who had served an
indentured apprenticeship or were the children of members. No member
was to take more than two apprentices besides his own children. No
journeyman who was not a member could be employed, but it was in
fact, like the west of England woollen manufacture, a trade in which
the characteristic worker was the taker-in of put-out work, and so there
were very few journeymen.[75]

The employers refused to countenance the existence of a 'box' club
with its strike fund potential. In the Spring of 1758 they attempted to
break the union, but their attempt led to a great strike of the check-
weavers which extended around Manchester from Ashton and Oldham
to Eccles involving thousands of weavers.[76] The demands were for a
wage increase, an exact specification of the size of the piece of cloth
upon which rates were calculated and an end to the employment of
'unfair' men. The strike lasted for four months before the employers
offered a degree of conciliation, but still steadfastly refused to recognise
the 'box' club.[77] Although the weavers later announced that their combination had been dissolved, the aftermath was the appearance of 18
leaders before the Lancashire assizes in 1759, who were fined after
hearing a much-quoted lecture on the evils of combinations from the
presiding judge, and after apologising for their actions. For the next 20
years during the continued expansion of the cotton industry, despite
some direct action against the use of spinning jennies in 1768/9, full
employment brought about a decline in labour unrest. With the severe

trade recession of 1779-81 more vigorous activity revived. Several Lancashire societies united in 1779 to present an address to the government requesting the regulation of wages and, amidst an atmosphere of riots and machine-breaking in protest against the growth of factories, came the first proposal for an all Lancashire Federation of Weavers' Societies. A new Combination Act reflected the increase of unionism among northern textile workers, and in 1781 the Oldham weavers issued a manifesto demanding regulation of the trade, and the small-ware weavers blacklisted employers in a lengthy strike over prices. Quiescence returned with the recovery of trade as in the 1790s the historical peak of handloom weavers wages was reached: the 'golden age' before the long decline brought about by machine weaving in the factories began.[78]

The trades selected for detailed examination in this chapter form a basis for the understanding of the nature and variety of labour organisation in eighteenth-century England. These trades are the best documented. In itself this may reflect a degree of unrepresentativeness in the impact they made and the resulting notice they attracted. Nevertheless by the last decades of the century, and especially in the 1790s, comparable levels of organisation are well-documented for many other trades. Place advised the carpenters and plumbers as well as organising the tailors. Shoemakers were organising effectively in London and in the provinces. Printers, both pressmen and compositors, had adapted their long-established 'chapels' into effective trade unions, with the latter group organising the different London works into combined action from their house of call, the *Hole-in-the-Wall* in Fleet Street. Papermakers and bookbinders were well organised. Calico printers had taken a pre-formed London union with them to Lancashire, and silk weavers had shown their combined capabilities in both Spitalfields and Coventry. In Sheffield combinations of workers in the various branches of the cutlery and file trades had brought contesting masters' associations into being. Shipwrights and other dockyard workers had habits of combined action going well back into the century. Most branches of the building trades had shown collective capabilities to affect their conditions, while coal-miners were organising in most of the coalfields, as they had long done in the north-east.[79]

Notes

1. Adam Smith, *The Wealth of Nations* (1776, edited by E. Cannan 1904, paperback edn, London, 1961), Vol. I, pp. 74-5.

2. Charles Hall, *The Effects of Civilisation on the People in European States* (1805, reprinted New York, 1965), p. 112 (footnote).

3. C.R. Dobson, *Masters and Journeymen. A Pre-history of Industrial Relations 1717-1800* (London, 1980), pp. 22, 26.

4. Ibid., pp. 22-6 and Appendix pp. 154-70.

5. Petition of the Master Tailors, 1721 reprinted in A.E. Bland, P.A. Brown and R.H. Tawney (eds.), *English Economic History Select Documents* (London, 1914), p. 622.

6. S. and B. Webb, *The History of Trade Unionism* (London, 1911 edn), pp. 1-2.

7. Mary Rhys Baker, 'Anglo-Massachusetts Trade Union Roots, 1130-1970', *Labor History*, vol. 14, no. 3 (1973), pp. 381-2.

8. H.A. Turner, *Trade Union Growth, Structure and Policy. A Comparative Study of the Cotton Weavers* (London, 1962), p. 45.

9. Ibid., pp. 77-8.

10. Ibid., pp. 87-9.

11. Ibid., pp. 79, 85.

12. This is the argument of his paper, 'English Trade Unionism and Other Labour Movements before 1790', *Bulletin of the Society for the Study of Labour History*, no. 17 (1968), pp. 19-24.

13. Webb & Webb, *Trade Unionism*, p. 2.

14. Ibid., p. 6.

15. F.W. Galton, *Select Documents Illustrating the History of Trade Unionism: The Tailoring Trade* (London, 1896), pp. 88-95.

16. Dobson, *Masters and Journeymen*, p. 39; Galton, *Tailoring Trade*, pp. 5-6.

17. Galton, *Tailoring Trade*, pp. 16, 7.

18. 8 George III Cap. 17.

19. Smith, *Wealth of Nations*, Vol. I, pp. 158-9.

20. Galton, *Tailoring Trade*, pp. 47-9.

21. Ibid., pp. 30, 59; Dobson, *Masters and Journeymen*, p. 69.

22. Galton, *Tailoring Trade*, pp. 7, 13, 30, 49.

23. *Calendar of Home Office Papers of the Reign of George III*, 15 May 1768, nos. 883-4.

24. Dobson, *Masters and Journeymen*, pp. 39-40, 60, 69.

25. *C.H.O.P. George III, 1760-5*, 27 July 1764, p. 429.

26. Galton, *Tailoring Trade*, p. 38.

27. R. Campbell, *The London Tradesman* (1747, reprinted Newton Abbot, 1969), pp. 192-3.

28. Dobson, *Masters and Journeymen*, p. 71.

29. Ibid., pp. 71-3.

30. *C.H.O.P. George III*, 15 May 1768, nos. 883-4; *Commons Journals*, XXXVI, 3 February 1778, p. 169.

31. *Second Report of the Select Committee on Artisans and Machinery*, P.P. 1824 (51), V, p. 45.

32. Galton, *Tailoring Trade*, pp. 71-3.

33. Ibid., pp. 23, 81; A.P. Wadsworth and J. de L. Mann, *The Cotton Trade and Industrial Lancashire 1600-1780* (Manchester, 1931), p. 361.

34. George Unwin, 'A Seventeenth-century Trade Union', *Economic Journal* (1900), X, pp. 394-403.

35. *Commons Journals*, XXXVI, pp. 118-19 Petition and pp. 192-3 Report of

the Committee on the Petition of the Hat Makers, 18 February 1777.

36. Wadsworth & Mann, *Cotton Trade*, pp. 381-2.

37. The House of Lords in fact modified the bill when it reached the house. *Commons Journals*, XXXVI, 28 April 1777, p. 447.

38. Wadsworth & Mann, *Cotton Trade*, p. 382; G.A. Chinnery (ed.), *Records of the Borough of Leicester Vol. VII* (Leicester, 1974), p. 151; Dobson, *Masters and Journeymen*, Appendix pp. 154-70.

39. *Second Report of SC on Artisans and Machinery*, P.P. 1824, V, pp. 80-1.

40. A. Aspinall (ed.), *The Early English Trade Unions. Documents from the Home Office Papers in the Public Record Office* (London, 1949), doc. nos. 212, 256, 327, 260.

41. *Instructions to Travellers* (1751), quoted in E. Lipson, *The Economic History of England, Vol. III, The Age of Mercantilism*, revised edn (Newton Abbot, 1943), p. 55.

42. M. Dunsford, *Historical Memoirs of Tiverton* (Exeter, 1790), p. 205.

43. *Commons Journals*, XV, 26 February 1707, p. 312.

44. Ibid., p. 313.

45. Dunsford, *Tiverton*, pp. 205-6, 208.

46. *Commons Journals*, XVIII, p. 715.

47. *Commons Journals*, XX, 3 March 1725, pp. 598-9, 602.

48. G.D.H. Cole and A.W. Filson (eds.), *British Working Class Movements. Selected Documents 1789-1875* (paperback edn, London, 1965), pp. 86-8.

49. Ibid., pp. 82-3.

50. Incidents from Dobson, *Masters and Journeymen*, Appendix pp. 154-70.

51. W.G. Hoskins, *Industry, Trade and People in Exeter 1688-1800* (Exeter, 1935, 2nd edn, 1968), p. 59.

52. Dobson, *Masters and Journeymen*, Appendix pp. 154-70; *Exeter Mercury*, 11 May 1764.

53. Hoskins, *Exeter*, pp. 60-1.

54. See the account in W.E. Minchinton, 'The Beginnings of Trade Unionism in the Gloucestershire Woollen Industry', *Transactions of Bristol and Gloucestershire Archaeological Society*, vol. 70 (1951), pp. 126-41 and the same writer's 'The Petitions of the Weavers and Clothiers of Gloucestershire in 1756', ibid., vol. 73 (1954), pp. 218-25.

55. Minchinton, 'Petitions', p. 225.

56. The case between the weavers and the clothiers (1739) reported by J. Smith, *Memoirs of Wool, II* (1747, reprinted Farnborough, 1968), p. 310.

57. Cole & Filson, *Working Class Movements*, p. 86; *Commons Journals*, XX, 31 March 1726, p. 648.

58. Minchinton, 'Trade Unionism', p. 130.

59. Diary of George Wansey of Warminster in J. de L. Mann (ed.), *Documents Illustrating the Wiltshire Textile Trade in the Eighteenth Century* (Devizes, 1964), doc. 172.

60. *Exeter Mercury*, 14 August 1767; *Sherborne Mercury*, 30 July 1781; Dobson, *Masters and Journeymen*, Appendix pp. 154-70.

61. *Sherborne Mercury*, 22 January 1798; 30 April 1798; 5 February 1798.

62. Minchinton, 'Trade Unionism', p. 135.

63. Smith, *Wealth of Nations, Vol. I*, p. 141.

64. Wadsworth & Mann, *Cotton Trade*, p. 341; A.F.J. Brown (ed.), *Essex at Work 1700-1815* (Chelmsford, 1969), p. 25; Dunsford, *Tiverton*, pp. 206, 208-9.

65. Rhys Baker, 'Trade Union Roots', p. 365 (footnote); Chinnery, *Records of Leicester*, pp. 31, 36, 49, 52, 90.

66. Webb & Webb, *Trade Unionism*, p. 31.

67. Dunsford, *Tiverton*, p. 205; *Commons Journals*, XLIX, 31 March 1794,

p. 395; 2 May 1794, p. 546.

68. E.J. Hobsbawm, 'The Tramping Artisan' in his *Labouring Men* (London, 1964), pp. 35, 28, 39-40.

69. Aspinall, *Early Trade Unions*, doc. 126, pp. 127-35 where the rules are printed.

70. See the list appended to Dobson, *Masters and Journeymen*, pp. 154-70.

71. H. Heaton, *The Yorkshire Woollen and Worsted Industries* (Oxford, 1920), pp. 317-19.

72. Aspinall, *Early Trade Unions*, doc. 65, p. 64.

73. For a discussion of the debate on Luddism see my introduction to the 1979 reprint of J.L. and B. Hammond, *The Skilled Labourer* (London, 1979).

74. Wadsworth & Mann, *Cotton Trade*, pp. 343-4.

75. Ibid., pp. 346-7.

76. Ibid., p. 362.

77. Turner, *Trade Union Growth*, p. 57.

78. Ibid., pp. 60-1.

79. For trade unionism in these industries see: J. Child, *Industrial Relations in the British Printing Industry — The Quest for Security* (London, 1967); G.I.H. Lloyd, *The Cutlery Trades* (London, 1913); E. Welbourne, *The Miners Unions of Northumberland and Durham* (Cambridge, 1923) as well as the Webbs' general history.

7 THE METHODS AND EFFECTIVENESS OF INDUSTRIAL ACTION

In commenting on the ineffectiveness of collective labour actions, Adam Smith was concerned only with their lack of success in raising or defending wage levels. In the passage of the *Wealth of Nations* in question he was not discussing issues such as the control of entry into a trade. His belief that the balance of strength lay with the employers cannot really be disputed, but a close examination of his reasoning suggests that workers' unions were not always as ineffective in wage contests as he supposed.

One of his reasons was the discrimination of the law against the men: 'We have no acts of Parliament against combining to lower the price of work; but many against combining to raise it'.[1] Certainly he was right to stress the effective immunity from prosecution of masters' combinations to disadvantage their employees, and to consider them a normal feature in manufacturing industry. Whoever thought that masters rarely combined was 'as ignorant of the world as of the subject'. They were always in a 'tacit but constant and uniform' combination not to allow wages to rise. More importantly in the context of industrial relations, they sometimes entered into 'particular combinations' to effect wage reductions. These were always conducted with 'the utmost silence and secrecy' until the moment of their execution. If the workmen did not resist, they were never publicly known at all, but frequently they became so when they were resisted by a 'contrary defensive combination of the workmen'.[2]

Such a combination of employers to lower wages lay behind the widespread disturbances in the west-country clothing districts in 1738/9, and significantly the weavers of Taunton complained in 1764 not of masters having lowered their wages, but of their being about to do so.[3] The historian has to accept Smith's assertion at face value because of the secret nature of such associations of employers, but there are times and contexts in which employers' combinations can be more evidently seen at work. Smith argued that when trade was brisk, profits high and markets expanding, the 'natural' combination of employers would break as they competed for scarce labour.[4] However employers were just as aware of this possibility and at times conscious enough of a common

172

interest to limit its impact. This could be done, for example, by an undertaking not to employ workers who were unable to produce certificates of discharge from previous employers, or by making employment conditional on the signing of agreements to accept proffered wages. The west-country clothiers in 1756 were trying to get weavers to sign such agreements to work below the 'legal' rates fixed by the justices in sessions.[5] The northern coal owners used discharge certificates in an attempt to prevent pitmen from forcing up their premium payments at the time of the annual bond renewal.[6]

When a strike actually broke out, or was regarded as imminent, or when a trade union was regarded as becoming too powerful, masters could combine purposely to alleviate the threat. The attempts of the employers in the London tailoring trades to break the journeymen's organisation have been described in the previous chapter. Combinations of employers directly to resist unions became increasingly frequent towards the end of the century, when, sure of the support and approval of the government, they contrasted with the secret and natural combinations of Adam Smith by being open and explicit about their existence and purpose. It has already been seen that the Worsted Committee formed to prosecute the embezzlers of materials turned its attention in the nineties to prosecuting trade unions. In the Sheffield cutlery trade an organisation calling itself the 'Sheffield Mercantile and Manufacturing Union' urged resistance to 'extensive combinations' of workmen to raise wages which had made: 'a progress so alarming as to threaten the most dangerous consequences to the trade' by seeking advances 'immoderate beyond all precedent' and by using violent and illegal means to secure them. They wanted a lock-out to break the workers' unions, and resolved that no member employer would agree to pay wages higher than those of the previous year nor employ any cutler without a certificate of discharge from his previous employer. The costs of prosecuting strikers would be collectively borne, and loans made to small employers if their resistance to their workers put them at financial risk. Pressure was to be put on parish overseers not to give relief to strikers, and a campaign was begun for the abolition of the trade's by-laws restricting the numbers of apprentices.[7] This employers' union was perhaps a more formal development of earlier attempts by masters in the individual branches of the cutlery trade. In 1796 a strike of spring-knife and table-knife makers had led to a meeting where 91 out of 96 firms resolved to resist wage demands and pledged not to employ each others' workmen without discharge certificates. Within months this had extended into a general combination of the employers manufacturing knives, sickles, shears, scissors, razors and scythes. Even before then, in 1790, 34 masters in the scissors-grinding branch had met to arrange collective finance for the prosecution of strikers.[8]

In the paper manufacture well-established unionism among the journeymen had produced a counter-organisation of employers by the end of the century. The journeymen had developed the tactic of striking against selected masters instead of calling a general turn-out. This had encouraged their employers to view a lock-out as the only effective way of combating this strategy. In 1796 the Buckingham-shire employers met at High Wycombe and resolved to give all their employees a fortnight's notice and close down their mills until those closed by the men's selective strike action had been re-opened. In 1801 the Kent and Surrey manufacturers formed themselves into the 'Society of Master Papermakers of the Counties of Kent and Surrey, associated for the purpose of resisting the illegal combinations amongst the journey-men paper-makers'. They aimed at extending the lock-out as a means of resistance and at refusing employment to those who belonged to the journeymen's union.[9]

Enough has been said to support Adam Smith's view that the ease and frequency of combinations by employers was an inhibiting factor on effective trade unionism. According to Francis Place the master type-founders had such a close organisation that by the use of character notes and dismissal of the recalcitrant they managed to keep labour unions out of their industry for many years, and in 1818 defeated the one strike they could not prevent.[10] Printing employers resisted the demands of their pressmen by suspending business after first securing the goodwill and support of their customers, the booksellers.[11] Perhaps Adam Smith had also in mind the way in which throughout the century, employers had combined effectively to secure from Parliament so many specific statutory prohibitions on workers' combinations and the repeal of such a substantial amount of labour-regulating restrictions on their own free-dom of action.

If there was no effective legal limitation on employers combining against the interests of their work people, there were a good many limit-ing the rights of employees to combine. At the time of the passing of the general Combination Acts in 1799 and 1800 there were already more than 40 acts prohibiting combinations of workmen to raise wages.[12] Instances have already been given of such acts applying to specifically the west-country clothing workers (1726), the London tailoring trade (1721), the hat manufacture (1777) and the paper manufacture (1794). These examples of legislation following the petitioning of employers are only the best known of a large number of such acts. What they offered was speedy and sometimes summary punishment from a clear proclamation of illegality. However the use of such adjectives as 'unlawful' or 'illegal' to precede 'club' or 'combination' did not await the passing of a general statute, nor was it confined to trades covered by such acts. The common law view of conspiracy and the rich reserves of the statute book offered ample support for those seeking a legal basis for moving against a trade union or less permanently organised group of striking workers. The proclamation issued against the combinations of weavers and combers in the West Country in 1718 referred not only to existing laws against riot, but also to an act of 1548, 'A Bill of Conspiracies of Victuallers and Craftsmen' against workers agreeing to withhold their labour until wages were advanced or hours decreased. Even this law of 1548 did not regard itself as making illegal actions which had previously not been so, for its preamble refers to the workers' actions as being 'contrary to the laws and statutes of this realm'.[13] This particular act was not much used, although the Liverpool magistrates reminded journeymen tailors of its existence during a dispute in 1765.[14] Prosecutions for leaving work unfinished (which could be brought under various acts including 5 Elizabeth) and prosecutions for conspiracy were more commonly used. The advantage of prosecuting for conspiracy at Common Law was that the 'justice' of the claims of the striking workmen was not a relevant issue. The fact of a combination which would have the effect of injuring another party, i.e. the employer was in itself sufficient. A specific act of 1721 applied only to tailors in London, but in that same year an appeal against conviction on behalf of some striking journeymen tailors at Cambridge was heard in the King's Bench. For the men it had been argued that they had been charged with a conspiracy not to work for less than so much per day which could not be an offence since 5 Elizabeth did not mention daily but only annual wages. The court rejected the appeal by ruling that the plea was irrelevant: 'It is not for refusing to work, but for conspiracy that they are indicted, and a conspiracy of any kind is illegal'. It was immaterial that their demands were not excessive: 'it is for a conspiracy which is an offence at common law'.[15] Cases through the century restated the principle. In 1783 seven Liverpool tailors were convicted of conspiring to impoverish one Henry Booth for preventing him by their strike action from carrying on his trade.[16] At the trial of journeymen printers in 1798 the Recorder's summing-up conveniently emphasises the point about actions for conspiracy. He held that for men to meet privately to do injury to another had 'at all times been considered by the law of this country, as a very heinous crime', and in his view this was proper for not only the 'peace of society', but the 'commerce of the country' was threatened. Very severe penalties were accordingly merited. Even if the combination had been intended to carry out 'a good and useful act', the mode taken to achieve that end was a conspiracy, and a strike could hardly be other construed than an attempt to injure the interests of another: 'upon this indictment supposing any one of them to have acted in concert with the other, the crime is made out against them'.[17] The extent to which conspiracy prosecutions were brought against striking workmen cannot be known since many are lost among local sessions records. Some cases brought before the London courts are well-known, for example, the successful one brought against seven wheelwrights in 1792, which has the interesting sidelight in that the employers had in this dispute also to censure the 'Father of the Company' who would appear to have been willing to pay the journeymen the wages they sought. The charge against the men was in the usual form that they: 'unlawfully and fraudulently did conspire, combine and confederate and agree together unlawfully and unjustly and oppressively to increase and augment the wages of themselves and other Journeymen'.[18] In Leicester successful cases were brought against the hatters in 1777 and the cordwainers in 1794.[19] Dr Dobson has compiled a list of 29 cases between 1720 and 1800, but the total population of such cases must remain unknown.[20]

The weapon of conspiracy proceedings was a powerful but a slow and costly one. Delay limited its effectiveness. The master-millwrights when they petitioned Parliament in 1799 for a combination act for their trade — incidentally starting the debate and process which led up to the passing of the general Combination Acts later in the year — were seeking a more speedy remedy. Indictment for conspiracy *after* the strike action left an interval during which offenders frequently removed themselves from the district, knowing that the time and cost of discovering them was as likely as not to lead to the dropping of the case.[21] Nevertheless even after the acts of 1799 and 1800 brought more speedy remedy to employers in general, there were still odd occasions when conspiracy proceedings seem to have been employed. The cotton spinners were so proceeded against in 1818 and the London fellmongers in 1813 conducted their activities so carefully and secretly that no evidence sufficient for prosecution under the Combination Acts could be obtained, and they were eventually prosecuted for leaving work unfinished.[22]

With such powers residing in the law, why was not collective labour action in the eighteenth century even more effectively inhibited? Part of the explanation certainly lies in the reluctance of employers to embark on slow and costly legal processes which could often not begin until the dispute in question was already over. Employers too often preferred to end a dispute on as good terms as possible with their workers rather than prolong a sullen and resentful aftermath. To this end the threat of prosecution was not infrequently remitted if public apology were offered, and promises of future 'good behaviour' secured. The bargemen on the River Tone were so let off in 1800 when 17 of them signed a public apology inserted in the *Sherborne Mercury*. In such cases the employers not only saved trouble and expense but were able to appear tolerant and merciful.[23]

Employers sometimes recognised that the leaders of well-organised combinations were likely to be men of such qualities as brought them respect from their fellows, and that to appear to victimise them by pro- secution could be counter-productive. A printing employer regretted in 1824 that leaders of a strike 'a great many years ago', had been im- prisoned for it had created a great deal of misunderstanding on the part of the rest of the journeymen for the imprisoned men had become 'some of the most respectable of the workmen'. Ill-blood had been created by the employers' action which had long persisted.[24] The United Friendly Society of Journeymen Bookbinders had an annual celebration of their 'martyrs' who had been imprisoned following a dispute in 1786.[25] Legal action against the striking Northumberland pitmen in 1765 was con- sidered pointless, not only because the imprisonment of a few out of 4,000 on strike could hardly have much effect, but also because it would be ill-advised to make 'martyrs for the good cause'.[26] Even if conviction of a striker were secured, public, press or even magisterial approval was not at all times with the employer.[27] In times when brisk trade was in the offing, the wish of the employers to resume profitable production as soon as possible could produce agreement to the workers' demands or compromise as being in the employer's best economic interest. Such occasions would be unlikely to leave documentation for the historian except when compromise was reached, as it sometimes was, through the mediation of a third party, perhaps a justice or local Member of Parlia- ment.[28]

The law was in any event only directly applicable to cases where combinations to raise wages or shorten hours were in question. Organ- isation for the purpose of petitioning Parliament for redress or to secure regulation of wages or apprenticeship were only illegal to the extent that they advocated strike action, or employed intimidating or riotous methods.[29] Masters were not always insensitive to the pressures of rising food prices and often compromised on wage demands based on cost of living grounds. This was especially evident during the highly inflationary years of the French Wars, 1793-1815, but in some such cases employers expected their journeymen to take a cut in wages when food prices came down again.[30]

The greater financial resources of the employers, Adam Smith considered, gave them the simple but often conclusive advantage of being able to hold out until exhausted and hungry workers were obliged to slide back to work: 'many workmen could not subsist a week, few could subsist a month and scarce any a year without employment'.[31] This was all too often true of *defensive* strikes against wage reductions since they tended to occur when market conditions were such that masters had no strong concern to maintain output of goods already in over-supply. But this disadvantage did not operate to the same effect on all occasions and in all circumstances. To argue that the employer could hold out for longer than striking workmen is not to insist that it was always in his interest to do so. High profits were available in times of expanding markets, and a premium was put on increased output even at a higher unit labour cost. Adam Smith thought that it was at such times that the 'natural' combination of employers broke down, and competition for scarce workers produced higher wages without any need for collective action on the part of the workmen.[32] Certainly this did often happen. Private letters from the west of England clothing districts illustrate this. A clothier wrote in 1761 that his work folk had taken advantage of a brisk trade to impose as much as they could on their masters and in the following year another wrote: 'I believe the masters will advance their prices soon, occasioned by the demand and scarcity of workmen'.[33] This may explain the relative quiescence of weavers during the intervals between their well-known peaks of agitation. But much evidence suggests that workmen did not always sit back and wait for 'natural' wage advances to manifest themselves. Market forces do not readily and promptly draw increased pay from reluctant employers whatever their eventual effect. In fact groups of workmen precipitated wage advances by chosing appropriate times to strike. This might involve little more than an appreciation of seasonal peaks of activity. Serge weavers at the beginning of the century knew enough to strike in the spring: 'When there is the greatest demand for goods and most plenty of work'.[34] The fellmongers chose Michaelmas for their strikes. That was the time of the pre-winter slaughter of sheep and was 'the worst time in the year for the master that the men should enter into such a combination'. The masters were vulnerable because of the large quantities of perishable hides they had rapidly to process, and the journeymen fellmongers succeeded in raising their wages by Michaelmas strikes in 1794 and in 1804, and almost did so in 1802.[35] Even the harvest could be used effectively as it was by weavers at Newbury in 1724 and at Norwich in 1752 who on refusal of increases simply stopped work and went into the fields where the harvest just beginning assured them of several weeks' support, until their employers offered an agreement.[36] Exeter wool-sorters seeking higher wages in 1787 chose a moment when their employers had exceptionally large wool stocks on their hands.[37] Suitable occasions might present themselves in many trades. Hansards suffered a strike in 1805 when, taking advantage of a backlog in parliamentary printing orders because of an unusually large number of bills pending, 24 pressmen left work without warning. Hansard was not, however, a master to give in. He sought and found unemployed men and supplied the necessary expertise by working at the press himself alongside his sons. When his compositors tried to restrict him in the number of apprentices he could take in 1807, he straightaway sacked them.[38] London coopers took advantage of the 'amazing business that was doing' while vessels were being provisioned for the War of 1812 to strike successfully. Wars always strengthened the bargaining power of the naval shipyard workers. There was a wave of strikes in 1739 during the Anglo-Spanish war, most of which were peacefully conducted and rapidly successful. At the outbreak of the American war a strike by Portsmouth shipwrights against the introduction of a new piecework scheme lasted for three months before being settled in compromise, while at the same yard shipwrights in 1801 chose the critical moment when the fleet was being prepared for the expedition to Denmark for a strike.[39] The demand for black ribbon following the death of Princess Charlotte in 1817 was used by Coventry weavers to force their employers to keep to an earlier arbitration agreement from which they had been straying.[40] One wonders how many church-going tailors or silk-weavers prayed with all their hearts for the health of the royal family.

Francis Place pointed out that, cases of desperation and defence excepted, organised workmen were not likely to embark upon ill-considered strike action. Journeymen dreaded a strike as did their wives who needed convincing and only in exceptional circumstances gave their encouragement to their menfolk. Above all to strike before a supportive fund had been built up was to invite defeat.[41] Adam Smith did not at all consider the strike-sustaining power of a previously built-up fund. If the timing was right and the fund sufficient then success was far from unobtainable. The Webbs saw eighteenth-century trade unionism as

springing not from any particular institution, but from 'every opportunity for the meeting together of wage earners of the same trade'.[42]
The importance of the houses of call, the tramping system, the formal-
isation of workshop practices and the extension of the functions of sick
and burial 'box' clubs to trade protection has already been indicated.
'Box' clubs of one form or another enabled the idea of contributions
for collective purposes to develop, and experience in financial administration to be gained. Dr Dobson suggests that early trade clubs should
not be regarded as disguised friendly societies, but as perfectly open
'box' clubs for trade-related purposes.[43] This is to an extent true. Concentration on the years when the general Combination Acts were in
force has produced in historians a tendency to over-stress the need for
a friendly society cover at all times and for all collective purposes. The
employers during the great cotton-weavers' strike of 1758 were adamant
despite the weavers' protestations that they subscribed only for benefit
purposes, that the 'boxes' must be put down as they would be the ruin-
ation of the trade. So long as they feared the building up of a strike
fund they refused recognition of the weavers' society. But although the
weavers denied that it was a strike fund, actual or intended, they had
not thought it necessary to conceal that one of its purposes was to op-
pose 'the unlawful practices of the masters'.[44] While the Combination
Acts of 1799 and 1800 were in force, the weavers of the West Country
did not think it necessary to hide the subscription to a fund in support
of 'an association to subscribe our mites to bring this before the honourable House of Commons'. A Huddersfield cloth worker could similarly
see no need to hide the fact that besides belonging to a sick club, he
belonged to another for 'bringing up the matter'. The matter was the
enforcement of the laws on apprenticeship.[45]

But in those years when the purpose was to support a strike, then
cover was needed. Place became a member of the Leather Breeches
Makers Benefit Society which although it actually was a benefit society
was also intending to support a strike. In the spring of 1793 with £250
accumulated, 'which was deemed sufficient', they struck. They had
chosen a time when the rate of hands leaving the trade to join the expanding stuff breeches trade had left their employers temporarily short
of labour at a time when trade was picking up: 'the leaders therefore
calculated, as they thought securely on obtaining it'.[46] The shoemakers
expressed their conviction in 1792 that: 'nothing short of a general fund
can lay the foundation of a lasting union among journeymen of any
trade'. The journeymen bookbinders took four years to build up a fund
to support a strike for a shorter week, while the master printers drew

attention in 1805 to the extent to which despite the Combination Laws, 'under the cover of friendly or benefit societies, journeymen printers, as well as various bodies of mechanics, and other workmen, separately associate in their respective callings, not so much for granting assistance to each other in case of sickness, as for the obvious purpose of compelling their employers to raise their wages'.[47]

There were ways in which funds could be stretched to support lengthy strikes. When Place found himself involved in the breeches-makers' strike of 1793, he quickly began to organise things. He found that strike pay of 7s a week was intended, at which rate the fund would last only three weeks. He proposed that all those willing to do so should take just one week's strike pay and a certificate and go from London on the tramp for a month. He further suggested that the fund could last even longer if ready-made breeches were made up and as many as were willing would take two pairs a week at 4s a pair i.e. 1s a week more than the proposed strike pay, and if these were sold at a loss of only 2s 6d the fund would last twice as long. He was elected to the strike committee, a shop was rented of which he was appointed manager at 12s a week, while those who worked to make the ready-made breeches got 9s. By such methods the strike managed to last for three months before the men were forced to return on the employers' terms. But it was not all for nothing. The masters fearful of another prolonged stoppage gave in to fresh wage demands presented to them under threat of strike the following spring.[48] In the period intervening Place had been refused employment by the masters and instead had worked full-time for the union reorganising the funding of their benefit society. He also formed societies for the carpenters and the plumbers and later claimed that all societies which he organised were successful in wage objectives.[49]

In trades with an effective tramping system it could be used to remove the single men from the fund. When the shoemakers turned out in 1804 in several towns it was without any real fund to back them, and it was reported from Bath, one of the towns involved that those men who were able to leave town were preparing to do so as soon as possible.[50] But by the 1820s they had learned the need both for proper funding and for national organisation, and had links running as far south as Exeter and as far north as Perth. Local clubs 'by general vote of the trade' decided whether or not to support colleagues in disputes in other towns.[51] The well-organised hatters began a strike in the early-nineteenth century with strike pay as much as £1 a week although it later dropped to 15s. Despite not having made special efforts in advance to build up their fund they managed to support a 15-week strike with the aid of contributions from clubs in other parts of the country.[52]

The most important tactical development was the use of the 'rolling' strike. By the end of the eighteenth century it is known to have been employed by calico printers, compositors, papermakers and bookbinders. The journeymen calico printers had taken a ready formed union with them when a group of them moved with their firm from London to Lancashire in 1783. Superior workmen, highly conscious of a scarce skill, they were said to have more 'the appearance of gentlemen' than workmen. But their security and confidence were threatened in the 1790s by employers' attempts to introduce machinery worked by apprentice labour. A strike in 1785/6 at one firm, the Mosney Turn-out, lasted with contributions from the trade in general for three months before the firm went bankrupt. In 1788 advantage was taken of a period of brisk trade to build up a sick fund which was really intended for strike support. Fund collecting went on as trade continued to go well in 1789. Demand for labour was so high at this period that employers were paying premiums to attract workmen. Realising that this practice was escalating labour costs to their ultimate disadvantage, the masters combined to limit the gain the journeymen could make from their scarcity by implementing a discharge certificate scheme and agreeing not to employ each other's men. The journeymen responded with a general strike which lasted for six weeks before the employment of 'new men' caused some to return on the masters' terms. Those who did so were dubbed 'knobsticks' by the 'flints', the name taken by the hard-liners who stayed out. The employers' refusal to discharge their 'new men' meant that many of the 'old' journeymen stayed out for four months before their funds, out of which they were reported to have paid nearly £5,000, were exhausted. The employers had taken on more than 200 so-called apprentices to replace them. On the surface the trade went on peacefully for the next few years, but underneath the men were rebuilding their resources for their desperate and ultimately fore-doomed resistance to machinery and cheap apprentice labour. It was during a brief period of resurgent confidence in the 1790s that they first put into practice the lesson painfully learned in their long general turn-outs, and adopted the strategy of striking one shop at a time with those remaining in work supporting those who were out. By this means they managed a four-month strike at one firm.[53]

The journeymen papermakers, a southern labour force working for the most part at mills in Berkshire, Hampshire, Kent, Buckinghamshire, Hertfordshire and Surrey, were well-organised by the 1790s. Backed by a well-established fund they were putting forward substantial wage demands. Their practice was to demand an increase at one mill at a time, and in the event of its being refused strike its labour force supporting them at full rates from the general fund.[54] It seems probable that the London compositors had also learned this tactic before the end of the century and had found it especially useful in disputes with newspapers:

> When workmen find it necessary to strike for an advance of wages that they should not do it *en masse* all the workmen striking at the one time, but that they should attack their employers in detail, selecting a few of the masters for which they will not work reduce them to submission, and then attack the remainder . . . The men who continue, at their work would be able to support those who had 'turned out'.[55]

Funds might be extended by appeals to the local population. In some circumstances 'extracted' would have been regarded as a more appropriate description. The weavers of Taunton in 1725 were supposed to have gone 'in great bodies about the country, extorting money from divers persons', while those of Melksham in 1738 remained in that town after demolishing a clothier's premises to 'live upon free quarter upon the town, and extort money'.[56] But contributions were not necessarily extracted by intimidation; the framework knitters of Leicester were thankful in 1819 for good support from the gentry, the public and the parish officers.[57] Support from other trades on any significant scale would presume a more prevalent consciousness, wider than the trade itself, than in fact existed. But contributions from other trade societies were sometimes made, if often at a level which was more token than crucial. The Manchester smallware weavers in 1781 thanked the silk weavers for their assistance in a long dispute.[58]

The chain effects of one group's strike upon another's employment so evident in a modern economy were obviously weaker in the less interdependent economy of the eighteenth century. Nevertheless inter-union conflict could arise. The woolcombers of Tiverton on strike in 1749 against the clothiers' importation of ready-combed wool from Ireland, aroused the hostility of the town's weavers waiting for combed wool on which to work, and quite ready to accept the Irish. A full-scale battle was fought between the two groups needing the reading of the Riot Act and the intervention of the military before order was restored. One weaver who sympathised with the combers and refused to weave the Irish wool was 'cool staffed' by his fellows and dragged through a river.[59] The compositors of London were less certain of what to do when the pressmen were bringing the printing trade to a halt in 1805, after agreement with themselves had already been reached:

> We lament the hostility which at present exists between the pressmen and their employers, of which we are likely to be the first sacrifices; and though we think every compositor ought, so far as possible, to refrain from working at press, or any other measure, which may be, or even appear to be, hostile to either party, if necessity drives the compositor to press, we cannot think he ought to be held culpable by his fellow-workmen.[60]

Adam Smith felt that the usual ineffectiveness of collective labour action led the disillusioned and desperate workers to acts of violence and destruction:

> They are desperate, and act with the folly and extravagance of desperate men, who must either starve, or frighten their masters into an immediate compliance with their demands. The masters upon these occasions are just as clamorous upon the other side, and never cease to call aloud for the assistance of the civil magistrate, and the rigorous execution of those laws which have been enacted with so much severity against the combinations of servants, labourers, and journeymen.[61]

Fifty years before that the clothiers of Wiltshire had been accused of starving the poor when they pleased and of working them up by their severities into riots and tumults. The results of their handiwork they then called 'rebellion' and shouted for the military.[62]

If concentration is placed less on the element of desperation and more on the purposeful notion of *intimidation*, we may find that, here too, Smith was underestimating the effectiveness of certain kinds of action, and come closer to an understanding of the role of violence and direct action in eighteenth-century labour disputes. The early historians of the labour movement, especially the Webbs and the Hammonds, could not reconcile the element of violent or destructive action with their view of a gradualist, legitimate trade union development. Violent action was therefore to be set apart. It was the resort of men other than those who were associated with proper trade unionism, or else it was a lapse into desperation when 'constitutionalist' means met with rebuff.[63] More recent historians take a rather different view and place machine-breaking and similar activities within a central context of early trade union methods. Professor Hobsbawm's 'collective bargaining by riot' has become a much quoted phrase, and Mr Thompson has emphasised that careful consideration of direct industrial actions, along with such manifestations of popular determination as food rioting, from a functional perspective is a necessary corrective to the Webbs' 'episodic' view of eighteenth-century disputes.[64]

We can consider 'intimidation' in several contexts: the sending of threatening letters to terrify employers; machine-breaking; the intimidation of masters by direct methods other than machine-breaking and the intimidation of blacklegs, those unwilling to join strikes or 'unfair' workmen. These categories are not always totally separable; for example the threat to destroy machinery may be intended to frighten or may have been a clear statement of intention subsequently carried out, while the intention behind the destruction of machines might in some contexts be the prevention of working them with 'blacklegs' or 'unfair' labour. The evidence also clearly shows that any or all of these methods could have been used not only by groups without established traditions of organised unionism, but also by groups whose collective organisation and methods were notably sophisticated. Thus the following threatening letter was sent by the calico printers of Manchester in 1786:

we are determined to destroy all sorts of Masheens for Printing in the Kingdom for there is more hands than is work for so no more from the ingerd Gurneman Remember we are a great number sworn nor you must not advertise the Men that you say run away from you when your il Usage was the Cause of their going we will punish you for that our Meetings are legal for we want nothing but what is honest and to work for selvs and familers and you want to starve us but it is better for you and a few more which we have marked to die then such a Number of Pore Men and there famerles to be starved.[65]

We have already seen that the calico printers were highly skilled, highly status-conscious and highly organised. Few trades had a longer history of organisation than the hatters, but one of their employers received a letter in 1809 threatening to burn his house and warehouses and murder him and his sons and claiming responsibility for the death of one master already found in the canal.[66]

Machine-breaking was also frequently preceded by the sending of anonymous letters, such as in the west-country shearmen's campaign against shearing frames in the 1790s and in the better known Luddite disturbances of the Regency period. The Wiltshire shearmen in 1799 threatened those who introduced dressing machinery: 'if you follow this practice any longer . . . we will keep som (sic) people to watch you About with loaded Blunderbuss or Pistols And will Certainly Blow your Brains out it is no use to destroy the Factorys But put you Dam'd Villions to death'.[67]

Destructive or violent action could be employed in contexts in which industrial action was inappropriate. Thus Tiverton weavers and combers rioted in 1738 and in 1749 against publicans who had made a practice of buying up sub-standard cloths rejected by the clothiers and spoiling the market by selling them off cheaply. Grimes, the publican concerned in 1738, was attacked by workers collected from six towns. His serges were cut and he was 'horsed on a staff' through the town and deposited at the mayor's door. In the ensuing battle with the constables one man was killed.[68] The journeymen carpenters of Liverpool believed their employment to be dependent upon the continuation of the slave trade and threatened in 1792 that if abolition took place they would pull down the houses of the town's abolitionists. Once again the threats were issued by journeymen who far from being an unsophisticated mob came from a trade which had developed locally a powerful delegated trade organisation.[69] The Spitalfields weavers twice influenced government to pass legislation in their favour by the serious level of their street rioting: in 1719 when the Calico Acts offered them some protection from the fashionable preference for printed cottons over silk and in the violent prelude to the passing of the Spitalfields Acts of 1773 regulating their trade.[70]

Professor Hobsbawm has emphasised an important distinction between machine-breaking where the machine itself was seen as a threat to employment (as in the misleading popular understanding of 'Luddism'[71]) and cases where the machine was destroyed simply as a means of putting pressure on an employer in disputes where the employment of machinery was not in itself an issue. The power of many eighteenth-century trade unions rested, in part at least, on their being able to apply this kind of pressure. It was a 'traditional and established part of industrial conflict in the period of the domestic manufacturing system and the early stages of factory and mine'. In such conflicts not only machinery, but also employers' houses, finished goods and raw materials could be destroyed. In their struggle against the clothiers in 1802 Wiltshire shearmen burned hay ricks, barns and kennels belonging to unpopular employers, cut down their trees, destroyed loads of cloth, as well as attacking and destroying their mills.[72] It is evident from the actions of miners in dispute that machinery itself was not resented. Miners could hardly disapprove of pumping or lifting gear that was a necessary condition of their employment. When the Wigan colliers threatened to pull up the engines, throw down the wheels and fill in the pits during the course of a strike over wages, they probably had two objectives in view: to put pressure on the mine owners and to prevent the pits being worked with 'blackleg' labour. Newcastle pitmen had in 1765 actually cut the gin ropes and thrown the lifting gear down the shaft at the mine of one owner who had got his pits working during a strike. Such action was similar to that of the Cornish tinners who before coming out in 1795 pulled up the ladders from the shafts. [73]

This wider awareness of the nature and purposes of 'riotous' actions by various groups of workers helps the understanding of why such methods were often employed alongside more 'legitimate' union activities. The weavers' and combers' clubs of the south-west had their 'flags, ensigns, banners, club houses, and by-laws' but in their dispute of 1725/6 they spoiled wool, cut cloth and roughly treated both employers and journeymen who resisted joining their combination. The 1738 riots in the Melksham district began with direct attacks on rate-cutting clothiers, but there must have been some degree of continuity between these actions and the 'legal' organisations for petitioning Parliament both previously in 1728 and subsequently in 1756. [74] The claim of Gravenor Henson, the framework knitters' leader, that Luddite and legal trade union activities such as petitioning Parliament were the actions of two separate groups was accepted by the Hammonds, but has not been so by more recent historians. [75]

Almost ritualistic forms of humiliation were used both against employers and, more commonly, against blacklegs, strike-breakers or 'unfair' men. 'Cool staffing' was the fixing of a man to a long pole and parading him through the town or village before depositing him in a convenient stream or duck pond. In the disputes of 1725/6 a master was thus treated at Callington while workmen refusing to strike were similarly disciplined at Taunton. [76] The weavers of Banbury who had 'of late years associated, formed laws of their own and set those of their country at defiance' dealt in similar manner with one of their number who broke a strike in 1793:

A body of about 200 paraded the streets with martial music, and then proceeded to a place two miles distant, the residence of the man so working, and violently took his piece of shag from the loom and triumphantly returned two and two, with each a green bough in his hat, one of them bearing the shag mounted on an ass, preceding the rest with fifes playing.

They finished their march by laying the cut cloth at the door of the master who had put it out.[77] Pressure was often simply a matter of numbers. During the dispute of 1756 in Gloucestershire, clothiers complained that weavers who wanted to work were being forced from their looms by the mob, while it would have taken a foolhardy collier to have insisted on remaining at work near Bristol in 1792 when the men of Kingswood made a tour in growing numbers of the mines for six to eight miles around the city persuading their miners to join in.[78] The pattern of hiring by the yearly bond in the north-east by putting all agreements up for renewal at the same time, placed considerable power in the hands of the pitmen to protect their interests by the sheer immensity of their combined numbers, as they did in 1765.[79] The most extreme form of treatment was meeted out to those who informed on their fellows. The whole of Spitalfields seethed with anger in 1769 when two men involved in cloth-cutting episodes were executed. After the execution a large mob seized a man named Clark who had been a witness against the cutters, stripped him, tied his hands behind him, threw him into a pond and stoned him to death.[80]

Apart from the attacks like those of the shearmen which were clearly motivated by hostility towards machinery, we can see several important motives and intentions underlying direct action in eighteenth-century disputes. Pressure on the employer could induce him to give in and thus shorten a strike. Pressure could be effective against individuals who were not employers but whose actions were believed to threaten employment. It was needed to maintain solidarity by drawing the reluctant into the strike and in holding them to it. Used against 'unfair' workmen it both discouraged others not apprenticed from interloping and masters from seeking to employ them. By taking grievances to the streets it could arouse the concern of magistrates or even of government, who might be disposed to offer remedy as well as order. As a pamphleteer on behalf of the silk weavers put it in 1719: 'The complaints of weavers we can know only by their murmurings in corners, and their riotous actions in the open streets'.[81] It is not difficult to accept Professor Hobsbawm's claim that 'collective bargaining by riot' was as effective as any other means available to eighteenth-century unions, especially where intermittent pressure had to be put on employers. Riot and machine-breaking backed workers in disputes with valuable reserve powers. The master was constantly aware that an intolerable action could produce not only a strike with temporary loss of profits, but the destruction of capital equipment.[82]

Adam Smith was concerned with the effectiveness of collective action in affecting wage levels. But there were other objectives of workers' combinations in the eighteenth century. Hours were not an issue in the large number of cases where employees were home-based piece-rate workers, but could be where they worked in workshops or on their employer's premises. The length of the working day was an issue in the tailors' disputes of the early-eighteenth century, and they did succeed in getting an hour off their statutory day in 1768. The London wheel-wrights combined their demands for higher piece rates in 1734 with one for two hours off the day, while Cornish miners insisted on their right to relieve shifts at the surface rather than underground at the place of work.[83] Even in the case of home-based workers attempts to cut rates were as much an attack on leisure as they were on earnings, and weavers fighting falling rates were well aware that more was at stake than a material standard of living.

In Chapter 4 we saw how closely early trade unionism among skilled workers was bound up with the enforcement of apprenticeship and how many and to what extent workers' organisations were able to exercise effective control in this area. Historians have tended to go along with Brentano's view of trade unionism as originating with the non-observance of 5 Elizabeth. Edward Thompson has pointed out that the Webbs underestimated the notion of 'the trade' and the way in which the demand for strict apprenticeship enforcement became increasingly a demand which the journeymen made their own, and serves as a bridge between old forms and new, qualifying to this extent the Webbs' rejection of any line of descent from the old guilds to the new trade unionism. It was the journeymen who in several London trades around 1750 fought the masters to preserve the old exclusiveness of the 'freedom'. The Masons Company was complaining in 1750 that its journeymen had 'entered into unlawful combination' and were more anxious to prevent others from entering the trade than to work hard at it themselves. Consequently although the freedom of the trade had once been 'a great and invaluable franchise' by securing employment to the 'honest citizen', they were using it 'to destroy subordination and to raise an intractable spirit in the lower class of freemen' and to make them 'negligent in their callings, exhorbitant in their demands and disrespectful to their superiors'.[84] At the same time the Painter-Stainers Company was having trouble with a 'club of journeymen painters that will not work nor let others'. The journeymen had brought a case against an employer for employing someone not free of the company. Before a hearing at the Lord Mayor's Court leading masters affirmed that in the summer the press of work was such as to need many temporary labourers to carry out orders in addition to the freemen, none of whom was ever refused work. The court found for the men and this assertion of their case as a recognised principle caused a wind of anxiety to blow through the incorporated trades of the City. Masters from several companies organised a petition to the Court of Common Council to propose a licensing system for the exercise of a trade by those not free. A strong attack on journeymen's clubs was mounted in the press:

> Even those freemen who have been taken apprentices, and kindly brought up from the meanest situations, and who are the most forward, and often leaders in combinations ... are according to the present system, MASTERS OF THE LIBERTIES OF LONDON, while the real citizen, who bears the great expense of rent, taxes, and the most burdensome offices, must be in some sort subject to the power and insults of these dictators, without being availed of his privileges as a citizen, or enjoying his natural right as an Englishman.

Petitions in support of the exclusive right of the freeman to follow his trade were received from the carpenters, masons and printers as well as the painters. The journeymen printers claimed not only to be determined to support the rights and privileges of the 'free' workmen, but to have been already in combination for that protective purpose. Early in 1750 the Court delivered its verdict. The exclusive right of exercising a trade within London had been a great and valuable franchise, but when journeymen made use of this right, they perverted it to 'promote idleness', destroy subordination, and raise 'an intractable spirit in the lower class of freemen'.[85]

The struggle was a foreshadowing of the greater struggle involving almost all the craft trades of London and a great many from the country which around 1809 began first to campaign for the better and wider enforcement of the apprenticeship clauses of 5 Elizabeth, a campaign which, as we have seen, had to turn into a hard-fought but ultimately unsuccessful resistance to their repeal in 1814. The employers' attempt to remove those clauses was a frontal attack on established trade unionism, perhaps a more direct one than the securing of the general Combination Acts of 1799 and 1800. The latter may have been an attempt to provide a general remedy of speedy and effective action against what was seen as a spreading problem of increasing strike action at a time of war, rising prices, and an increasingly disseminated popular jacobinism, but the attack on statutory apprenticeship was an attempt to root out the very basis of existing and effective trade unionism in the skilled trades.

Notes

1. Adam Smith, *The Wealth of Nations* (1776, edited by E. Cannan, London, 1904), Vol. I, p. 74.

2. Ibid., p. 75.

3. *Exeter Mercury*, 11 May 1764.

4. Smith, *Wealth of Nations*, I, p. 77.

5. W.E. Minchinton, 'The Petitions of the Weavers and Clothiers of Gloucestershire in 1756', *Transactions of the Bristol and Gloucestershire Archaeological Society*, vol. 73 (1954), p. 219.

6. *Annual Register* (1765), p. 130. Reprinted in G.D.H. Cole and A.W. Filson (eds.), *British Working Class Movements. Selected Documents 1789-1875* (paperback edn, London, 1965), pp. 15-16.

7. *Fifth Report of the Select Committee on Artisans and Machinery*, P.P. 1824, V (51), p. 401.

8. G.I.H. Lloyd, *The Cutlery Trades* (London, 1913), pp. 242-5.

9. D.C. Coleman, *The British Paper Industry 1495-1860: A Study in Industrial Growth* (Oxford, 1958), pp. 264, 272-3.

10. J. Child, *Industrial Relations in the British Printing Industry – The Quest for Security* (London, 1967), p. 49.

11. E. Howe, *The London Compositor: Documents relating to Wages, Working Conditions and Customs of the London Printing Trade* (London, 1947), docs. xvii and xviii, pp. 100-2.

12. A. Aspinall (ed.), *The Early English Trade Unions. Documents from the Home Office Papers in the Public Record Office* (London, 1949), Introduction, p. ix.

13. Cole & Filson, *Working Class Movements*, p. 86.

14. A.P. Wadsworth and J. de L. Mann, *The Cotton Trade and Industrial Lancashire 1600-1780* (Manchester, 1931), p. 375.

15. Cole & Filson, *Working Class Movements*, pp. 88-9.

16. F.W. Galton, *Select Documents Illustrating the History of Trade Unionism: The Tailoring Trade* (London, 1896), p. 81.

17. Cole & Filson, *Working Class Movements*, pp. 89-90.

18. E. Bennett, *The Worshipful Company of Wheelwrights of the City of London 1670-1970* (Newton Abbot, 1970), pp. 53-5.

19. G.A. Chinnery (ed.), *Records of the Borough of Leicester Vol. VII* (Leicester, 1974), pp. 150-1, 207.

20. C.R. Dobson, *Masters and Journeymen: A Pre-history of Industrial Conflict 1717-1800* (London, 1980), p. 127.

21. Cole & Filson, *Working Class Movements*, pp. 90-1.

22. S. and B. Webb, *The History of Trade Unionism* (London, 1911 edn), p. 60; *Report from the Committee on the Apprentice Laws*, P.P. 1812/13, IV (243), p. 54.

23. *Sherborne Mercury*, 2 December 1800.

24. *Second Report of the Select Committee on Artisans and Machinery*, P.P. 1824, V, p. 52.

25. Child, *Printing Industry*, p. 57.

26. *Calendar of Home Office Papers of the Reign of George III 1760-1765*, 13 September 1765, p. 599.

27. Pamphlets written by 'Gentlemen' sympathetic to oppressed workers are not uncommon.

28. For the use of 'third party' mediators see the Chapter 'The Magistrate as Mediator' in Dobson, *Masters and Journeymen*, pp. 74-92.

29. See for example the advice given by the Home Office to a local justice on

the Cotton Weavers' Association in Lancashire in 1799. Their object in petitioning Parliament was 'not contrary to the Act of 39 George III, c. 81, or any other laws affecting the same'. It did, however, go on to urge careful watching as such associations 'contain within themselves the means of being converted into a most dangerous instrument to disturb the public tranquillity' (Aspinall, *Early Trade Unions*, doc. 28, pp. 26-7).

30. As happened to the printers in 1816 (*Second Report on Artisans and Machinery*, P.P. 1824, V, p. 52).

31. Smith, *Wealth of Nations*, Vol. I, p. 75.

32. Ibid., p. 77.

33. J. de L. Mann (ed.), *Documents Illustrating the Wiltshire Textile Trades in the Eighteenth Century* (Devizes, 1964), docs. 207, 217.

34. *Commons Journals*, XX, 31 March 1726, p. 648.

35. *Report on Apprentice Laws*, P.P. 1812/13, IV, p. 53.

36. Dobson, *Masters and Journeymen*, p. 30.

37. W.G. Hoskins, *Industry, Trade and People in Exeter 1688-1800*, 2nd edn (Exeter, 1968), p. 54.

38. Howe, *London Compositor*, footnote to pp. 129-30.

39. *Report of the Select Committee on the Combination Laws*, P.P. 1825, IV (417, 437), p. 34; J. Stevenson, *Popular Disturbances in England, 1700-1870* (London, 1979), pp. 126-7.

40. *Report of the Committee on the Silk Ribbon Weavers' Petitions*, P.P. 1818, IX (134), p. 8.

41. *Second Report of Select Committee on Artisans and Machinery*, P.P. 1824, V, p. 47; Aspinall, *Early Trade Unions*, doc. 70, p. 66.

42. Webb & Webb, *Trade Unionism*, p. 22.

43. Dobson, *Masters and Journeymen*, p. 45.

44. Thomas Percival, *A letter to a friend: occasioned by the late disputes betwixt the clock-makers of Manchester, and their weavers and the check-weavers ill usage of the author* (1758), p. 10. Reprinted in K. Carpenter (ed.), *Labour Disputes in the Early Days of the Industrial Revolution* (New York, 1972).

45. *Minutes of Evidence before the Committee on the Laws Relating to the Woollen Trade*, P.P. 1802/3, VII (95), pp. 25, 226.

46. *Autobiography of Francis Place* (edited by M. Thale, Cambridge, 1972), pp. 112-13.

47. Aspinall, *Early Trade Unions*, doc. 83, p. 84; Child, *Printing Industry*, p. 62; Howe, *London Compositor*, doc. xv, p. 103.

48. Place, *Autobiography*, pp. 113-16.

49. Ibid., pp. 125-6; *Second Report on Artisans and Machinery*, P.P. 1824, V, p. 44.

50. Aspinall, *Early Trade Unions*, doc. 80, p. 78.

51. *Third Report on Artisans and Machinery*, P.P. 1824, V, p. 135.

52. Ibid., p. 148.

53. This account is based on *A History of the Combination of Journeymen Calico Printers* (1807), pp. 13-15. Reprinted in K. Carpenter (ed.), *Trade Unions under the Combination Acts* (New York, 1972).

54. *Commons Journals*, LI, 21 April 1796, p. 595.

55. Child, *Printing Industry*, p. 63.

56. *Commons Journals*, XX, 7 March 1725 (6), p. 602; Diary of George Wansey, 28/30 November 1738, reprinted in Mann (ed.), *Documents on Wiltshire Textile Trade*, doc. 172.

57. *Fourth Report on Artisans and Machinery*, P.P. 1824, V, p. 271.

58. Wadsworth & Mann, *Cotton Trade*, p. 371.

59. M. Dunsford, *Historical Memoirs of Tiverton* (Exeter, 1790), p. 230.

60. Howe, *London Compositor*, doc. xi, p. 90.

61. Smith, *Wealth of Nations*, Vol. I, pp. 75-6.

62. *The Devil Drove out the Warping-bar* (1727), pp. 12-13. Reprinted in K. Carpenter (ed.), *Labour Problems before the Industrial Revolution* (New York, 1972).

63. See my introduction to the 1979 edition of J.L. and B. Hammond, *The Skilled Labourer* (London, 1979), pp. xx-xxiii.

64. E.J. Hobsbawm, 'The Machine-breakers' in his *Labouring Men: Studies in the History of Labour* (London, 1964), p. 7; E.P. Thompson, 'English Trade Unionism and other Labour Movements before 1790', *Bulletin of the Society for the Study of Labour History*, no. 17 (1968), pp. 19-24.

65. E.P. Thompson, 'The Crime of Anonymity' in D. Hay, P. Linebaugh, J.G. Rule, E.P. Thompson and C. Winslow, *Albion's Fatal Tree. Crime and Society in Eighteenth-century England* (paperback edn, Harmondsworth, 1977), Appendix p. 318.

66. Aspinall, *Early Trade Unions*, doc. 102, p. 105.

67. Thompson, 'Crime of Anonymity', pp. 275, 320.

68. Dunsford, *Tiverton*, pp. 226, 228.

69. Aspinall, *Early Trade Unions*, doc. 2, p. 2.

70. The most recent account of both the 1719 and the 1773 agitations is in A. Plummer, *The London Weavers' Company 1600-1970* (London, 1972).

71. See J.G. Rule, Introduction to 1979 edition of Hammond & Hammond, *Skilled Labourer*, pp. xx-xxi.

72. Hobsbawm, 'Machine-breakers', p. 7.

73. Aspinall, *Early Trade Unions*, doc. 8, p. 7; *Sherborne Mercury*, 23 September 1765; J.G. Rule, 'The Labouring Miner in Cornwall c. 1740-1870', unpublished PhD thesis, University of Warwick, 1971, p. 382.

74. Hobsbawm, 'Machine-breakers', p. 7.

75. See Rule introduction to *The Skilled Labourer*, p. xxii.

76. *Commons Journals*, XX, 31 March 1726, p. 648.

77. Aspinall, *Early Trade Unions*, doc. 22, p. 19.

78. Ibid., doc. 7, pp. 6-7.

79. E. Welbourne, *The Miners Unions of Northumberland and Durham* (Cambridge, 1923), pp. 21-2.

80. *Calendar of Home Office Papers of the Reign of George III 1770-72*, p. 273.

81. *The Weavers' Pretences Examined* (1719) reprinted in J. Smith, *Memoirs of Wool* (1747, reprinted Farnborough, 1968), p. 184.

82. Hobsbawm, 'Machine-breakers', p. 17.

83. Galton, *Tailoring Trade*, p. 60; Bennett, *Wheelwrights*, p. 52; Rule, 'Labouring Miner', p. 85.

84. J.R. Kellet, 'The Breakdown of Guild and Corporation Control over the Handicraft and Retail Trade in London', *Economic History Review*, X (1958), p. 388.

85. Dobson, *Masters and Journeymen*, pp. 50-3.

8 CUSTOM, CULTURE AND CONSCIOUSNESS

The keelmen of the Tyne struck work in 1719, 'on pretence their accustomed wages are too small'. The Chatham ropemakers of the naval yard petitioned the king in 1717 that their four holidays of the king's birthday and coronation anniversary, November 5 and Shrove Tuesday should continue: 'as has been customary for over fifty years past', and in 1718 when the employers in the south-west attempted to lengthen the cloth piece by half-a-yard, they were acting: 'contrary to law, usage and custom from time immemorial'.[1] In the preceding chapters the importance of custom in determining the expectations from work of men; in conditioning their attitudes and practices in performing it and in defining their relationships with their employers has been stressed. Such attitudes persisted well into the nineteenth century, when it has been suggested that the strength of customary expectation was still so strong that with skilled groups calculating their wages on a customary rather than a market calculation, employers at times got their skilled labour at less than market cost.[2]

Employers were not the only persons with whom working relations were needed. Even a weaver working at home was daily in face-to-face contact with his wife and children. In a small cottage or set of rooms, this could, as Francis Place knew so well, engender a special claustrophobic feeling of strain as working and living were not easily separable. Even when the circle was widened by the addition of an apprentice or journeyman, the relationships were not always as harmonious as those idealised in the poem on the Yorkshire clothiers.[3] Those who worked away from home in workshops, or factories, construction sites, mines or shipyards worked with other workmen, often as members of 'gangs' or teams or pairings involving a high degree of interdependence. A man might have to trust his very safety to a colleague, or the level of his earnings might depend upon the collective productivity of the group.

Whether groups were self-formed gangs contracting collectively with employers, or whether their composition was determined by their employers, co-operation for mutual benefit demanded a customary sanction to ensure that the individual did not seek to follow his own interests at the expense of the group's. Most eighteenth-century labour groups were of equal adult partners with a supplementary lad or two.

194

The emergence of middle men, like the hated 'butties' of the midlands coalfields, was a nineteenth-century development. Some groups, however, worked under foremen, as the shipwright gangs in the dockyards did under 'quartermen'. Shipwrights worked in gangs of 20. The 'task gangs', the more skilled, were pre-selected for efficiency, but the bulk of the shipwrights on the more routine work, the 'day gangs', were 'shoaled', that is dissolved and reselected from time to time. The purpose was to mix good and bad workmen. The men preferred this as the earnings of each depended upon those of the whole, and shoaling guaranteed that the wages of those getting older, or less physically able would be maintained and all could expect reasonable, level earnings through their working life.[4]

Customary control of a fair sharing of work among men in the same shop or yard was an important aspect of mutuality. The compositors had long practised it. When Charles Manby Smith entered his first London printing works in the early-nineteenth century, he was a self-confessed 'stranger to the customs of the trade'. Expecting to be able to put in as many hours as he chose to maximise his earnings, he found that by agreement with the compositors' union, London masters had forbidden touching the type before 8 am or after 8 pm. Manby Smith complained that the amount of work allowed to be done by one man was, in his view, 'limited to the capacity of the meanest ability'. No man was allowed to be paid for more than 60 hours work in a week. In his first week he put in 82 hours and expected £2 14s 8d; instead he received £2, the pay for 60 hours, and was told he had been allowed 22 hours 'on the shelf', which meant he need only work 40 hours the next week: 'you must take what comes and, mike [be idle] a bit now and then, if you are such a fast man'. Manby Smith was an ambitious, and unpopular man who could see little merit in any of the customs of his trade. He even railed against the tramping system:

> The practice of tramping had . . . risen to a most disgraceful climax. A regular tide of lazy and filthy vagabonds, professedly of various trades, but virtually living without work, or the intention of working, flowed through the kingdom . . . The greatest misfortune that could befall a regular tramp was the finding of employment.[5]

By this time, the 'customs' of the trade had in many cases become incorporated into trade union rules. In printing this went back to 1801, when the compositors established a society to correct 'irregularities' and to bring 'the modes of change from custom and precedent into

one point of view, in order to their being better understood by all concerned'. In 1805 they were complaining that in too many instances the
employer had taken advantage of ignorance on the part of the journeymen by 'disputing or denying custom, and by refusing to acknowledge
precedents, which have been hitherto the only reference'.[6]

Accounts of the customary work practices of printers survive from
the seventeenth century. The origin of calling a printing house 'the
chapel' is unknown, but a senior compositor in each works known as
the 'father of the chapel' was the pivotal figure in ensuring the observance of good, mutual, work habits. Within each chapel the compositors
were usually organised into a 'companionship' of three to six men under
a leader, 'the clicker', who apportioned the work among the men, who
earned a lump sum collectively, usually on the basis of lines set. The
'fat', the half-printed pages, titles etc. were customarily paid as if fully
printed, and these were by custom evenly divided among the compositors.[7] Discipline among the journeymen was based on the chapel. When
a member had a complaint against a fellow, the 'father' held a trial
('called a chapel') before the 'imposing stone' and if found against the
offending compositor was fined (a solace). A long list of rules were
backed by this sanction. For the most part they were designed to ensure harmonious relations among the men, and encourage working
habits which were for the collective good. Thus fines were levied for,
among other things, swearing, fighting or defaming; drunkenness or
gambling; dropping or leaving tools or type dirty or in the wrong place
and for leaving a candle burning at night. The fines were usually paid,
but refusal could bring eleven strokes with a board across the backside.[8]

Among shipwrights too, the formation of a union on the Thames at
the end of the century led to the exertion of control over the amount
of work an individual might take on at the expense of his fellows:

> Previous to the union it was nothing uncommon for men to take
> such a quantity of work that many men were left destitute; that I
> am sure many a man died a premature death for want of sustenance,
> because the greater part of this employ was engrossed by a few hands.
> The union provides against it . . . that no man is to engross or take to
> himself a greater quantity of work than what he can accomplish. The
> result is, it throws it open for other people to come in. By that means
> many a man gets a job who would not get a job, supposing the old
> system of working was adopted.[9]

The claim was made by John Gast and it may have taken his skills, perhaps the equal of any union leader of his day, to improve the working practices of the Thames yards. However at Liverpool there is a strong impression that the union there was, like the printers', adding its strength to an old custom among the shipwrights. Those who offended there were 'drilled', that is their fellows refused to work with them for a period of time, thus effectively keeping them out of work. For drunkenness or bad language a man might be drilled a week, but for taking more than his share of work, for as much as three weeks. By 1823 this had been implemented for some time by the decision of the union committee, although it probably did not appear as a formal entry in the rule book. In fact it seems most likely to have been a long established practice of generally sanctioning unpopular workmates. Asked what 'drilling' meant one shipwright replied, 'They do not like to work with him, because he is a very droll character; a proper idle character; then people refuse to work with him; that is the meaning of it'. Certainly the feeling of mutuality at Liverpool seems to have been a strong one, for the young and fit agreed to abandon a piece-rate scheme in 1817 and insist on day wages with all getting the same:

It was proposed on account of the old men; when piece work was brought in, they were mostly put off work, and the members thought it very hard to see the old men walking about, without being able to get a day's work.[10]

A miner's earnings depended upon the potential of the part of the mine in which he worked: its mineral or coal quantity and quality as well as the ease with which it could be dug. In order that fortune was shared as fairly as possible, the hewers of the north-east drew lots four times a year (known as 'cavilling') so that a good or bad place came by luck not by the allotment of officials to favoured workmen.[11] Portions of the mine were, as we have seen, allocated to the Cornish tributers on the basis of a 'Dutch Auction', the lowest rate offered securing the bargain. However a strong convention prevailed, probably at least from the late-eighteenth century, of not bidding against 'the old pare'. That is the other miners would recognise the right of 'a pare' of tributers to continue working their old 'pitch' if they so wished, even if others might wish to have it. This did not mean that the mine captain was forced to accept any rate the men then offered, for he always kept a reserve price above which he would not 'set' the pitch. In effect the rest of the miners were allowing the 'old pare' the priority of agreeing terms with the captain.[12]

A craftsman's self-confidence in his own skill and status, even a labourer's pride in his strength and prowess, or the special feeling which miners shared for their extreme occupation which, by taking them underground, set them apart from all others, were all founded on shared experiences, beliefs and attitudes. This customary consensus revealed itself most clearly when a newcomer joined, a stranger arrived, or a determined deviant who refused to conform (such as a boss's man or a self-interested one) came into conflict with the collective mores. When the ending of an apprenticeship brought a new recruit to the ranks of the skilled, initiation ceremonies of an elaborate nature marked his admission to the full 'mystery' of the craft. The old word in itself conveys something of the ritual needed to establish the significance of being allowed into the craft group and to share in its exclusive exercise of its trade.

Elaborate 'rites of passage' marked the graduation of a printer from his first binding. Before being admitted a 'Chapellonian' he had to be made a 'Cuz' or 'Deacon':

> The Chapellonians walk three times round the room, their right arms being put through the lappets of their coats, the boy who is to be made a 'Cuz' carrying a wooden sword before them. Then the boy kneels, and the Father of the Chapel, after exhorting him to be observant of his business, and not to betray the secrets of the workmen, squeezes a sponge of strong beer over his head and gives him a title, which is generally that of Duke of some place of the least reputation near which he lives, or did live before; such as those of Rag Fair, Thieving Lane, Puddle Dock, P-ssing Alley, and the like. This being done, the Father of the Chapel gives the boy an account of the safety he will enjoy by being made a Cuz, which is that whatever accident may happen to him, no ill consequence will attend it, such as *Falling from an house*, or into the *Thames*, etc. Whilst the boy is upon his knees, all the Chapellonians . . . walk round him, singing the Cuz's Anthem, which is done by adding all the vowels to the consonants in the following manner. Ba-ba; Be-be; Bi-bi; Bo-bo; Ba-be-bi-bo; Bu-bu; Ba-be-bi-bo-bu — and so through the rest of the consonants.[13]

Coming out of his time, the apprentice had to endure 'banging out'. He was smeared with printers' ink and led in procession through the various departments of his firm, promising beer money to all the workers. Even more messy is the centuries-old, still surviving, 'trussing the cooper'. The newly-qualified man stands in a barrel of his own making and is first of all heated. He then gets down in the barrel and is covered with a mixture of soot, shavings, feathers, treacle and beer. He is rolled around the workroom three times, before being taken out and tossed three times in the air.[14]

Newcomers who had served their time elsewhere at another firm or in another town, were expected to show their good feeling towards their new colleagues by buying drinks: 'a maiden garnish'. In a large shop this could amount to a sizeable sum. A hatter told Professor W.J. Ashley of such customs being well-established by the time he arrived to work in London in 1856. His 'maiden garnish' came to 9s 8d among the 32 members of the shop. If the foreman of the shop had not passed his first week's work, he would have been turned off, and if that had happened the men who had taken of his garnish would have subscribed twopence each to another 'kitty' as 'treatings' to drink with them and drown his sorrow. If there was a vacant 'plank' and a man wished to move to it he had to pay a 'plank gallon', if he put on a silk 'under' for the first time he paid a 'fancy gallon'.[15] Among the printers the maiden garnish was known as the *bienvenue*, and was of a fixed sum of 2s 6d. Those returning to a shop where they had previously worked paid half.[16]

The deviant who ignored or set himself against the customs might expect sanctions. Benjamin Franklin in his time in a London printing house in the early-eighteenth century, was hardly courting popularity. By never keeping 'Saint Monday' and by running up stairs carrying twice the load of the others, he seemed a 'prig'; an impression strengthened by his preaching against their beer drinking. When he was promoted from the press to compositor, his fellows demanded a *bienvenue*. Having already paid one when he had first joined the firm, Franklin refused. He stood out for two or three weeks, while being subjected to 'little pieces of private malice'. His lines were transposed, his letters mixed etc. All this was attributed to the 'chapel ghost', which the men said ever haunted those 'not regularly admitted'. He had in the end to give in and pay up, 'convinced of the folly of being on ill terms with those one is to live with continually'.[17] We have already noted Manby Smith's dislike of the customs of the trade. Understandably unpopular with the other compositors, they dubbed him 'the Professor' because of his ability to read Latin and his generally superior manner. His opinion was asked on sham disputes and listened to with exaggerated respect. Goaded into a fight, he was 'chapelled' and fined 5s, which was gleefully spent on three hours' drinking. He had been equally unpopular when working in Paris with other English compositors some years before. There he had been sent on false errands, and had to hold back his resentment, which had he displayed it would have resulted in his being 'sent to Coventry'.[18] Not only printers acted in such a way. When William Lovett came from Cornwall and took work in London as a cabinet-maker, a trade to which he had not been apprenticed, his shopmates talked of 'setting Mother Shorney at him'. By this they meant to hide his tools and injure his work in such a way as to drive him from the shop.[19] The tailors had a more civilised and practical way of deciding whether a country lad fresh to London was worthy of being employed alongside them. He was required to accomplish 'the log', an amount of work fixed by the union to be completed in a day, and from accounts of those so tested it was a fair but demanding task.[20]

The calling of a 'chapel' in printing was not the only example of disciplining through 'workshop' courts. William Lovett, when he found his new workmates determined to drive him from the shop, was able to invoke another custom of the trade: he called a shop-meeting. This was done by first sending out for a quantity of ale and then striking one's hammer and holdfast together to produce a ringing sound which would assemble the shop around your bench. A chairman was then appointed and the caller asked to present his case. Lovett argued that he had spent the prime of his life learning a trade, ropemaking, which he had found comparatively useless, and appealed to their sense of justice to determine whether it was 'right to prevent me from learning another'. After some discussion it was agreed to let him stay:

But the demands made upon me for drink by individuals among them, for being shown the manner of doing any particular kind of work, together with fines and shop scores, often amounted to seven or eight shillings a week out of my guinea.[21]

Among the hatters a system of shop jurisdiction persisted until the end of the nineteenth century, although by then in decay. An account of how it was working in the 1850s survives:

When workman A called B by an opprobrious name, which the latter resented, B could 'weigh out the caulker', by declaring, 'If your name is A, a man of this shop and a shopmate of mine, I caulk you: prove me (to be so and so) before you hat, or pay sixteen pence for larking'. At this time the 'constable of the shop' called out, 'Gentlemen, the caulker is out'. Everyman in that battery had ceased work. Now A could either 'call his words in again' or 'give the wrong insist'. If he did the latter, the constable at once said, 'a garrett in ten minutes'.

The garrett was formed by the men of the battery; and if they decided that A deserved the reproach, he was fined four shillings, which was spent in that battery. The case could, however, have been taken to the higher court — 'the dozening', the men for which would have been selected from a dozen shops.[22]

Drinking evidently played an important part in workshop customs. Its role went beyond simple conviviality. Treating confirmed symbolically a wish to belong. As a means of spending fines it allowed a point about expected behaviour to be made in a way which re-emphasised the harmony and fellowship which the deviant had disturbed. Even on normal occasions beer drinking was a feature of working men's lives during work as well as leisure time. Franklin was surprised to find when he entered a London printing works in the 1720s that an alehouse boy was employed in constant attendance to supply the workmen. The pressmen drank a pint before breakfast, a pint at breakfast, a pint between breakfast and dinner, a pint at dinner, a pint in the afternoon, and another at the end of the day's work. This cost around 4s or 5s a week from their wages.[23] Coopers did not have to buy their own beer. An employer told a committee of enquiry in 1825, that 'for years', the men were provided with tools and as much beer as they could drink besides other privileges: 'They will have as much beer as they please if we only happen to be out of beer for ten minutes all the yard is in a ferment'.[24] Beershops or gin-shops are recorded as having existed on the premises at both royal dock-yards and Cornish mines.[25] A persistent complaint of those concerned with working-class intemperance was the habit of settling wages in public houses on Saturday nights. Publicans allowed pay tables to be set up and it was a normal practice for wages to be given out in this manner, with the result, as Sir John Fielding pointed out, that tradesmen went home drunk and empty-handed. In 1764 it was said to be a common sight in London between midnight and 1 am on a Sunday morning to see victuallers carrying the 'scores' of coachmakers, carpenters, smiths, plasterers, plumbers, builders etc. to get payment, while wives hung about waiting. Wilberforce's Proclamation Society proposed in 1789 that an undertaking not to allow the setting-up of a pay table should be made a condition for licensing. Place described the practice in 1825 as having only died out 'of late years'.[26]

The truly independent craftsmen, in the sense of owning the materials on which they worked, and marketing the produce of their own labour were, we have seen, much in a minority by the mid-eighteenth century.

There are, however, other aspects of 'independence'. The control of the out-working artisan, or small-workshop craftsman over the pace and intensity of their working week was one important one, which we have seen survived until the coming of factory regularity and discipline. What an eighteenth-century worker would have most likely himself meant by a proud assertion of independence was the capability of supporting himself and his family at a proper standard without having recourse to charity or the poor law. When the cotton weavers were forced to work 16 hours or more a day in 1808 to make even a bare subsistence, they complained bitterly: 'there never was a time before the present when the workman could not live by his trade'.[27] 'Living by his trade' meant more than surviving. It meant the right to educate and supervise his own children, rather than be driven by desperation to send them to the factory, and to preserve a customary lifestyle. The compositors put the matter very clearly in 1810:

> The profession of a man should always be equal to the support of himself and family in a decent way. They should be supplied with not merely what will preserve animation, but what custom has rendered necessary for their comfort.[28]

In watchmaking in the crisis of 1817/18 the trauma of falling into dependence on poor relief was evident. The watchmakers of Clerkenwell were proud of the fact that they *paid* the poor rate and had 'lived in respectability and credit'. Many had been housekeepers in their own right: 'men who had formerly appeared independent in their way as workmen, seemed to be depressed to the lowest state of poverty'. One who had earned 30s a week had been rapidly reduced to 9s 6d.[29] The watchmakers of Coventry were equally demoralised; nearly all were said to be either in the workhouse or on out-relief to supplement the two or three days a week work, which was all they could get. Independence was threatened in a further sense. It was the proud boast of such people that through their subscription clubs they could take care of the distressed among them without going outside the trade. The Clerkenwell watchmakers were proud of the fact that they 'supported their own', while at Coventry:

> Persons [around 1800] . . . were enabled by their skill and industry to maintain themselves and families in a state of comfort and respectability, and to keep their own houses and pay taxes, scot and lot, and contribute toward the maintenance of other persons in their

profession, who were either sick or in distress, so that it was scarcely known that any person in this trade ever applied for parochial relief.[30]

Asked if his profession thought relief from the parish 'dishonourable' because the trade was deemed 'the profession of a gentleman, and the highest order of mechanics', a watchmaker simply replied, 'Yes'. Watchmakers lived 'in respectability': no person of the trade was known to take parish relief. Those in distress were supported by a subscription on the trade: 'as it was thought dishonourable to allow a watchmaker to be in distress'.[31]

The two watchmakers' benefit societies were in serious difficulties. They had between them 90 members who paid 1s a week into a fund for 14s a week sick relief, ten guineas death benefit to their widows and five to themselves if their wives died. After leaving £100 in the 'box' as 'a bond of compact', the surplus was shared every Christmas. The decline of the trade had cut the flow of subscriptions by a half, and the benefits likewise. One of the societies had already divided up its stock to relieve the poverty of its members, and was expected to dissolve at Christmas, there being no longer any inducement to its members to remain.[32]

Clearly any notion of an 'artisan culture' is a dependent one. As a description of a lifestyle and expected standard it is applicable to normal and good earnings periods, but may lose its distinctive characteristics in some trades under pressure of falling incomes: not only because of poverty, but also because such times were invariably associated with the necessity of working such long hours for maintenance, that leisure elements could not survive. Leisure as well as income marked the 'golden' times. Radcliffe's description of the period 1788 to 1803 for the handloom cotton weavers intermingles experience and myth, but nevertheless conveys meaning:

> Their dwellings and small gardens clean and neat – all the family well clad – the men each with a watch in his pocket, and the women dressed to their own fancy – the church crowded to excess every Sunday – every house well furnished with a clock in elegant mahogany or fancy case – handsome tea services in Staffordshire ware . . . Birmingham, Potteries, and Sheffield wares for necessary use and ornament . . . many cottage families had their cow.[33]

Samuel Bamford's father worked in this period as a muslin-weaver. He was imbued with book knowledge, interested in maths and astronomy. He could play the flute and composed verses. Bamford remarks that such talents, both natural and acquired, were 'not often possessed by men of his condition in society' at that time and that he 'stood far above his rustic acquaintance in the village'. Before experiencing a Methodist conversion, Bamford Senior had been drinker, dancer and a wrestler of renown, but even during that time had had a taste for books.[34] He may well have been unusual but that may have been rather from the range of his talents than from any individual one. It was during periods of adequate earnings that weavers could allow their children to acquire an education. Indeed in this region an historian has commented on the decline in literacy which came with the Industrial Revolution, the collapse of 'the golden age' and the systematised and regular labour of children at the factory.[35]

It may well be possible to talk of an 'artisan culture' with characteristics of independence, leisure interests which could embrace the 'improving', a high level of literacy, general awareness and mutuality expressed through clubs. William Hutton in his account of artisan Birmingham published in 1781, described the 'low amusements' of the 'humbler class': the Wakes ('completely suited to the lowest of tempers'), bull baiting, foot races, skittles and ale. He also describes 'perhaps hundreds' of clubs among the artisans which were not only for the support of the sick. There was a building club, where the subscribers paid 2 guineas a month and balloted for the fund each time it reached £100 to build a house. There was the capital club when subscribers balloted when the fund reached £50 for capital for business. Below these were the breeches club where small subscriptions were paid and a pair of breeches value a guinea made and balloted for each time the subscriptions reached that level. Clock clubs, watch clubs, book clubs and rent clubs were organised on a similar basis. Francis Place has described a similar custom among London artisans.[36] Such lifestyles were fluctuating in two senses. For any trade a period of bad times could destroy them and, secondly, a particular trade could so decline in status permanently that its members were left with only a fading memory of better days. Professor Hobsbawm's idea of an 'aristocracy of labour' for the nineteenth century depends upon the same characteristics as those we have tried to identify, but he recognises that fluctuations in fortunes and status may make the idea less firmly applicable to the eighteenth century.[37]

If a 'respectable' artisan culture was emerging in late-eighteenth century England was it doing so by a process of separation from a broader 'culture of poverty' which embraced the casual labourer, the unemployed, the vagrant and the criminal? The culture of deprivation and poverty, of violence, crime, casual employment and prostitution, was an evident feature of eighteenth-century London, but how far removed from it were the tradesmen and craft workers of the city? Place was the very model of the journeyman striving for status and respectability, but he held off a distinctly less reputable culture at barely more than arm's length. Place's father had been something of a 'rough diamond'. Bred a baker, he could sign his name but manage little else in the way of literacy and excelled instead in 'drinking, whoring, gaming, fishing and fighting'. The young Francis was educated with, and to the level of, the better class of tradesmen. Their sons were the companions of his apprenticeship days:

> The class to which I belonged was by no means the lowest. The boys with whom I associated would not keep company with Journeymen excepting in their workshops, nor with lads whose fathers were not housekeepers.

Such youths would not associate with parish apprentices. Yet of the fellow members of the cutter club (rowing) which he joined, the stroke was hanged for a murder he did not commit, having been unable to establish an alibi because he had been engaged on a burglary at the time and the cox was transported for robbery. He, like the stroke, was a printer. Most of the other members either robbed their masters or other persons, and this club was 'no better than many others'. His first master had three daughters who were prostitutes, although with different specialisations, one son who was a pick-pocket and another who had been a thief. Place's sister married a butcher who in fact was the son of a family keeping a shop only as a cover for fencing. His brother-in-law was a go-between for the thieves and the shop, and sometimes thieved himself. Eventually he was hanged for highway robbery.[38]

Place believed that it was only since his youth, that the London craftsmen began to 'improve' into a respectable class. He warned the reader of his recollections:

> The circumstances which it will be seen I have mentioned relative to the ignorance, the immorality, the grossness, the obscenity, the drunkenness, the dirtiness, and depravity of the middling and even of a large portion of the better sort of tradesmen, the artisans, and the journeymen tradesmen of London in the days of my youth, may excite a suspicion that the picture I have drawn is a caricature.

Improvement he put down to better policing, education, including

Sunday schools, stricter moral values and the availability of cotton underwear.[39] He was sure too of the decline of intemperance, remarking of the tailors:

> I should say, they like all other journeymen, are greatly improved in morals. Twenty years ago few tailor shops were without a bottle of gin: the men drank as they liked; one kept the score, and the publican came at certain times to replenish the gin bottle. I suppose there is not a shop in London that has one now.[40]

'Now' was 1824 and Place was not the only witness before the *Committee on Artisans and Machinery* to make the point. Printing workers were said to have improved in character: 'a printing office was like a public house on a Monday when I was an apprentice, and now we have no drinking at all'. While the engineers were said to have become cleaner, better dressed, improved in their conduct and their manners and much less given to drunkenness: 'they are decidedly better men'.[41]

There was a dissenting opinion on behalf of the hatters, one of whose leading employers could see no 'general moral improvement', and they still were notorious for drink.[42] William Lovett thought that any improvement among the cabinet-makers and indeed among the London working classes in general had only taken place since he had arrived there in 1821, but that the subsequent improvement was very great.[43]

Although Place thought that the improvement he described extended into the country as well as London, it is clear that we must be careful about reading too far back into the eighteenth century, nineteenth-century identifications of a separable, 'respectable' craftsman class.[44]

One of the difficulties is that the idea of a 'working-class culture' applied to the nineteenth or twentieth centuries conveys an essentially urban meaning. It is evident that any attempt at establishing an urban/rural dichotomy would split the manufacturing workers of the eighteenth century. The urban culture of the eighteenth century recently discussed by historians, was not a manufacturing one however distinctive its 'commercial' characteristics.[45] True London, Birmingham, Manchester or other large towns could have had few points of familiarity for the newly arrived farm-boy, but neither would they have had for the rural weaver or knitter, let alone miner. In many respects, however, the contrast can be exaggerated. Surface differences concealing fundamental similarities. The way-goose dinner of the printers marking the date at which they began working by candlelight was as much a calendar custom as the harvest-home. The saints' days kept by different groups of workers: St

Crispin for the shoemakers, St Clement for the smiths, St Blaise for the woolcombers etc. had their equivalent in the keeping of village saints' days and Plough Mondays. The begging licence allowed to village children on certain days had its direct parallel with those allowed to manufacturing apprentices.[46] The 'cool staffing' or 'stang riding' of strike breakers was another form of the rural 'rough music' sanction on those who offended community mores. One is not surprised to see that the rural weavers of Bamford's Lancashire kept the calendar of feasts, celebrations and ceremonies alongside their agricultural neighbours, but even Francis Place's London was still keeping up customs and rituals derived from rural origins.[47]

Miners wherever they lived were regarded as communities apart. When John Wesley first began preaching to the colliers of Kingswood in 1739 he found them as he had expected them to be: 'neither fearing God nor regarding man'. 'If he will convert heathens', people used to say tauntingly of George Whitefield, 'why does he not go to the colliers of Kingswood?'[48] Proverbially riotous, drunken and rough, they shared their reputation with the miners of other districts. The pitmen of the north-east were described in the eighteenth century as a: 'rude, bold, savage set of beings, apparently cut off from their fellow men in their interest and feelings', sharing the same occupation, they stood out as 'a sturdy band apart from the motley mixture of common humanity'.[49] Readers of a London newspaper in 1776 would not have been attracted to Cornwall by reading:

> The common people here are a very strange kind of being, half savages at the best. Many thousands of them live entirely underground, where they burrow and breed like rabbits.[50]

A strange impression indeed! But instructive in that it was not atypical of the kind of thing the unfamiliar were prepared to believe of miners. James Silk Buckingham spent his boyhood at Flushing, a mere handful of miles from the mining district of Cornwall, nor was he a man given to extreme language, but here is his description of a body of tinners who came through his village in the 1790s during a period of food-rioting:

> they were all dressed in the mud-stained frocks and trousers in which they worked underground, and all armed with large clubs and sticks of various kinds, and speaking an uncouth jargon, which none but themselves could understand, they struck terror wherever they went,

and seemed like an eruption of barbarians invading some more civil-
ized country than their own.[51]

Superstition was especially rife in mining communities, and, until the
remarkable success of John Wesley in evangelising mining areas they
were generally regarded as little troubled by religion. So far as literacy
went they certainly were considerably behind most other workers in
manufacturing, and may even have been behind the rural labourer in
general.[52]

 The amazing rapidity with which Wesleyan Methodism was taken to,
and spread among, miners was the most striking cultural change they
underwent in the eighteenth century. By the beginning of the nineteenth
century, the connection of mining with Methodism had become so
established that methodistical traits had imparted themselves on the
behaviour patterns of the mining communities, to be commented on by
outsiders almost as readily as they had earlier commented on barbarity
and roughness. In fact Methodism made far more impact on manufacturing communities in general than it did in agricultural villages. One
thing which could with certainty be said about a miner or a manufacturing worker in eighteenth-century England, was that he was far more
likely to have been a Methodist or dissenter of some other kind than
was a farm labourer or small farmer.[53] This fact, whatever the anti-
radical views of the early leaders of Methodism, at least represented the
weakening of the hold of one of the arms of the establishment: the
church. As such it is one of the factors which explain the weaker hold
of paternalism and deference over the manufacturing worker.

Few historians would maintain that the horizontal class divisions of the
nineteenth century are directly applicable to the lines of social cleavage
in the eighteenth. Class consciousness in the sense of recognising the
collective interest of a 'working class' as opposed to a 'capitalist class',
and expressed in terms of the ideologies which both form and develop
from that consciousness, are inappropriate to the analysis of eighteenth-
century society. Instead of 'class conflict' historians have tended to
offer suggestions that *paternalism* or some similarly ill-defined 'social
quantum',[54] produced a consensus society which lasted until industrialisation. Within manufacturing we are urged to think not of horizontal
class consciousness separating masters from men, but instead of vertical
consciousness of 'the trade' embracing the mutual interests of the employee. Quarrels between them were like quarrels in a 'family', squabbles
which did not prohibit recognition of an overall common interest. *Within*

a trade horizontal fissures arose because the component levels did not live up to reciprocal expectations. Thus *some* masters might be seen as acting in an *unmasterlike* manner, or at *some* times masters in general might forget their obligations sufficiently to act solely in their own interest. This would produce temporary conflict along horizontal lines implying perceived separation of interest. This happened frequently enough in some trades for some historians to accept that class conflict was *latent* in eighteenth-century manufacturing.[55] Professor Hobsbawm has pointed out that whereas under industrial capitalism class is an immediate and directly experienced reality, in earlier periods it may be viewed as an analytical construct which makes sense of a complex of facts otherwise inexplicable.[56] Again we come to the main point: social class was manifest in the nineteenth century, and latent in the eighteenth.

Perception of a separate labour interest distinct from and opposed to that of capital was not widespread enough to talk of a conscious working class in any formed or remotely homogeneous sense. The expression of separate interest was, however, sufficiently evident in some areas, for example in industrial relations, where it formed the basis of Adam Smith's views on wage bargaining, and, indeed, created the formative basis for the development of trade unionism. Professor Perkin has remarked on the fact that class feeling was nearer to the surface in industrial relations, than anywhere else in the eighteenth century.[57] That view is one with which I find myself in substantial agreement. Nevertheless the belief that the perception of an overall trade interest was much stronger is a persuasive one, even when events and evidence seem sometimes to suggest otherwise. Thus a period of hostility might produce a flourish of rhetoric which sounds like the instinctive reaction of class, but which might be straightaway followed by expressions of a desire to return to a properly ordered world in which masters and men alike know both their place and their obligations. A pamphlet of 1739 in sympathy with the hardships of 'starving workpeople' ascribes their misery to the actions of 'unmasterlike masters' who lower wages and increase oppressions.[58] The disputes which preceded the passing of the famous Spitalfields Act of 1773 were extremely violent, but very soon after them a poem was inserted in a rate book, from which the following lines are taken:

And may no treacherous, base, designing men
E'er make encroachments on our rights again;
May upright masters still augment their treasure,
And journeymen pursue their work with pleasure,

> May arts and manufactories still increase,
> And Spitalfields be blest with prosperous peace.[59]

The journeymen papermakers had a well-organised trade union with a strategy sufficiently evolved to include the 'rolling' strike. After a bitter period of strikes and counter-offensive lock-outs, they nevertheless concluded their rule book for 1803 with these verses:

> May masters with their men unite,
> Each other ne'er oppress;
> And their assistance freely give
> When men are in distress.
>
> We covet not our master's wealth
> Nor crave for nothing more
> But to support our families
> As our fathers have before
>
> Then may the God that rules above
> Look on our mean endeavour
> And masters with their men unite
> In hand and hand for ever.

The journeymen stressed their wish for 'sentiments of peaceful co-operative and conservative rectitude'.[60] The Compositors' Society in 1801 had as one of its declared objectives the promotion of 'harmony between the employers and the employed'. When the framework knitters petitioned Parliament in 1778, 'real necessity' had driven them to beg for redress, but not 'ill will to the masters'. The wrath of General Ludd was discriminate: it was, in 1811, 'entirely confined to wide frames/And to those that old prices abate'.[61]

The ribbon weavers of Coventry in distress in 1818 sent a 'respectful address' to their employers entreating them to act as Christian masters should:

> Suppose you were the journeymen, and they your masters; would you like the treatment they now receive from you? No! no! Then adopt the maxim which has received the sanction of heaven and earth, of angels and men, of philosophers and patriots, of all but the worthless and vile — 'Therefore all things whatsoever ye would that men should do unto you, do ye even so to them.[62]

The 'old-fashioned master', like the old-fashioned squire is part of the strand of paternalism, which as a broad idea covers those 'powerful bonds and loyalties' Professor Perkin sees as overlying 'latent class' and effectively preventing its 'overt expression'.[63] The 'old-fashioned master' like the ideology of paternalism of which he is part, tended to look ever backwards: 'Always paternalist actuality appears to be receding into an ever more primitive and paternalist past. And the term forces us into confusions of actual and ideological attributes'.[64] Samuel Bamford recalled the old 'bearing home' day when the out-working weavers went to fetch their cotton yarn from their employer. Business was done in an amicable manner and a reasonable atmosphere: 'No captious fault-finding, no bullying, no arbitrary abatement, which have been too common since, were then practiced'. After putting-out the work the master's agent would join the men at the inn for a drink (after first dining separately in the parlour). Even so there were those who remembered still earlier days when relations had been even closer. Then a weaver might take a bite and smoke a pipe with the master himself, not simply a post-lunch drink with his agent.[65]

Even in dispute with their employers, the manufacturing workers' characteristic ideology was a conservative one. 'Paternalism' in its broadest sense governed not just relationships between gentry and plebians and between masters and men, but ran through the social structure at all levels. Edward Thompson has pointed out that apprenticeship was more than simply an instruction into particular skills, but an induction into the 'social experience or common wisdom of the community'. Each new generation stood then in a relation of apprentice to its seniors: 'Although social life is changing and although there is much mobility, change has not yet reached the point at which it is assumed that the horizons of each generation will be different'. Practices and norms were reproduced down the generations within the 'slowly differentiating ambience of "custom"'.[66]

Despite the fact that, as Lipson has remarked, the whole industrial outlook was being permeated by a growing economic individualism, to the extent that *The Wealth of Nations* largely succeeded because Adam Smith gave an articulate expression to ideas towards which the leaders of industry had long been feeling their way,[67] the paternalist legal inheritance, symbolised above all by the Statute of Artificers (5 Elizabeth), retained a special meaning for the skilled workers. They did not cease to act as if regulatory redress for their grievances was obtainable. At crisis points in the relations between labour and capital from the woollen weavers' petitions of 1727 to the Luddite disturbances of the Regency,

workers from a wide variety of employments sought help from government. They kept a powerful vision of the past when their well-being
had been preserved by custom and by paternalist legislation. The Act
of 5 Elizabeth had a reality in the notion of what *ought* to be, and to
it, artisans, journeymen and small masters alike appealed. The repeal
of the apprenticeship clauses of that statute in 1814 may be viewed as
marking an end to the final crisis of paternalist protection.[68]

Even among manufacturing workers and miners, the most frequent
disturbances did not arise out of industrial relations issues, but over food
prices. So much research has now been published on food-riots that no
one could doubt that one clear consciousness which the eighteenth-
century industrial worker did most emphatically have, was a consumer
one. They were predominant in those disturbances over rising food prices
which marked the grain-crisis years of the century. The account of more
than 40 such riots in the *Annual Register* for 1766 amply illustrates the
involvement of industrial workers: cloth workers in Gloucestershire and
Wiltshire destroyed mills and distributed corn among themselves, while
at Exeter they took cheese and sold it below price. Tin miners in Cornwall forced farmers and butchers to lower their prices. At Wolverhampton
farmers were forced to sell their wheat at 5s a bushel, and the butchers
their meat at 2½d a pound. Colliers from Bedworth plundered warehouses of cheese and sold it out at low prices, while cloth workers at
Norwich rose in a general riot against mills, malt houses and bakers'
shops. At Birmingham bread and cheese were taken and sold at prices
fixed by the rioters, while the framework knitters of Nottingham were
controlled enough to seize all the cheese offered for sale at the fair by
middle men, while leaving that being sold directly by the farmers alone.[69]
Mr Thompson has convincingly written of a 'moral economy' of the
English crowd in the eighteenth century, which with its fixing of 'just'
prices on seized corn and other foodstuffs, saw itself as acting legiti-
mately within the context of Tudor and Stuart paternalist regulation
of the corn trade in the interests of the poor consumer. If justices were
no longer so willing to enforce those old regulations against forestalling,
regrating or engrossing, and other market practices which enhanced the
price in years of scarcity, then there was no resort but to direct action
in resistance to those who would have no laws other than those of the
market determine the price of corn.[70]

The protest of the manufacturing poor was conservative in its forms:
in its appeal to custom, paternalist legislation and in its seeking to rein-
force traditional usage. But it was also a 'rebellious traditional culture'[71]
because it resisted in the name of custom, the economic innovations

and rationalisations which the employers, and increasingly the rulers, were seeking to impose and make a new orthodoxy. In other words they were resisting an ever-encroaching and growing capitalism. Ironically while the employers and rulers professed to see dangerous tendencies towards insubordination and a threat to the established order developing among the manufacturing poor as a result of the influence of the French Revolution, the watchmakers of London in 1817 regretting the ending of statutory apprenticeship, and lamenting the distress which this repeal, in the name of economic freedom, had brought to their trade, resolved:

That the pretensions to the allowance of universal uncontrolled freedom of action to every individual, founded upon the same delusive theoretical principles which fostered the French Revolution, are wholly inapplicable to the insular situation of this kingdom, and if allowed to prevail, will hasten the destruction of the social system so happily arranged in the existing form and substance of the British Constitution, established by law.[72]

Notes

1. *Calendar of State Papers Domestic of the Reign of George I, 1714-19* (Mss. Public Record Office) p. 211; ibid., p. 71; State Papers Domestic 35/14 Petition of the Weavers of the South West (1718).
2. E.J. Hobsbawm, 'Custom, Wages and Work-load in Nineteenth-Century Industry' in his *Labouring Men* (London, 1964), p. 348.
3. See above pp. 38-9.
4. D. Wilson, 'Government Dockyard Workers in Portsmouth 1793-1815', unpublished PhD thesis, University of Warwick, 1975, pp. 153-5.
5. Charles Manby Smith, *The Working Man's Way in the World* (1853, reprinted, London, 1967), p. 171, pp. 184-6, pp. 12-13.
6. E. Howe (ed.), *The London Compositor: Documents Relating to Wages, Working Conditions and Customs of the London Printing Trade* (London, 1947), pp. 84-5.
7. J. Child, *Industrial Relations in the British Printing Industry* (London, 1967), pp. 42-3.
8. Based on the account in William Hone, *The Every Day Book* (London, 1864), Vol. I, pp. 572-3.
9. *Report from the Select Committee on the Combination Laws*, P.P. 1825 (417, 437), IV, p. 318.
10. *Report from the Select Committee on Artisans and Machinery*, P.P. 1824 (51), V, pp. 212-13; pp. 222-8; p. 31.
11. E. Welbourne, *The Miners' Unions of Northumberland and Durham* (Cambridge, 1923), p. 11.
12. J.G. Rule, 'The Labouring Miner in Cornwall, c. 1740-1870: A Study in Social History', unpublished PhD thesis, University of Warwick, 1971, p. 42.

13. An account of 1740 from Howe, *London Compositor*, p. 29.

14. A. Smith, *Discovering Folklore in Industry* (Tring, 1969), pp. 15-16.

15. W.J. Ashley, *Surveys: Historic and Economic* (London, 1900), pp. 260-1.

16. Hone, *Every Day Book*, Vol. I, p. 573.

17. *Autobiography of Benjamin Franklin* (London, 1903 edn), pp. 56-8.

18. Manby Smith, *Working Man's Way*, p. 61.

19. William Lovett, *Life and Struggles in pursuit of bread, knowledge and freedom etc.* (1876, reprinted London, 1967), p. 25.

20. M. Dorothy George, *London Life in the Eighteenth Century* (Harmondsworth, 1966 edn), p. 210.

21. Lovett, *Life and Struggles*, p. 25.

22. Ashley, *Surveys*, p. 261.

23. Franklin, *Autobiography*, p. 56.

24. *SC on Combination Laws*, P.P. 1825, Minutes p. 35.

25. Rule, 'Labouring Miner', p. 19; D. Baugh, *British Naval Administration in the Age of Walpole* (Princeton, 1965), p. 314.

26. George, *London Life*, pp. 287-9.

27. *Report of the Committee on the Petitions of Several Cotton Manufacturers and Journeymen Cotton Weavers*, P.P. 1808 (177), II, p. 6.

28. Howe, *London Compositor*, p. 391.

29. *Report from the Select Committee on the Petitions of the Watchmakers of Coventry*, P.P. 1817 (504), VI, pp. 6-14.

30. Ibid., p. 73.

31. Ibid., pp. 75, 78.

32. Ibid., p. 87.

33. Quoted in E.P. Thompson, *The Making of the English Working Class* (Harmondsworth, 1968 edn), pp. 304-5.

34. Samuel Bamford, *Early Days* (reprinted London, 1967), p. 2.

35. This is the argument of M. Sanderson, 'Literacy and the Industrial Revolution', *Past & Present*, no. 56 (1972), pp. 75-104.

36. William Hutton, *A History of Birmingham* (Birmingham, 1781), pp. 130-9; Francis Place, *Autobiography* (edited by M. Thale, Cambridge, 1972), p. 106.

37. E.J. Hobsbawm, 'The Labour Aristocracy in Nineteenth-century Britain' in his *Labouring Men*, p. 273.

38. Place, *Autobiography*, pp. 17, 40, 71, 73-4, 121-2, 133-4.

39. Ibid., pp. 14-15.

40. *SC on Artisans and Machinery* P.P. 1824, *Second Report* V, p. 46.

41. Ibid., *First Report*, p. 25; *Second Report*, p. 55.

42. Ibid., *Second Report*, p. 86.

43. Lovett, *Life and Struggles*, p. 26.

44. Place, *Autobiography*, p. 16.

45. See, for example, P. Borsay, 'The English Urban Renaissance: The Development of Provincial Urban Culture c. 1680-1760', *Social History*, 5 (1977), pp. 581-603.

46. For the observance of saints' days by manufacturing workers see: Hone, *Every Day Book*, Vol. I, pp. 108 (Bishop Blaize), 113 (Shrove Tuesday, Apprentices), 296-7 (May Day, chimney sweeps), 571 (Bartholomew tide, printers' waygoose feast), 705 (St Crispin, shoemakers), 753 (St Clement, smiths and dockyard workers). For some interesting insights into village observances see R.W. Bushaway, 'Ceremony, Custom and Ritual: Some Observations on Social Conflict in the Rural Community, 1750-1850' in W. Minchinton (ed.), *Reactions to Social and Economic Change 1750-1939* (Exeter, 1979), pp. 9-29. For a useful survey of industrial folklore see Smith, *Discovering Folklore in Industry*.

47. Bamford, *Early Days*, Chapter XIV; Place, *Autobiography*, pp. 64-70.

48. John Wesley, *Journal* (Everyman edn, London, 1906), Vol. I, p. 250. On Kingswood see R.W. Malcolmson, '"A Set of Ungovernable People": The Kingswood Colliers in the Eighteenth Century' in J. Brewer and J. Styles (eds.), *An Ungovernable People. The English and their Law in the Seventeenth and Eighteenth Centuries* (London, 1980), pp. 85-127.
49. Welbourne, *Miners' Unions*, p. 15.
50. Rule, 'Labouring Miner', p. 80.
51. Ibid., p. 160.
52. See, for example the low rating scored by miners in Lancashire in Sanderson, 'Literacy and the Industrial Revolution', p. 90.
53. This is stressed by H. Perkin, *The Origins of Modern English Society 1780-1880* (London, 1969), pp. 33-7.
54. The phrase is E.P. Thompson's from his penetrating analysis 'Eighteenth-century English Society: Class Struggle without Class', *Social History*, vol. 3, no. 2 (1978), p. 134.
55. Ibid., pp. 134-5; Perkin, *Origins*, pp. 26-8. For a short, but useful critique of views of the 'classlessness' of eighteenth-century society see R.J. Morris, *Class and Class Consciousness in the Industrial Revolution 1780-1850* (London, 1979).
56. Quoted in Thompson, 'Eighteenth-century English Society', p. 148 (footnote).
57. Perkin, *Origins*, p. 31. Dr Morris would put it rather more strongly: 'Evidence of the behaviour and consciousness of the eighteenth-century labour force is fragmentary, but it is enough to leave a question mark against the "classlessness" of the eighteenth century', *Class and Class Consciousness*, p. 18. Professor Perkin suggests that it was in the 1810s and 1820s 'that class and class antagonism became a fact' (*Origins*, p. 28), while Mr Thompson writes of a 'structural re-ordering of class relations and of ideology' in the 1790s, which makes it 'possible for the first time, to analyse the historical process in terms of nineteenth-century notations of class' ('Eighteenth-century English society', p. 165). A recent study has stressed the importance of the 1820s for the development of a wider consciousness among Birmingham artisans: C. Behagg, 'Custom, Class and Change: The Trade Societies of Birmingham', *Social History*, vol. 4, no. 3 (1979), p. 456.
58. 'Gentleman of Wiltshire', *Miseries of the Miserable* (1739), reprinted in K. Carpenter (ed.), *British Labour Struggles* (New York, 1972), volume entitled *Labour Problems before the Industrial Revolution*, p. 6.
59. A. Plummer, *The London Weavers' Company* (London, 1972), p. 326.
60. D.C. Coleman, *The British Paper Industry 1495-1860: A Study in Growth* (Oxford, 1958), pp. 266-7.
61. Howe, *London Compositor*, p. 84; *Commons Journals*, 36, 25 February 1778, p. 741; song entitled 'General Ludd's Triumph' printed in J.L. and Barbara Hammond, *The Skilled Labourer* (edited by J.G. Rule, London, 1979), p. 212.
62. *Report from the Committee on the Silk Ribbon Weavers' Petitions*, P.P. 1818 (134), IX, p. 27.
63. Perkin, *Origins*, p. 37.
64. Thompson, 'Eighteenth-century English Society', p. 136.
65. Bamford, *Early Days*, pp. 117-19.
66. Thompson, 'Eighteenth-century English Society', pp. 152-3.
67. E. Lipson, *The Economic History of England Vol. III The Age of Mercantilism* (revised edn, London, 1943), p. 265. See also the comment of Sidney and Beatrice Webb, 'The next few years [after 1756] saw a revolutionary change in the industrial policy of the legislature which must have utterly bewildered the operatives. Within a generation the House of Commons exchanged its policy of medieval protection for one of "Administrative Nihilism"' (*The History of Trade Unionism* (London, 1911 edn), p. 44).

68. I developed this argument at a little greater length in my introduction to the 1979 edition of the Hammonds' *Skilled Labourer*, pp. xvi-xvii.

69. The relevant report from the *Annual Register* is reprinted in G.D.H. Cole and A.W. Filson (eds.), *British Working Class Movements: Selected Documents 1789-1875* (paperback edn, London, 1965), pp. 20-5.

70. The extensive literature on eighteenth-century food riots can be reached through the footnotes to E.P. Thompson's seminal article: 'The Moral Economy of the English Crowd in the Eighteenth Century', *Past & Present*, no. 50 (1971), pp. 76-136. In a recent regional study, Dr Wells has made interesting comments on the role of industrial workers. He has shown that the Wellington woolcombers met before the riots in the west in 1800 to draft a set of resolutions on food prices and sent them for adoption to their colleagues in other woollen towns (R. Wells, 'The Revolt of the South-west, 1800-1: A Study in English Popular Protest', *Social History*, 6 (1977), p. 742).

71. Thompson, 'Eighteenth-century English Society', p. 153.

72. *SC on Petitions of Coventry Watchmakers*, P.P. 1817, VI, p. 18.

SELECT BIBLIOGRAPHY

(A) Primary Sources

(1) Government and Parliamentary Publications and Papers

Calendar of State Papers Domestic 1633-4

Calendar of Home Office Papers of the Reign of George III, 1760 to 1775 (4 volumes, 1878-99)

Journals of the House of Commons

Report from the Committee on the Woollen Clothiers Petition. P.P. 1802/3, V (30), p. 243

Report from the Committee on the Woollen Manufacturers Petition. P.P. 1802/3, V (71), p. 305

Minutes of Evidence taken before the Committee to whom the Bill respecting the laws relating to the Woollen Trade is committed. P.P. 1802/3, VII (95), p. 495

Minutes of Evidence taken before the Committee on the Petition of the Journeymen Calico Printers. P.P. reprinted in 1807, II (129), p. 107 (first printed 1804)

Report from the Committee on the petitions of several Cotton Manufacturers and Journeymen Cotton Weavers. P.P. 1808. II (177), p. 95

Report from the Committee on the Apprentice Laws, P.P. 1812/13, IV (243), p. 941

Report from the Committee on the petition of the Watchmakers of Coventry. P.P. 1818, VI (504), p. 285

Report from the Committee on the Laws relating to Watchmakers. P.P. 1818, IX (135), p. 203

Report from the Committee on the Silk Ribbon Weavers Petitions. P.P. 1818, IX (134), p. 5. Second Report. IX, p. 53

Reports from the Select Committee on Artisans and Machinery. P.P. 1824, V (51), p. 589 (6 reports)

Report from the Select Committee on the Combination Laws. P.P. 1825, IV (417) (437), p. 499, 565

(2) Newspapers etc.

Exeter Mercury
Hampshire Chronicle

Sherborne Mercury
The Times
The Gentleman's Magazine

(3) Printed Primary Sources Including Collections

Aikin, J. *A Description of the Country from Thirty to Forty Miles round Manchester* (London, 1795; reprinted New York, 1968)

Aspinall, A. *The Early English Trade Unions. Documents from the Home Office Papers in the Public Record Office* (London, 1949)

Bamford, Samuel *Autobiography Volume I. Early Days* (1848-9, reprinted London, 1967)

Bland, A.E., P.A. Brown and R.H. Tawney (eds.), *English Economic History Select Documents* (London, 1914)

Brown, A.F.J. *English History from Essex Sources 1750-1900* (Chelmsford, 1952)

— *Essex at Work 1700-1815* (Chelmsford, 1969)

Burn, Richard *The Justice of the Peace and Parish Officer* (13th edn, London, 1776)

Campbell, R. *The London Tradesman* (1747, reprinted Newton Abbot, 1969)

Carpenter, K. (ed.), *British Labour Struggles* (New York, 1972). Facsimile reprints of contemporary pamphlets. Volumes entitled: *Labour Problems before the Industrial Revolution*; *Labour Disputes in the Early Days of the Industrial Revolution*; *The Spread of Machinery*; *Trade Unions under the Combination Acts 1799-1823*

Chinnery, G.A. (ed.), *Records of the Borough of Leicester. Vol. VII* (Leicester, 1974)

Cole, G.D.H. and A.W. Filson, *British Working Class Movements, Selected Documents 1789-1875* (1957, reprinted London, 1965)

Cornish, J.B. (ed.), *The Autobiography of a Cornish Smuggler* (Truro, 1894, reprinted 1971)

Defoe, Daniel *A Plan of the English Commerce* (1728, reprinted Oxford, 1928)

— *A Tour through the Whole Island of Great Britain* (Everyman edn, two volumes, reprinted London, 1962)

Drew, J.H. *Samuel Drew, M.A. – The Self-Taught Cornishman* (London, 1861)

Dunsford, M. *Historical Memoirs of Tiverton*, 2nd edn (Exeter, 1790)

Eden, F.M. *The State of the Poor* (three volumes, London, 1797)

Felkin, W. *History of the Machine-wrought Hosiery and Lace Manufactures* (1867, reprinted Newton Abbot, 1967)

Finer, Ann and G. Savage (eds.), *The Selected Letters of Josiah Wedgwood* (London, 1965)

Franklin, Benjamin *Autobiography* (London, 1903 edn)

Galton, F.W. *Select Documents Illustrating the History of Trade Unionism. Volume I. The Tailoring Trade* (1896)

Hall, Charles *The Effects of Civilization on the People in European States* (1805, reprinted New York, 1965)

Hone, William, *The Everyday Book* (London, 1864 edn)

Howe, E. (ed.), *The London Compositor: Documents Relating to Wages, Working Conditions and Customs of the London Printing Trade 1785-1900* (London, 1947)

Hutton, William *A History of Birmingham* (Birmingham, 1781)

— *Life of William Hutton F.A.S.S.* (London, 1817 edn)

— *History of Derby* (2nd edn, London, 1817)

J.C., *The Compleat Collier* (1708, reprinted Newcastle, 1968)

Lovett, William *My Life and Struggles in pursuit of Bread, Truth and Knowledge etc.* (1867, reprinted London, 1967)

Manby Smith, C. *The Working Man's Way in the World* (1853, reprinted London, 1967)

Mann, J. de L. *Documents Illustrating the Wiltshire Textile Trades in the Eighteenth Century* (Devizes, 1964)

Maton, W.G. *Observations on the Western Counties of England* (Salisbury, 1794-6)

Minchinton, W.E. 'The Petitions of the Weavers and Clothiers of Gloucestershire in 1756', *Transactions of the Bristol and Gloucestershire Archaeological Society*, vol. 73 (1954), pp. 218-25

Origin, Object and Operation of the Apprentice Laws; with their application to Times Past, Present and to Come. Addressed to the Committee of General Purposes of the City of London (1814, reprinted in the *Pamphleteer*, vol. III)

Place, Francis *Autobiography* (edited by M. Thale, Cambridge, 1972)

Pryce, W. *Mineralogia Cornubiensis* (Oxford, 1778; reprinted Truro, 1972)

Ramazzini, Bernard *De Morbis Artificum* (1700, translated by W. Cave Wright, Chicago, 1940)

Shaw, Rev. S. *A Tour to the West of England in 1788* (London, 1789)

Smith, Adam *The Wealth of Nations* (1776, edited by E. Cannan, 1904, paperback edn, two volumes, London, 1961)

Smith, John (ed.), *Memoirs of Wool. Volume II* (1747, reprinted Farnborough, 1968)

Turner Thackrah, C. *The Effects of the Principal Arts, Trades and Pro-*

fessions and of Civic States and Habits of Living on Health and Longevity with a particular reference to the Trades and Manufactures of Leeds (London, 1831)
Wesley, John *Journals* (Everyman edn, four volumes, London, 1906)
Young, Arthur *The Farmer's Tour through the East of England* (1771)
— *A Six Months' Tour through the North of England* (2nd edn, 4 volumes, London, 1771)
— *A Six Weeks' Tour through the Southern Counties of England and Wales* (London, 1768)
— *Tours in England and Wales selected from the Annals of Agriculture* (London, 1932)

(B) A Note on Secondary Authorities

The most useful introduction to the social history of the period remains M. Dorothy George, *England in Transition* (1931; Penguin Books, Harmondsworth, 1953) which conveys as much information as many books twice its size. There is still much value in W. Bowden, *Industrial Society in England towards the end of the Eighteenth Century* (1925; 2nd edn, Frank Cass, 1965). It is especially useful for its copious quotation from contemporary sources as is the classic study of Paul Mantoux, *The Industrial Revolution in the Eighteenth Century* (1928; 2nd edn, Methuen, 1961, paperback 1964) and that of L. Moffit, *England on the Eve of the Industrial Revolution* (1925; 2nd edn, Frank Cass, 1963).

The standard economic history of the period is T.S. Ashton, *An Economic History of England: The Eighteenth Century* (Methuen, 1955). It can be supplemented by the statistical information available from P. Deane and W.A. Cole, *British Economic Growth 1688-1959* (Cambridge University Press, paperback edn, 1969). The extensive documentation of E. Lipson, *The Economic History of England. Volume III, The Age of Mercantilism* (revised edn, Adam and Charles Black, 1943) makes it indispensable for the serious student. Of the many textbooks which discuss the first part of the eighteenth century as a continuation of the sixteenth and seventeenth centuries, B.A. Holderness, *Pre-Industrial England – Economy and Society from 1500-1750* (Dent, 1976) provides the best organised and most detailed coverage.

T.S. Ashton, *Economic Fluctuations in England 1700-1800* (Oxford University Press, 1959) is the best guide to its subject. The irregularity of labour before the factory system is best treated in the seminal article of E.P. Thompson, 'Time, Work-discipline and Industrial Capitalism',

Past & Present, no. 38 (1967), pp. 56-97. A good case-study is D.A. Reid, 'The Decline of Saint Monday 1766-1876', *Past & Present*, no. 71 (1976), pp. 76-101 which looks at Birmingham. P. Mathias discusses the question usefully in 'Leisure and Wages in Theory and Practice' reprinted in his *The Transformation of England: Essays in the Economic and Social History of England in the Eighteenth Century* (Methuen, 1979). On wages the most detailed published study is still that of Elizabeth W. Gilboy, *Wages in Eighteenth-century England* (Harvard University Press, Cambridge, Mass., 1934).

Historians have written little on occupational health in the century, but the historical chapters of D. Hunter, *Health in Industry* (Penguin, Harmondsworth, 1959) are very useful. Apprenticeship has also been neglected and Jocelyn O. Dunlop, *English Apprenticeship and Child Labour – A History* (T. Fisher Unwin, 1912) is the only truly comprehensive treatment. T.K. Derry, 'The Repeal of the Apprenticeship Clauses of the Statute of Apprentices', *Economic History Review*, III (1931/2), pp. 67-86 provides the details of the campaign of 1814.

The history of crime is a developing area, but as yet there is no published study of its industrial context. A paper by P. Linebaugh summarised in the *Bulletin of the Society for the Study of Labour History*, no. 25 (1972), pp. 11-14 indicates some of the important insights in his unpublished PhD thesis on the subject. D.A. Baugh, *British Naval Administration in the Age of Walpole* (Princeton University Press, 1965) is the most accessible source for dockyard perquisites and pilfering. The passing and implementation of the Worsted Acts of 1777 are covered in H. Heaton, *The Yorkshire Woollen and Worsted Industries from the earliest times up to the Industrial Revolution* (1920; 2nd edn Clarendon Press, Oxford, 1965).

C.R.Dobson, *Masters and Journeymen: A Prehistory of Industrial Relations 1717-1800* (Croom Helm, 1980) is the first detailed study of trade unionism since the early chapters of Sidney and Beatrice Webb, *The History of Trade Unionism* (1894 and many subsequent editions and reprints). The Webbs' interpretation is still central to any discussion of eighteenth-century trade unionism and it is briefly discussed by E.P. Thompson, 'English Trade Unionism and Other Labour Movements before 1790', *Bulletin of the Society for the Study of Labour History*, no. 17 (1968), pp. 19-24. *Labouring Men* (Weidenfeld, 1964) a collection of essays by E.J. Hobsbawm, contains essential studies of machine-breaking and of the 'tramping artisan'. Two books on industrial relations whose historical chapters are very useful are: H.A. Turner, *Trade Union Growth, Structure and Policy. A Comparative Study of the Cotton*

Unions (Allen and Unwin, 1962) and J. Child, *Industrial Relations in the British Printing Industry – The Quest for Security* (Allen and Unwin, 1967). For the end of the century and the continuing story, E.P. Thompson, *The Making of the English Working Class* (1963; Penguin edition with added postscript, Harmondsworth, 1965) has become an established, if controversial, classic which is essential reading.

The recreational culture of the lower orders is discussed in R.W. Malcolmson, *Popular Recreations in English Society 1700-1850* (Cambridge University Press, 1973). A convenient introduction to industrial folklore, A. Smith, *Discovering Folklore in Industry* (Tring, 1969) is a pamphlet, but we lack larger studies of this important subject. On the question of 'consciousness' see the recent study by E.P. Thompson, 'Eighteenth-century English Society: Class Struggle without Class?', *Social History*, vol. 3, no. 2 (1978), pp. 133-65 and the early chapters of H. Perkin, *The Origins of Modern English Society 1780-1880* (Routledge and Kegan Paul, 1969). Popular disturbances over food prices have produced an extensive literature and for an introduction to it see J. Stevenson, *Popular Disturbances in England 1700-1870* (Longmans, 1979). The central article to recent debates over the consumer consciousness of the poor and their use of the food riot is E.P. Thompson, 'The Moral Economy of the English Crowd in the Eighteenth Century', *Past & Present*, no. 50 (1971), pp. 76-136.

The student of this subject will very soon wish to turn to some of the studies which deal with specific localities and occupations and have some information or insight to offer on the various themes discussed in this book. Many of these have earned a reputation for their interest and scholarship over many years. Among such 'classics' are: M.D. George, *London Life in the Eighteenth Century* (1925; paperback edn, Penguin, Harmondsworth, 1966); A.P. Wadsworth and J. de L. Mann, *The Cotton Trade and Industrial Lancashire* (Manchester University Press, 1931); G.I.H. Lloyd, *The Cutlery Trades: An Historical Essay in the Economics of Small Scale Production* (1913; new edn, Frank Cass, 1968); A.K. Hamilton Jenkin, *The Cornish Miner* (Allen and Unwin, 1927); T.S. Ashton and J. Sykes, *The Coal Industry of the Eighteenth Century* (1929; revised edn, Manchester University Press, 1964); F.A. Wells, *The British Hosiery and Knitwear Industry: Its History and Organisation* (1935; reprinted, Newton Abbot, 1972); W.G. Hoskins, *Industry, Trade and People in Exeter 1688-1800* (1935; 2nd edn, Exeter University Press, 1968) and Herbert Heaton, *The Yorkshire Woollen and Worsted Industries from the Earliest Times to the Industrial Revolution* (1920; reprinted, Clarendon Press, Oxford, 1965).

More recent studies include: C.J. Hunt, *The Lead Miners of the Northern Pennines* (Manchester University Press, 1970); A. Plummer, *The London Weavers' Company 1600-1970* (Routledge and Kegan Paul, 1972); D. Hey, *The Rural Metalworkers of the Sheffield Region* (Leicester University Press, 1972); J. de L. Mann, *The Cloth Industry in the West of England from 1640 to 1880* (Oxford, Clarendon Press, 1971) and D.C. Coleman, *The British Paper Industry 1495-1860: A Study in Industrial Growth* (Oxford, Clarendon Press, 1958).

INDEX

absenteeism 52-4, 56-7
acts against embezzlement of materials 130-1; Worsted Acts (1777) 131-2
apprenticeship: among calico printers 115-16, carpenters 109, cotton weavers 112-13, dockyard workers 109-10, framework knitters 104, 106, 113, 116, hatters 34, 111-12, printers 100-1, saddlers 97, shoemakers 110-11, silk weavers 105, woolcombers 96, woollen weavers and shearmen 98-9, 109, 112-15; and adolescence 102-3; and social control 100-4; connection with trade unionism 118-19; indentures 97-100; 'outdoor' 100-1; overstocking 105-6; 'property of skill' 106-7; remuneration 104-5; see also Statute of Artificers and Apprentices
artisan: definition 22; independence 203; clubs 204

Bamford, Samuel 18, 43, 203-4, 211
Banbury 24, 112, 187
Barnsley 19
Birmingham 11, 19-20, 26-7, 36, 67-8, 78, 108, 156, 204
Bolton 13, 24
box clubs 150, 167
Bristol 19, 29, 50, 108-9, 158, 188; Kingswood 28, 188, 207
building trades 51; see also carpenters, masons
Burslem 29

calico printers: apprenticeship 115-16; health 79; trade unionism and strikes among 182, 185
Camborne 13, 18
carpenters 111, 200; apprenticeship 109
cheating by workers: in coal mines 134, copper mines 134-5, dockyards 135, potteries 135
check weavers 112-13, 114, 166

child labour: in factories 43, pre-industrial economy 42-3
chips see embezzlement of materials
class consciousness in eighteenth century 208-13
Coalbrookdale 27
coal heavers 40, 142
Colchester 11, 19, 23, 126
combination acts 174-6, 180-1
conspiracy, cases against strikers 175-6
'cool-staffing' 183, 187-8
Cornwall 15, 17, 29, 30, 56, 79, 103-4, 134, 200, 207-8
cotton manufacture 13, 18, 24, 49, 53; apprenticeship in 112-13; see also calico printers, check weavers, factories, Lancashire, Manchester
Coventry 19, 100-1, 119, 133, 165, 168, 179, 202-3, 210
crime: industrial 125-34; in London 103, 205
customs 194-201, 206-7; among carpenters 200, coopers 198-9, 201, hatters 199, 200-1, keelmen 194, miners 197, 201, shipwrights 195-7
cutlers 56, 67-8; health 80, 86; see also Sheffield

Defoe, Daniel 11, 13, 16-19, 22-3, 32, 36-7, 42, 49, 54, 84
Derby 30, 41, 43
Derbyshire 29, 58, 67
Devon, 23, 138, 158-60
dockyards 28, 58, 109-10; see also Plymouth and Portsmouth
drinking: and absenteeism 52-4; customs 199, 201, health 77-8, Saint Monday 55-6
Durham see Northumberland and Durham coalfield

embezzlement of materials 124-34; among cloth workers 126-7, 130-3; among knitters 133; and putting-out system 130-3, 143;

dockyard chips 128-30; in craft trades 125-6; involving pawnbrokers 133; punishment for 133-4; *see also* acts against embezzlement of materials
Essex 17-19, 23-4, 42, 65, 96, 110-13, 126-7, 165
Exeter 11, 16, 108, 181

factories 30, 61, 90-91
family economy 37-9, 42-4, 53
fellmongers 58, 61, 118, 178-9
fines and stoppages 139-42; coal heavers 142; miners 142; framework knitters 141-2; woollen workers 140
food riots 212
framework knitting (stocking manufacture) 25-6; apprenticeship 104, 106, 113, 116; embezzlement by knitters 133; stoppages by employers 141-2; wages 69; *see also* machine breaking
Franklin, Benjamin 56, 199
friendly and benefit societies 87, 150, 180-1, 203
Frome 17, 19, 50

George, M. Dorothy 69, 109
Gilboy, Elizabeth 68-9
Gloucestershire 23, 127, 132, 137, 158, 161-4, 188
guilds and companies 109, 189-91

Halifax 36-7, 132
Hall, Charles 75, 78, 147-8
Hammond, J.L. and Barbara 22, 187
hatters 28, 34, 200-1; apprenticeship 111-12; embezzlement of materials by (bugging) 125-6; health 79; trade unionism 156-8
health: and drink 77-8, manufactures 75; overwork 77; evidence for 75-6; factories 90-91; of bakery workers 80, building workers 81, 85, calico printers 79, chimney boys 89, copper refiners 79, craft workers 82, gilders 79, glaziers 79, grinders and filers 80, 86, hatters 79, iron forgers 81, 85, lead workers 79, miners 79-81, 84-5, 86-7, 89, pottery workers 79, 85, shipwrights 87-8, shoemakers 82-3, tailors 82-3, 88,

weavers 82, 88-9, woolcombers 80
Hobsbawm, E.J. 165, 184-6, 188, 204, 209
house of call: among tailors 154-5, printers 168
Hutton, William 20, 30, 43-4, 53, 78, 103, 105, 141, 204

indentures 97-100
independence 22; from poor relief 202-3; and artisan attitudes 203-6
industrial workforce, size of 11-12
iron workers 27, 81, 85

journeyman, defined 32-3
justices, wage fixing by 153, 161-2

keelmen 40, 194
King, Gregory 12

labour: hours of 57-61; irregularity of 52-7
Lancashire 49, 167; size of towns 18; *see also* cotton manufacture
leather-breeches makers 61, 104; strike of 181-2
Leicester 17, 19, 26, 108, 157
Leeds 24, 83, 166
Lipson, E. 31, 211
Liverpool 24, 28-9, 108
London: manufacturing in 20-1, 28, 33-6, 57-8; population 20-1; wages in 62-3
Lovett, William 111, 200, 206
luddism 26, 116, 166; *see also* machine breaking

machine breaking 50, 167-8, 184-7; *see also* luddism
Manchester 13, 18, 20, 24, 43, 53, 61, 65, 106, 111-12, 115, 133, 157, 166-7, 185
manufacturing population 11-12; dispersion 16-21
Massie, Joseph 12, 23, 61-2
masons 21, 51, 61, 189
Mather, Joseph 55-6, 138
metal workers 26-7; wages of in Birmingham and Sheffield 67-8
Methodism 208-9
mines: accidents 84-5; bad air 86-7
miners and mining 28-9; coalminers 14-15, 23, 28-9, 30-1, 40-1,

absenteeism 56-7, hours 58-9,
    wages 65; Cornish miners 13, 15,
    23, 29-30, 54, absenteeism 56-7,
    hours 59-60, wages 65 *see also*
    tribute and tutwork systems;
    health of miners 79-80, 84-5,
    86-7, 89; perquisite coal 127-8
mixed occupations 11-16; and family
    economy 15-16

nail making 26, 32
Newcastle 11, 19, 27, 65, 84, 187
Norfolk 16, 42
Northumberland and Durham coal-
    field 23, 28, 40, 58, 65
Norwich 11, 17, 19, 24, 50, 179
Nottingham 17, 26, 141

oppression by employers, accusations
    of: in cutlery manufacture 138; in
    west country cloth trade 135-7

painters 51, 58, 189-90
papermakers 58, 63, 210; strike of
    182-3
pinmakers 35
Place, Francis 33, 44, 103-5, 155-6,
    179, 180-1, 194, 201, 205-6
Plymouth 19-20, 28, 30, 129
poor relief, independence from 202-3
Portsmouth 28, 30, 50-1, 61, 88,
    129, 179
pottery manufacture 29, 56; health
    of workers 79, 85; *see also*
    Burslem and Wedgwood, Josiah
Prescott (Lancs) 14
printing workers 21, 34-5, 179, 206,
    210; apprenticeship 101; customs
    195-6, 198, 199-201; strikes
    183-4; wages 62-3
proto-industrialisation 53
putting-out system 22, 31-2; and
    embezzlement of materials 130-3,
    143

Ramazzini, Bernard 74, 82-3
razor polishers 68
Redruth 13
redundancy: and trade cycle 49-50;
    and wars 50-1; seasonal 51-2
regulation of wages: by Act of
    Parliament for tailors 152-3, 175;
    see also Spitalfields Act; by
    Quarter Sessions 153, 161-2

riots: against unapprenticed workers
    111, 187-8; against merchants
    186; *see also* food riots and
    machine breaking
Rudé, George 103

saddlers 36, 63, 97
sawyers 126
serge weavers and combers: trade
    unionism among 158-161
shearmen 65, 114-15, 163, 166, 185
Sheffield 16, 18-19, 26-7, 36, 56, 68,
    85, 130, 138, 168
shipwrights 19, 27-8, 30; apprentice-
    ship 109-10; customs of working
    195-7; health 87-8; hours of work
    58; perquisite of chips 128-30;
    wages 63
shoemakers 21, 28, 33-4, 104;
    apprenticeship 110-11; health
    82-3; embezzlement of materials
    by 130
Shropshire 27, 80
silk weavers 21, 24, 52, 210;
    apprenticeship 105; embezzle-
    ment of materials by 130; *see also*
    Spitalfields, Spitalfields Act and
    Coventry
Smith, Adam: on apprenticeship 96,
    99, 106, 114, combinations of
    employers 137, combinations of
    workmen 147, 152-3, 172-4,
    178-9, 184, division of labour 35,
    health of labourers 75, 77-8, 87,
    irregular working 57, separation
    of capital from labour 31, wages
    62, 65, 87
Somerset 23, 138, 161-4
Spitalfields 14, 21, 25, 130, 133, 188
Spitalfields Act (1777) 111, 114, 186
Statute of Artificers and Apprentices
    (1563) 95-6; campaign against
    repeal of 114-19; modification by
    lawyers 107-8; prosecutions under
    110-11; *see also* apprenticeship
strikes: and tactics 178-9, 182-3, the
    law 174-7, violence 184-8; of
    calico printers 182, 185, coopers
    179, cotton weavers 150-1, 166-8,
    183, cutlery workers 138, 173-4,
    dockyard workers 179, fell mon-
    gers 178-9, framework knitters
    183, hatters 156-8, 181-2,
    leather-breeches makers 181-2,

miners 177, 186-7, paper makers 182-3, printers 179, 181, 183-4, silk weavers 179, 188, shoemakers (cordwainers) 176, 181, tailors 152-6, wheelwrights 176, wool-combers 164-5, 183, woollen and worsted weavers 158-64, 183, 187-8
strike funds 179-81

tailors 28, 51-2, 32-3; embezzlement of materials (cabbage) 126; health 82-3; hours of work 57, 142-3; strikes and trade unionism 140, 152-6; wages 62; *see also* regulation of wages
Taunton, 23, 42, 61, 159-61, 164, 172
Temple, William 43, 53, 88-9, 139-40
Thompson, E.P. 55, 151, 185, 189, 211-12
threatening letters 185-6
Tiverton 18, 159-60, 183
trade unions: Adam Smith on 147, 172; and apprenticeship 189-90; and the law 174-8; and the tramping system 164-5, 181; definitions of 149-51; for references to individual occupations *see* strikes
Trowbridge 17, 19
truck payments 138-9
Turner-Thackrah, Charles 76-7, 79, 82, 86, 90-1

violence in industrial disputes 184-8; *see also* riots and machine-breaking

wages 61-70; Birmingham 67-8; 'golden age' of 69; London 62-4, Table 2.1; miners 65-7, tribute and tutwork in Cornwall 59, 65-7; movement over eighteenth century 68-9; provincial 63-5, 68-9; slow payment of in dockyards 129-30; stoppages from 139-42
watchmakers 35, 50, 202-3, 213; apprenticeship 100; embezzlement of materials by 133; health 82
Webb, Sidney and Beatrice 95, 149-50, 179-80, 189
Weber, Max 52
Wedgwood, Josiah 29, 56, 79, 85, 135

Wesley, John 137, 208-9
wheelwrights 12, 21, 189
Wiltshire 23, 140, 158, 161-4, 185-6
Wolverhampton 27, 108
women: craft trades 41; in textiles 24-5; in the family economy 26, 41-2; in factories and mines 41-2
woolcombers 54; apprenticeship 96; health 80; trade unionism and strikes among 164-5
woollen manufacture 18-19, 23-4; in East Anglia 24, 42; in the south west 13, 22, 32; in West Riding 13-14, 16, 36-9; *see also* Essex
woollen and worsted weavers: apprenticeship 98-9, 109, 112-15; embezzlement of materials by 126-7, 130-3; *see also* Worsted Acts; health 82, 88-9; hours 60; trade unionism and strikes among 158-164, 183, 187-8; wages 61, 63-5
Worsted Acts (1777) 131-2
workshop 31, 61

Yorkshire 13-14, 17, 24, 30, 32, 36-7, 58, 109, 194
Young, Arthur 13-15, 20, 26-8, 30, 41-2, 53, 58, 65, 67-8, 85-6